Danish

An Essential Grammar

2nd Edition

Danish: An Essential Grammar is a reference guide to the most important aspects of current Danish as it is used by native speakers.

It presents a fresh and accessible description of the language, focusing on those areas of Danish that pose particular problems for English speakers, but at the same time, provides a broad general account of the language.

The *Grammar* is the ideal source of reference for the learner of Danish in the early and middle stages. It is suitable for independent study or for students in schools, colleges, universities and adult classes of all types.

This new edition has been fully updated to reflect changes in current language use and recent cultural developments. Features include:

- clear, jargon-free explanations
- many tables and diagrams for extra clarity
- separate glossary of linguistic and grammatical terms
- detailed index with key Danish and English words.

Tom Lundskær-Nielsen is Senior Lecturer in Danish at University College London, UK.

Philip Holmes is Reader Emeritus in Scandinavian Studies at the University of Hull, UK and is now a freelance translator.

Routledge Essential Grammars

Essential Grammars are available for the following languages:

Arabic
Chinese
Czech
Danish
Dutch
English
Finnish
Georgian
German
Modern Greek
Modern Hebrew
Hindi
Hungarian
Korean
Latvian (forthcoming)
Norwegian
Polish
Portuguese
Romanian
Serbian
Spanish
Swedish
Thai
Turkish
Urdu

Danish

An Essential Grammar

2nd Edition

 **Tom Lundskær-Nielsen
and Philip Holmes**

 Routledge
Taylor & Francis Group

LONDON AND NEW YORK

First published 2000
by Routledge

This second edition published 2011
by Routledge
2 Park Square, Milton Park, Abingdon OX14 4RN

Simultaneously published in the USA and Canada
by Routledge
711 Third Avenue, New York, NY 10017

Routledge is an imprint of the Taylor & Francis Group, an informa business

© 2000, 2011 Tom Lundskær-Nielsen and Philip Holmes

Typeset in Times New Roman and Gill Sans
by Florence Production Ltd, Stoodleigh, Devon

British Library Cataloguing in Publication Data
A catalogue record for this book is available from the British Library

Library of Congress Cataloging in Publication Data
A catalog record for this book has been requested

ISBN13: 978–0–415–49688–9 (hbk)
ISBN13: 978–0–415–49689–6 (pbk)
ISBN13: 978–0–203–87800–2 (ebk)

Contents

Chapter 5 Pronouns 71

Chapter 6   Verbs   97

Chapter 12   Word formation   223

Preface to the first edition

We have two aims with this book. First, we want to provide learners of Danish with a concise description of the structure of Danish phonology, morphology and syntax, as well as with a brief account of orthography, punctuation and word formation. Second, we try to describe in greater detail those areas of Danish structure that, in our experience, tend to pose special problems for learners whose first language is English. To help learners, most of the examples have been translated.

The 'new comma', as recommended by the Danish National Language Council, has been used throughout the book.

The book is largely traditional in its approach and terminology, but a number of the terms used are explained in a separate glossary of linguistic terms at the end of the book.

The various tables and diagrams are intended to make the book easy to use; in many cases, it will be possible for the learner to predict word forms and clause patterns from just a few rules. The index contains paragraph references to both linguistic concepts and to some Danish and English keywords and their uses, and, together with the table of contents, this should normally serve as a starting point for any search.

Learners progressing to an intermediate level or simply wanting more thorough explanations of specific points may wish to consult our much more detailed *Danish: A Comprehensive Grammar* (Routledge, 1995), reprinted with changes in 1998.

We would like to thank Henrik Galberg Jacobsen for his invaluable help, not least in helping prepare the chapter on pronunciation, and we are extremely grateful to Dinah Bechshøft at the Danish Ministry of Education for financial support in the preparation phase. Other colleagues and students have provided helpful suggestions, but any errors are ours alone.

The authors primarily responsible for the individual chapters of the book are as follows: Chapters 1, 2, 3, 4 (PH); Chapters 5, 6 (TLN); Chapter 7 (RA); Chapters 8, 9 (TLN); Chapters 10, 11 (RA); Chapters 12, 13, 14 (PH).

Robin Allan, Philip Holmes and
Tom Lundskær-Nielsen
November 1999

Preface to the second edition

This second edition has been prepared by Tom Lundskær-Nielsen and Philip Holmes. Our previous co-author Robin (Bob) Allan decided not to be part of it this time, so we would like to take this opportunity to thank Bob for his past contribution and to acknowledge the great help it was to be allowed to build on Bob's work in Chapters 7, 10 and 11, for which he was chiefly responsible in the first edition. We are pleased to say that much of the structure and data from these chapters has survived in this new edition.

The authors primarily responsible for the individual chapters of the book are as follows: Chapters 2, 3, 4 (PH); Chapters 5, 6, 7, 8, 9, 10 (TLN); Chapters 12, 13, 14 (PH), while the preparation of Chapters 1 and 11 has been a combined effort. For more detailed information on specific grammatical issues, the reader is referred to our *Danish: A Comprehensive Grammar*, 2nd edition (Routledge, 2010).

The first edition of this book appeared in 2000. While this second edition involves no major changes to the structure of the book, there are, nevertheless, some significant alterations, most visibly: an entirely new paragraph numbering system has been used and there have been numerous changes to the content of the book, both in the explanatory text and in the examples. Some new material has also been incorporated. Among the more substantial changes are the following:

- changes to Chapter 2 regarding plural forms and the genitive;
- a rearrangement of, and additions to, parts of Chapter 6;
- a rearrangement of parts of Chapter 7;
- a revision of Chapter 11, including the addition of a section on phrases;
- alterations to the assimilation of foreign loans in Chapter 12;
- a new section on the guidelines for use of the comma in Chapter 14;

- use of the traditional comma (including 'startkomma') in the relevant examples; and
- an update of the bibliography.

For this second edition, we have greatly benefited from the advice offered by a few anonymous readers whose opinions were sought by Routledge. We are immensely grateful to Martin Fiedler for his painstaking labours on our behalf and have adopted many of his numerous suggestions and recommendations. Finally, we wish to express our thanks to Samantha Vale Noya, Assistant Editor at Routledge, for her support and cooperation.

Tom Lundskær-Nielsen and Philip Holmes
Cambridge and Kineton, September 2010

Symbols and abbreviations used in the text

[ ]	phonetic script
[iː]	long vowel
2+ syllables	two or more syllables
kolleg(a)er, (at)	letter, syllable or word may be omitted
ringer	stem **ring** plus ending **-er**
der/som	alternatives
'kalde, stu'd<u>e</u>re	stressed syllable
x → y	**x** becomes **y** (e.g. when an ending is added)
MC, SC	main clause, sub-ordinate clause
hv-question	question introduced by an interrogative pronoun (**hv-**)
pron.	pronunciation
⊗	'plus zero' (i.e. no ending is added to a word form)
*	incorrect form or ungrammatical construction
S	subject
FS	formal subject
RS	real subject

InfS	subject of an infinitive
Subj.Comp.	subject complement
O	object
DO	direct object
IO	indirect object
V	verb
FV	finite verb
NFV	non-finite verb
intrans.	intransitive verb
trans.	transitive verb
prep.	preposition
Prep.Comp.	prepositional complement
sub. conj.	subordinating conjunction
a	clausal adverbial (position)
A	sentence adverbial (position)
F	front position
k	link position (conjunctions)
X_1, X_2	extra positions
FE	first element (in compounds)
SE	second element (in compounds)

Chapter 1

Pronunciation and spelling

This brief account of Danish pronunciation uses a modified version of IPA (International Phonetic Alphabet).

1.1 Vowel sounds

1.1.1 *Vowels and their pronunciation*

1.1.1.1 Unrounded vowels

I		E			Æ	
[iː]	[i]	[eː]	[e]	[ə]	[ɛː]	[ɛ]
smile	lille	dele	hedde	pibe	kæle	tælle

A						
[aː]	[a]	[ɑː]	[ɑ]			
male	bal	vare	pragt			

1.1.1.2 Rounded vowels

- Rounded front vowels

Y		Ø				
[yː]	[y]	[øː]	[ø]	[œː]	[œ]
hyle	fylde	føle	øl	gøre	børn

• Rounded back vowels

U		O		Å			
[u:]	[u]	[o:]	[o]	[å:]	[å]	[ɔ:]	[ɔ]
bule	kulde	skole	foto	måle	bombe	åre	bånd

Notes:

The pronunciation of the letters **i, o, u, y** when representing short vowels is often more open than is usually associated with these letters:

finde [fenə], **bombe** [båmbə], **kul** [kål], **skylle** [sgølə]

The pronunciation of **e, æ, a, ø, å** before and after **r** is more open than in other positions:

long vowels: **ren, træ, fare, frø, gøre, får**

short vowels: **fred, fræk, fra, var, krølle, børste, rådhus**

1.1.1.3 The position of Danish vowels

Unrounded vowels

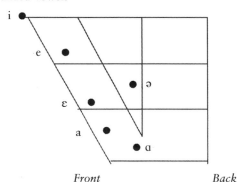

Front   *Back*

Rounded vowels

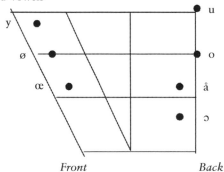

Front   *Back*

1.1.1.4 Vowels by articulation

	Front		Back	
	Unrounded	*Rounded*	*Unrounded*	*Rounded*
Closed	i	y		u
Half closed	e	ø		o
Half open	ɛ/a	œ		å
Open			ɑ	ɔ

1.1.1.5 Approximate equivalent to pronunciation

(Here, 'English' = Standard British English)

Long i	[iː]	ee in English 'bee'
Short i	[i]	i in English 'sin'
Long e	[eː]	No equivalent in English, cf. es in French 'les'
Short e	[e]	i in English 'if'
Unstressed e	[ə]	initial a in English 'again'
Long æ	[ɛː]	ai in English 'said'
Short æ	[ɛ]	e in English 'pet'
Long a	[aː]	a in English 'bad', but slightly more open
Short a	[a]	a in English 'hat'
Long (open) a	[ɑː]	a in English 'card'
Short (open) a	[ɑ]	ea in English 'heart', but shorter
Long y	[yː]	No equivalent in English, cf. ü in German 'Bühne'
Short y	[y]	No equivalent in English, cf. ü in German 'Glück'
Long ø	[øː]	No equivalent in English, cf. ö in German 'schön'
Short ø	[ø]	No equivalent in English, cf. eux in French 'deux'
Long (open) ø	[œː]	No equivalent in English, cf. eu in French 'leur'
Short (open) ø	[œ]	No equivalent in English, cf. eu in French 'neuf'
Long u	[uː]	oo in English 'room'
Short u	[u]	u in English 'full'
Long o	[oː]	No equivalent in English, cf. o in German 'froh'
Short o	[o]	No equivalent in English, cf. eau in French 'beau'
Long å	[åː]	No equivalent in English, French or German
Short å	[å]	No equivalent in English, French or German
Long (open) å	[ɔː]	a in English 'all'
Short (open) å	[ɔ]	o in English 'hot'

Notes:

The pronunciation of **e** is very variable and difficult to predict. In unstressed syllables, the letter **e** is pronounced as schwa [ə]:

gribe [griːbə], **flue** [fluːə], **gammel** [gaməl], **billede** [beləðə], **værelse** [vɛːrəlsə], **fælles** [fɛləs]

-er often merges and is pronounced [ɔ]: **sommer** [sɔmɔ], **søster** [søsdɔ]

-re and **-rer** are pronounced [ɔ]: **lære/lærer** [lɛːɔ]

For the loss of **e** in the pronunciation of some words, see 1.2.6.

1.1.2 | *Vowel length and spelling*

1.1.2.1

A double consonant or consonant group between two vowels usually indicates that the preceding vowel is short; a single consonant that it is long (but see 2.2).

Long	*Short*
VCV	VCCV
læse	**læsse**
lyse	**tyske**
kæle	**vælte**
smile	**lille**
lune	**kunne**
skrabe	**krabbe**

Exceptions:

Long vowel + double consonant is found in some words in -æ- (which is long): **æg** – **ægget**, **æt** – **ætten**, some words in -**dd**, -**tt**: **bredde, vidde, otte, sjette** and a few others: **hoste, påske**.

Vowels before -**gl**, -**gn** where the **g** is silent are long: **fugle, ligne**.

1.1.2.2

The single final consonants **b** and **n** usually follow a long vowel: **reb, gren**. But if the single final consonant is **m, p, t, k, g** (pronounced hard as [g]) or **f**, the preceding vowel is usually short: **lam, krop, hat, blik, bryg, stof**. It is not always possible to predict whether the vowel is long or short from the written form, as one of the two consonants is usually dropped in final position in Danish. This is especially true in the case of **l, s**:

Long	Short
sal	smal
sol	øl
stil	til
hus	bus
las	glas

Only when these words are inflected (i.e. when a vowel is added after the consonant) can we determine from the single or double consonant what the vowel length is:

Long	Short
salen	smalle
solen	øllet
huset	bussen
lasen	glasset

1.1.2.3

Final stressed vowels are usually long:

se, sy, tro, gå

Exceptions:
These include some words usually unstressed in the sentence, e.g. personal pronouns: **du, vi, I, de**, adverbs **nu, så** and the interjections **ja, jo**.

1.1.3 Diphthongs

Danish diphthongs are of two kinds. Notice the spelling of these sounds.

- Diphthongs with [i] as their second component:

ej, aj, eg, ig	[ɑi]	**hej, maj, leg, mig, dig, sig**
øj, øg	[ɔi]	**høj, tøj, fløjte, løg, nøgle**

  Rarely:

uj	[ui]	**huje**

- Diphthongs with [u] as their second component:

iv	[iu]	**ivrig, livlig, tvivl**
ev	[eu]	**blev, hev**
ev	[ɛu]	**evne, brev**
yv	[yu]	**syv, tyv**
øv	[øu]	**øvre, støv**
øv	[œu]	**støvle, vrøvl**
ov	[ɔu]	**lov, skov**
ag	[ɒu]	**hagl**
av	[ɑu]	**hav** (sea)
av	[au]	**gav**
og	[åu]	**bog, sprog**

1.2 Consonant sounds

1.2.1 Stops: p, t, k

1.2.1.1

There are nine stops in Danish.

	Unvoiced		Voiced
	Aspirated	Unaspirated	
Lip sounds (bilabial)	p	b	m
Tongue tip sounds (alveolar)	t	d	n
Tongue root sounds (velar)	k	g	ŋ

1.2.1.2

p, t and k in initial position before a full vowel are aspirated stops:

p	[p]	**passe, pose**
t	[t]	**tand, til**
k	[k]	**kirke, komme**

In all other positions (including after s- and when doubled), **p, t, k** are unaspirated stops and pronounced [b], [d], [g]:

p	[b]	**spille, tæppe, stop**
t	[d]	**støj, rotte, kat**
k	[g]	**sko, lokke, tak**

This produces homophones, so that **lappe** and **labbe** are both pronounced [labə].

1.2.1.3

Notice the following special pronunciations and spellings in loanwords:

p- is silent in the group **ps-**		**pseudo'nym, psyko'log**
qu	[k]	**en'quete, manne'quin**
	[kv]	**quickstep, quiz**
-t is silent in some French loans		**buf'fet, de'but, fi'let**
-ti-	[ʃ] or [sj]	**funk'tion, informa'tion, sta'tion**

1.2.2 Stops: b, d, g

1.2.2.1

The letter **b** is pronounced [b] in all positions:

bil, briller, dyb, skæbne, åben

1.2.2.2

The letter **d** is usually pronounced in one of three ways:

- 'hard' **d**   [d]   initially and before a full vowel:

  dag, dusin, dø, djærv, drama, sol'dat, stu'dent, heldig

- 'soft' **d**   [ð]   after a vowel and when doubled:

  mad, møde, tredive, smedje, bedre, sødme, hedde, sidde

Exceptions:

d is [d] in **ad'dere, middag, bredde, vidde**

moder, mother; **fader**, father; and **broder**, brother, are usually abbreviated **mor, far, bror** in both pronunciation and spelling.

7

- silent **d**

  d is silent in the combinations:

  -ld: ild, sild, kildre, melde

  -nd: mand, vind, dundre, kende

  d is, therefore, silent in words ending in **-ende**:

  spændende, søskende, tyvende

  -rd: bord, gård, gærde

Exceptions:

- **ld, nd, rd** are pronounced [ld], [nd], [rd] respectively when they are followed by -ig, -isk:

heldig, mandig, værdig	(cf. silent **d** in **held, mand, værd**)
he'raldisk, indisk, nordisk	(cf. silent **d** in **alder, ind, nord**)

- **ld** is pronounced [ld] in the following frequent words incorporating **-ldr-**:

  aldrig, ældre, for'ældre, skildre

- **nd** is pronounced [nd] in many words incorporating **-ndr-**:

  andre, hindre, ændre

- **d** is also silent in the combinations:

  -ds: spids, klods, kryds, vidste

  -dt: skidt, fedt, godt, rødt

1.2.2.3

The letter **g** is usually pronounced in one of three ways:

- 'hard' **g** [g]

  before a full vowel: **gæst, gade, liga**

  when doubled: **kigge, lægge**

  before -t: **vigtig, vægt**

  following a short vowel: **mug, myg, ryg**

  (cf. inflected forms: **muggen, myggen, ryggen**)

- 'soft' **g** [j] (or silent) after **i, e, æ, a, y, ø**:

  krig, steg (from the verb **stege**), **læge, dag, syg, søge**

- silent **g**

    (a) **g** is silent in the combinations **-lg** in some cases:

    salg, valg

    (b) **g** is silent after **u**:

    rug, uge, kugle

    (c) **g** becomes [u] after **ra, r, o, å**:

    krage, sorg, bog, tåge

Note:

Adjectives normally do not have hard **g** in the neuter: **klogt** [klåud].

Note also the following loanwords involving the letter **g**:

g	[dj] in some English loans	**gentleman, manager**
g	[dʃ] in some English loans	**image, management**
g	[ʃ] in some French loans	**aubergine, logi, regi**
g	[ʃ] before e	**bagage, budget, garage, genere, ingeniør, prestige**
-gn	[nj] in some French loans	**champagne, cognac**

1.2.3 *s, c, sc, x, z*

s	[s]	**se, sol, spille, glas, vise**
s	is usually silent in French loans	**apropos, en gros, pommes, frites, succes**
-si-	[ʃ] or [sj]	**division, pension**
c	[s] before i, e, æ, y, ø	**cirkus, præcis, pjece, cæsar, cykel, cølibat**
c	[k] in other cases and before a, o, u	**café, computer, curling, picnic**
sc	[s] before i, e	**science fiction, scene**
	[sg] in other cases	**scoop, score, mascara, screene**
x	[s] initially	**xenofobi, xylofon**
x	[gs] after a vowel	**sex, taxa**
z	[s]	**benzin, jazz, ozon, zoologi**
zz	[ds] in some Italian loans	**pizza, mezzosopran**

| 1.2.4 | *f, h, j, sj, sh, ch* |

f	[f]	fem, fisk, kaffe
f	is silent in	af
f	[u] in af-	affald, afsked
h	[h]	hest, hotel, hus
h	is silent in **hj-, hv-**	hjul, hjem, hjælpe, hjørne (15 words in all)
		hvid, hvis, hvem, hvad, hvor, hvordan (some 30 words in all)
j	[j] before a vowel	jakke, jord, kjole, stjæle
j	[ʃ] in some French loans	jalousi, jargon, journalist
j	[dj] in some English loans	jazz, jeans, jeep, job, juice
j	is silent in	vejr
sj	[ʃ]	sjov, sjuske, sjælden
sh	[ʃ] in English loans	shampoo, shorts, sherry, finish
ch	[ʃ]	chef, chok, chauffør, match

| 1.2.5 | *l, n, ng, nk, r, v, w* |

l	[l]	lille, luft, plante, folk
	often silent in	til, vil, skal, skulle
n	[n]	nabo, sne, skinne, ven
ng	[ŋ]	seng, bange, finger, synge
ng	[ŋg] stressed g or before **a, u, o**	fungere, tangent, tango
nk	[ŋk] stressed **k** or before a consonant or **a, u, o**	blanket, Frankrig, banko
nk	[ŋg]	tank, enke, synke, tænke

Note:

an	[ɑŋ] in the following:	ambu'lance, branche, chance, restau'rant
en	[ɑŋ] in the following:	konkur'rence, enga'gere, pen'sion
on	[ɔŋ] in the following:	be'ton, jar'gon, per'ron, konkur'rere

r	[r]	ravn, ride, rose
r	[ə] in endings: vowel + r(e), -er	være, roser, sender
-r	is silent in French loans	ate'lier, fo'yer
v	[v]	vask, kvinde, svare, avis
v	[u] (see 1.1.3)	hævn, tavle, sovs
v	is silent in the ending -lv	selv, sølv, tolv, halv, gulv

Exceptions:

lv is pronounced [lv] in **hvælv**, **ulv** and in inflected forms: selve, halve.

w	[v] or [w]	sweater, weekend, whisky
w	[u]	cowboy, bowle, show

1.2.6 Syllable loss and vowel merger

1.2.6.1

Unstressed e [ə] in a medial syllable is often not pronounced:

interessant [intrə'san'd], **elleve** (or **elve**) ['ɛlvə], **mærkelig** ['maɔgli], **husene** [huː'snə], **lugtede** ['lågdð], **faldende** ['falnə], **cykelen** (or **cyklen**) ['syglən]

This also occurs in the present tense of certain common verbs, where a consonant + unstressed e is not pronounced:

beder ['beʼɔ], **klæder** ['klɛːɔ], **tager** [tɑʼ], **bliver** ['bliʼɔ], **giver** ['giʼɔ], **siger** ['siːʼɔ], **bruger** ['bruːɔ], **spørger** ['sbœɔ], **bærer** ['bɛɔ], **skærer** [sgɛɔ], **rører** ['rœɔ]

1.2.6.2

In rapid speech, unstressed e [ə] tends to merge with adjacent vowels:

	Normal tempo	*Rapid tempo*
stue	[sduːə]	[sduːu]
pige	[piːə]	[piːi]

Pronunciation of some frequent words

Some words of high frequency are not pronounced phonetically. They include the following, which are often found in unstressed positions in the clause (see 1.4.1).

Pronouns:

jeg	[jɑ]	**de**	[di]	**De**	[di]
mig	[mɑi]	**dig**	[dɑi]	**sig**	[sɑi]

Modal verbs:

kan	[ka]	**skal**	[sga]	**vil**	[ve]
kunne	[ku]	**skulle**	[sgu]		

Verbs:

have	[ha]	**blive**	[bliː]	**tage**	[ta]
var	[vɑ]				

Adverbs:

ikke	[eg]

Conjunctions, etc.:

og	[ɔ]	**at**	[ad] or [a]

Han lå og sov. / Hun sagde, at hun ville komme i dag.

at as an infinitive marker [ɔ]

Glem ikke at skrive! Don't forget to write!

Prepositions:

med	[mɛ]	**til**	[te]	**ved**	[ve]

1.3 The glottal stop

1.3.1 *The glottal stop (stød)*

'Stød' (marked ') is a peculiarly Danish phenomenon, not found in other North or West European languages. In English, it comes closest to the glottal stop (a sound like that found in Cockney 'bottle' [bɔ'l], 'water' [wɔː'ə] or 'little' [li'l]). However, in the glottal stop there is complete closure of the vocal cords (glottis), whereas the Danish 'stød' is more of a 'creaky voice', produced by irregularities in the vibration of the vocal cords, but without complete closure. 'Stød' is a functional phoneme that is sometimes able to distinguish words that are otherwise pronounced identically. Note the following words with and without 'stød':

No 'stød'		'Stød'	
man	one	**mand'**	man
hun	she	**hund'**	dog
mig	me	**maj'**	May
møller	miller	**Møll'er**	(surname)
maler	painter	**ma'ler**	paints
byger	showers	**by'er**	towns
(plural of **byge**)		(plural of **by**)	
tanken	the thought	**tan'ken**	the tank
(definite of **tanke**)		(definite of **tank**)	

Notice that, in the last two cases, 'stød' is used to indicate a monosyllabic stem (**by, tank**) and distinguish it from a bisyllabic stem without 'stød' (**byge, tanke**).

Note:
The 'stød' is not found in some southern Danish dialects.

1.3.2 | *General rules for 'stød'*

'Stød' is related to syllables, not words, and can normally only be present:

- in *stressed* syllables (though not all stressed syllables); and
- in *voiced* syllables.

It must have a '*stød* base', so only two types of syllable can have 'stød':

- syllables *with a long vowel* (with or without a following consonant); the long vowel then carries the 'stød':

  i's, bi'l, li'v, bageri', be'n, café', æ'g, hu's, ny', bå'd

- syllables *with a short vowel + voiced consonant*; the voiced consonant then carries the 'stød' (but 'stød' is not present in all cases):

  ler', mand', kam', skal', bord', grøn'

13

A word such as the adjective **let**, therefore, cannot have 'stød', as it has a short vowel and voiceless consonant. Nor can, for example, **hat, kop, hest, snaps.**

Notice that [b], [d], [g] are voiceless in Danish and *do not* take stød:

hoppe, otte, lægge

It is primarily monosyllables that have stød:

mund', grøn', frem', gå', barn'

1.3.3 | Inflected forms – 'stød' variations

1.3.3.1

The general rule is that inflection does not alter the 'stød' pattern in inflected forms:

with 'stød': **hu's, hu'set; vej', vej'en; bo', bor'**

without 'stød': **drage, drager; fare, farer**

1.3.3.2

In the summary below, the focus is, however, on those cases where the pattern *does* change.

- 'Stød' in nouns

  Plural forms:

  -r plurals – these normally end in **-e** in the singular and do not have 'stød':

  en rose, roser

  -er plurals – 'stød' is often lost in the plural of nouns in **-l, -m, -n, -r** + consonant:

  en form', former

  'stød' is lost in the plural of nouns ending in **-nd** where the **d** is silent:

  en stund', stunder

  'stød' is lost in the plural of nouns ending in **d** [ð]:

  en tid', tider

-e plurals – 'stød' is often lost in the plural:

et hu's, huse

Zero-plurals – the same rule applies in the singular and the plural (either with or without 'stød' throughout):

mu's, mu's

Nouns with end article:

Nouns ending in a voiced consonant may add 'stød':

gulv, gulv'et

- 'Stød' in adjectives

Neuter form in **-t** – most adjectives do not change.

Adjectives ending in a stressed vowel lose 'stød' when adding the neuter ending:

fri', frit

Adjectives ending in **d** [ð] lose 'stød' when adding the neuter ending:

dø'd, dødt

Plural forms in **-e** – monosyllables generally lose 'stød' in the plural:

dum', dumme

Comparatives and superlatives:

Adjectives with 'stød' generally lose it in the comparative and superlative:

nem', nemmere, nemmest; ung', yngre, yngst; se'n, senere, senest

- 'Stød' in verbs

Weak verbs (Conjugations I, II, III):

These tend to lose 'stød' in the past tense if they already possess it in the infinitive or present tense:

Infinitive	Present	Past	Past participle	Meaning
bo'	**bor'**	**boede**	**bo'et**	live, stay
tale	**ta'ler**	**talte**	**ta'lt**	talk
dø'	**dør'**	**døde**	**død'**	die

Strong verbs (Conjugation IV):

Those with 'stød' in the infinitive or present/past tense tend to lose the 'stød' in the past participle:

stå'	**står'**	**stod'**	**stået**	stand
finde	**find'er**	**fand't**	**fundet**	find

-**r** stem verbs only have 'stød' in the past tense:

bære	**bærer**	**bar'**	**båret**	carry
fare	**farer**	**for'**	**faret**	hurry

Imperatives:

If the infinitive has a long vowel, 'stød' appears in the imperative:

købe, kø'b!

If the infinitive has a short vowel + a voiced consonant, it takes 'stød' in the imperative:

kalde, kald'!

1.4 Stress

1.4.1 Stress – introduction

In Danish – as in English – there is an important distinction between words that have stress in the clause and those that do not. All the words that are significant for the meaning of a clause are stressed (see the list in 1.4.2). This is called *clause stress*. But different syllables within these stressed words may also be stressed. This is known as *word stress*. The method shown for marking is illustrated here:

Han er 'tredive 'år og fri'sør.
He is 30 years old and a hairdresser.

Below are examples of:

- types of words in the clause that have clause stress;
- types of words that are usually unstressed;
- phrases with two-word stress;
- stressed and unstressed syllables within words; and
- stressed and unstressed prefixes and suffixes within words.

1.4.2 | Stressed in the clause

Nouns

Nouns are usually stressed:

'Lisa har 'købt et 'hus.   **'Huset 'har en al'tan.**
Lisa has bought a house.   The house has a balcony.

Exceptions:

Nouns expressing quantity:

et antal 'børn   a number of children

Titles before proper nouns:

redaktør 'Nielsen   (the) editor Nielsen

Verbs

Simple verbs are usually stressed:

'Eva 'løber og 'svømmer 'hele 'ugen.
Eva runs and swims all week.

'Palle 'læser en 'bog.
Palle reads a book.

But verbs are unstressed when followed by a complement:

Hun blev 'syg.   She fell ill.
            Subj.Comp.

Han er poli'tibetjent.   He is a policeman.
            Subj.Comp.

Note:

er is pronounced [ɛɔ].

Expressions of manner, place, time (MPT-expressions):

These expressions usually have stress:

'Nu bor hun i Kor'sør.   Now she lives in Korsør.
MPT   MPT

'Lukker bu'tikken 'tidligt i 'dag?   Is the shop shutting early today?
              MPT   MPT

| 1.4.3 | *Unstressed in the clause* |

Modal verbs and modal equivalents

'Sven kan blive pro'fessor.　　　Sven can become a professor.

'Lene gider 'ikke lave 'mad.　　　Lene can't be bothered to cook.

Pronouns and hv-words (interrogatives)

jeg [jɑ], **du, han, hun, den, det** [de], **vi, I, De, de** [di]
I, you, he, she, it, it, we, you, they

mig [mɑj], **dig** [dɑj], **sig** [sɑj], **ham, hende, os, jer, Dem, dem**
me, you, himself, etc., him, her, us, you, them

Hvad 'sagde du?　　　What did you say?

Hvem 'så hende?　　　Who saw her?

Exception:

When the object pronoun is in initial position or is contrasted, it acquires stress:

'Hende elsker jeg, men 'ham synes jeg 'ikke om.
(cf. **Jeg elsker hende.**　　　I love her.)
Her I love but him I do not like.

Possessive pronouns when used with a noun

min, din, sin, hans, hendes
my, you, his, etc., his, her

dens, dets, vores, jeres, Deres, deres
its, our, your, their

Det er vores 'søn.　　　It's our son.

Conjunctions

og [ɔ], **men, at**
and, but, that

da, når, om, hvis
when/since, when, whether, if

Han 'sagde, *at* han var 'træt　　　He said that he was tired and hungry.
og 'sulten.

1.4.4 | *Two-word stress*

Where two or more words belong together in one semantic unit, the last word in the phrase is stressed.

Preposition + noun

(Kig) i 'bogen.
(Look) in the book.

(De kommer) i 'dag.
(They're coming) today.

Indefinite article + noun

en 'bil
a car

et 'hus
a house

Verb + particle

smide 'ud
throw out

vende 'om
turn round

Verb₁ + Verb₂

Jeg skal 'gå.
I must go.

De var 'rejst.
They had left.

Infinitive marker + verb

at 'se
to see

at 'vente
to wait

Verb + complement

(Han) er 'høj.
(He) is tall.

(Hun) er gra'vid.
(She) is pregnant.

end/som + the word compared

(Hun er højere) end 'Ole.
(She is taller) than Ole.

(Hun er lige så 'gammel) som 'ham.
(She is as old) as he is.

Pronoun + adverb

dette 'her
this

de 'der
those

Time, measurement

klokken 'tre
three o'clock

to kopper 'kaffe
two cups of coffee

First name + surname

Anders 'Hansen

1.4.5 | **Stressed and unstressed syllables**

1.4.5.1

Many indigenous non-compounds with more than one syllable, and all those with unstressed e [ə], have stress on the first syllable, and either secondary stress or no stress on the following syllables:

Stress on the first syllable:

'cykel, 'venlig, 'huse, 'eng,lænder, 'al,tid, 'ejen,dom, 'skrive, 'skriver, 'skrivende

Stress on another syllable:

- words with the prefixes **be-, er-, for-**:

  be'retning, account; **be'tale**, pay; **er'fare**, experience; **for'nemmelse**, feeling

- words with the suffix **-ere**:

  par'kere, park; **stu'dere**, study

- many foreign loans:

  restau'rant, restaurant; **re'vy**, revue; **universi'tet**, university

- words with foreign suffixes:

  regis'sør, stage manager; **gym'nast**, gymnast; **musi'kant**, musician

1.4.5.2

Compounds usually have stress on the first syllable:

'arbejds,plads, 'læse,bog, 'morgen,mad, 'skrive,bord

1.4.5.3 Some problem words

Many words that are familiar from English are, however, stressed differently from English:

chauf'før, choko'lade, demo'krat, demonstra'tion, direk'tør, fa'milie, fi'gur, institu'tion, interes'seret, journa'list, 'juli, ka'tolsk, kul'tur, littera'tur, milli'on, mi'nut, mo'del, na'tur, ner'vøs, passa'ger, poli'tik, por'tion, pri'vat, pro'gram, refe'rence, religi'on, restau'rant, stu'dent, toi'let, traditio'nel, universi'tet, vegeta'tion

1.4.6 Stressed prefixes

These include amplifying, negating and contrasting prefixes.

a-, ante-, anti-, eks-, hyper-, mis-, pseudo-, semi-, super-, ultra-, und-, van-, vice-, ærke-:

'asocial, 'antedatere, 'antisemitisk, 'eksmand, 'hyperaktiv, 'mistanke, 'pseudovidenskabelig, 'semifinale, 'supernova, 'ultrakort, 'undgå, 'vanvittig, 'vicedirektør, 'ærkedansk

1.4.7 Stressed suffixes

Many of these were originally loan suffixes.

-abel, -al, -ance, -ant, -ast, -at, -ere, -esse, -graf, -ik, -isme, -ist, -sion, -tet, -tion, -ør, -øs, -øse:

vari'abel, origi'nal, tole'rance, konso'nant, gym'nast, appa'rat, koncen'trere, stewar'desse, foto'graf, repu'blik, tu'risme, receptio'nist, ekspan'sion, universi'tet, sta'tion, konduk'tør, gene'røs, mas'søse

1.4.8 Unstressed prefixes

These include many loan prefixes.

ab-, be-, de-, er-, for-, ge-, in- (il-, im-, ir-), intro-, kom-, kon- (kol-, kor-), mono-, pan-, para-, peri-, poly-, trans-:

ab'norm, be'tale, degra'dere, er'hverv, for'stå, ge'mytlig, inva'lid, introduk'tion, kompag'ni, kon'cern, mono'pol, pante'isme, para'doks, peri'fer, poly'krom, trans'port

Exceptions:

'in- to express negation:	**'ineffektiv, 'intolerant**
'for- meaning 'before', 'front':	**'forstad, i 'forgårs**

1.4.9 | *Unstressed suffixes*

-de, -else, -ig, -(n)ing, -isk, -me, -ske:

'højde, 'følelse, 'rolig, 'regning, 'nordisk, 'sødme, 'sygeplejerske

Chapter 2

Nouns

2.1 Gender

Danish nouns are either common gender (**en**- words) or neuter gender (**et**- words). The corresponding indefinite article (see 2.4.1) is **en** or **et**, 'a(n)'. About 75 per cent of nouns are **en**- words and 25 per cent **et**- words:

Common gender		*Neuter gender*	
Indefinite		*Indefinite*	
en **mand**	*en* **uge**	*et* **hus**	*et* **æble**
a man	a week	a house	an apple

Gender determines the form with end article (definite article) singular (see 2.4.1):

Common gender		*Neuter gender*	
Definite		*Definite*	
mand**en**	ug**en**	hus**et**	æbl**et**
the man	the week	the house	the apple

Gender also determines the form of the adjective and some pronouns, as these agree in gender and number with nouns (see 3.2.1–3.2.5, 5.1.2, 5.4):

en stor by	**et stort hus**
a big town	a big house
byen er stor	**huset er stort**
the town is big	the house is big

2.1.1 | Gender rules

2.1.1.1 Common gender by meaning

Personal names and nouns denoting human beings, animals, plants, trees, festivals and months, and names of rivers are generally common gender:

en dreng, a boy; **en pige**, a girl; **en lærer**, a teacher; **en søster**, a sister; **en udlænding**, a foreigner; **en gås**, a goose; **en hund**, a dog; **en kat**, a cat; **en ko**, a cow; **en laks,** a salmon; **en rose**, a rose; **en birk**, a birch; **en eg**, an oak; **i julen**, at Christmas; **Themsen**, the Thames

Gender in proper names is normally only shown by congruence with other words:

Bo er ung endnu.   Bo is still young.   (**ung** = common gender)

Januar var kold.   January was cold.   (**kold** = common gender)

Cf. also:

Danmark er ikke stort.   Denmark is not big.   (**stort** = neuter gender)

Exceptions:

et **barn**, a child; et **bud**, a messenger; et **individ**, an individual; et **medlem**, a member; et **menneske**, a human being; et **vidne**, a witness; et **dyr**, an animal; et **egern**, a squirrel; et **føl**, a foal; et **kid**, a kid; et **får**, a sheep; et **lam**, a lamb; et **møl**, a moth; et **svin**, a pig; et **æsel**, a donkey; et **bær**, a berry; et **frø**, a seed; et **træ**, a tree; compounds in -bær, -frø, -træ.

2.1.1.2 Common gender by form

-ance	**en ambulance**, an ambulance
-ans	**en substans**, a substance
-ant	**en repræsentant**, a representative
-de	**en bredde**, a breadth; **en længde**, a length
-dom	**en ejendom**, a property; **en sygdom**, an illness
-é	**en allé**, an avenue; **en café**, a café
-else	**en bevægelse**, a movement; **en skuffelse**, a disappointment

Exceptions:
et **spøgelse**, a ghost; et **værelse**, a room.

-en	verbal nouns: **en formåen**, an ability; **en kunnen**, a capacity; **en væren**, (a) being; **en kommen og gåen**, coming and going
-ence	**en konference**, a conference
-ens	**en frekvens**, a frequency
-er	**en lærer**, a teacher
-hed	**en lejlighed**, a flat; **en tavshed**, a silence
-ik	**en grammatik**, a grammar
-ing	**en regning**, a bill; **en slægtning**, a relative; **en yndling**, a favourite
-ion	**en diskussion**, a discussion; **en situation**, a situation
-isme	**socialisme(n)**, socialism
-ør	**en direktør**, a director

For feminine suffixes, see 2.1.1.7.

2.1.1.3 Neuter by meaning

Nouns denoting substances, areas and localities, letters of the alphabet and nouns formed from other word classes (e.g. pronouns, interjections) are generally neuter:

(et) brød, bread; **glas**, glass; **jern**, iron; **kød**, meat; **papir**, paper; **snavs**, dirt; **vand**, water; **et kontinent**, a continent; **et sogn**, a parish; **et torv**, a square; **et langt i**, a long i; **et ja**, a yes; **jeget**, the ego.

Exceptions:
en by, a town; en ø, an island; verden, the world.

This also applies to proper nouns (names) for geographical locations. In the case of countries, the word **land(et)** is assumed:

England er dejligt om sommeren.	England is lovely in summer.
det lille Danmark	little Denmark

Exceptions:
Notice that, for towns, the word **by-en** is assumed: (Byen) **København er stor.**

2.1.1.4 Neuter by form

-dømme	**et omdømme**, a reputation
-ed	**et hoved**, a head
-ende	**et udseende**, an appearance

Exceptions:
These include people: **en gående**, a pedestrian; **en studerende**, a student.

-ri	**et bageri**, a bakery; **et batteri**, a battery
-um	**et gymnasium**, an upper secondary school; **et museum**, a museum

2.1.1.5 Suffixes where gender varies

-al	**en lineal**, a ruler; BUT: **et ideal**, an ideal
-ar	**en bibliotekar**, a librarian; BUT: **et eksemplar**, a copy
-at	usually neuter: **et certifikat**, a certificate; BUT: (people) **en demokrat**, a democrat
-i	**en industri**, an industry; BUT: **et parti**, a political party
-sel	**en trussel**, a threat; BUT: **et fængsel**, a prison
-skab	**en egenskab**, a quality; BUT: **et ægteskab**, a marriage

2.1.1.6 Compound nouns

These nearly always take the gender of the second element in the compound:

en skole	+ **et køkken**	→	**et skolekøkken**, a school kitchen
et køkken	+ **en kniv**	→	**en køkkenkniv**, a kitchen knife

Exceptions:
et måltid, a meal, cf. en tid, a time; et bogstav, a letter of the alphabet, cf. en stav, a stave.

2.1.1.7 Masculines and feminines

Feminine suffixes include: **-esse, -inde, -ske, -øse**

Matrimonial feminines are now rare: **baronesse**, baroness; **grevinde**, countess

Functional feminines in -inde, -ske, -trice, etc. have recently been curtailed as a result of a desire for gender equality: e.g. **lærer** and **lærerinde** → **lærer**, teacher; **nabo** and **naboerske** → **nabo**, neighbour

Some gender-neutral terms have also been introduced recently: **folketingsmand** → **folketingsmedlem**, Member of the Danish Parliament

In a few cases where the gender is important, these distinctions have been retained: **elsker** and **elskerinde**, lover; **samlever** and **samleverske**, cohabitee; **ven** and **veninde**, (male/female) friend

2.2 Plurals and declensions

2.2.1 *Plurals – introduction*

2.2.1.1 Plural endings

Danish nouns have three ways of forming regular plurals, namely by adding one of the following endings:

-(e)r, -e, zero (i.e. no plural ending)

About 75 per cent of nouns end in -(e)r, 15 per cent in -e and 10 per cent in **zero**. Note that nouns of both genders are found in all groups.

2.2.1.2 Declensions

Nouns are grouped into declensions according to their plural form:

First declension *-(e)r*		*Second declension* *-e*		*Third declension* **zero** *plural*	
en by a town	**to byer** two towns	**en lærer** a teacher	**to lærere** two teachers	**en fisk** a fish	**to fisk** two fish
et sted a place	**to steder** two places	**et land** a country	**to lande** two countries	**et lys** a light	**to lys** two lights

2.2.2 | Predicting plurals

Most plural forms can be predicted accurately from the form of the singular:

2.2.2.1 | Structure and gender

Monosyllabic en-nouns ending in a consonant:

add **-e**   **en hund**   **to hunde**

Polysyllabic en-nouns ending in -e:

add **-r**   **en pige**   **to piger**

Polysyllabic nouns ending in a consonant:

add **-er**   **en regning**   **to regninger**

Polysyllabic nouns with stress on the last syllable:

add **-er**   **en appelsin**   **to appelsiner**

2.2.2.2 | Form of the final syllable

Nouns ending in -dom:

add **-(m)e**   **en ejendom**   **to ejendomme**

Nouns ending in unstressed -er:

add **-e**   **en dansker**   **to danskere**

Nouns ending in -hed:

add **-er**   **en nyhed**   **to nyheder**

Nouns ending in -i:

add **-er**   **et konditori**   **to konditorier**

Nouns ending in -ion:

add **-er**   **en station**   **to stationer**

Nouns ending in -skab (with abstract sense):

add **-er**   **et venskab**   **to venskaber**

(But with literal sense: et skab, a cupboard/wardrobe:

add **-e**   **et køkkenskab**   **to køkkenskabe**)

Nouns ending in -um   drop **-um**

add **-er**   **et museum**   **to museer**

2.2.3 | *Plurals in -(e)r (en gade – gader; et billede – billeder)*

This group (known as the first declension) includes:

2.2.3.1 | Almost all nouns ending in a vowel

(a) Nouns ending in unstressed -e (which add -r in the plural):

en krone – kroner, crown; **en lampe – lamper**, lamp; **et menneske –
mennesker**, human being; **et vindue – vinduer**, window

Exception:

et øje – øjne, eye.

(b) Nouns ending in a stressed vowel:

en by – byer, town; **en ske – skeer**, spoon; **et træ – træer**, tree;
en ø – øer, island; **en å – åer**, river

Exception:

en sko – sko, shoe.

2.2.3.2 | Polysyllabic nouns, especially derivatives and loanwords, many of which have end stress

en avis – aviser, newspaper; **en hilsen – hils(e)ner**, greeting; **et køkken
– køkkener**, kitchen; **en måned – måneder**, month; **en paraply –
paraplyer**, umbrella; **en station – stationer**, station; **en tangent –
tangenter**, tangent, key; **en telefon – telefoner**, telephone; **en turist
– turister**, tourist; **et universitet – universiteter**, university

2.2.3.3 | Polysyllabic nouns ending in **-hed, -skab** (but cf. 2.2.2.2)

en enhed – enheder, unit; **et landskab – landskaber**, landscape

2.2.3.4 | Many monosyllabic common gender nouns ending in a consonant

en blomst – blomster, flower; **en flod – floder**, river; **en slægt – slægter**,
family; **en ven – venner**, friend

2.2.4 | *Plurals in -e (en dag – dage; et hus – huse)*

This group (known as the second declension) includes:

2.2.4.1 | Many monosyllabic common gender nouns ending in a consonant (cf. 2.2.3.4)

en del – dele, part; **en dreng – drenge**, boy; **en fugl – fugle**, bird; **en krig – krige**, war; **en løgn – løgne**, lie; **en stol – stole**, chair; **en vej – veje**, road

2.2.4.2 | Some monosyllabic neuter nouns

et bord – borde, table; **et brev – breve**, letter; **et land – lande**, country

2.2.4.3 | Nouns ending in unstressed **-er** (often denoting people)

en arbejder – arbejdere, worker; **en kunstner – kunstnere**, artist; **en lærer – lærere**, teacher; **en svensker – svenskere**, Swede; **en Århusianer – Århusianere**, inhabitant of Århus

2.2.4.4 | Nouns ending in **-dom, -(n)ing**

en ejendom – ejendomme, property; **en sygdom – sygdomme**, illness; **en udlænding – udlændinge**, foreigner; **en slægtning – slægtninge**, relative

2.2.5 | **Zero-*plural* (en sko – sko; et år – år)**

This group (known as the third declension) includes:

2.2.5.1 | Many monosyllabic neuter nouns

et bær – bær, berry; **et dyr – dyr**, animal; **et glas – glas**, glass; **et kort – kort**, card; **et par – par**, pair/couple; **et sprog – sprog**, language; **et tal – tal**, number; **et æg – æg**, egg; **et år – år**, year

2.2.5.2 | Some polysyllabic neuter nouns ending in a consonant

et fjernsyn – fjernsyn, television; **et spørgsmål – spørgsmål**, question

2.2.5.3 Some monosyllabic common gender nouns

en fejl – fejl, mistake; **en mus – mus**, mouse; **en sko – sko**, shoe; **en sten – sten**, stone; **en ting – ting**, thing

2.2.5.4 Nouns (for temporary occupations) ending in **-ende**

en rejsende – rejsende, traveller; **en studerende – studerende**, student

2.2.6 *Plurals with a vowel change (en tand – tænder)*

2.2.6.1 Vowel change + **er** (first declension)

A → Æ

en hovedstad	hovedstæder	capital
en kraft	kræfter	power
en nat	nætter	night
en tand	tænder	tooth

O → Ø

en bog	bøger	book
en bonde	bønder	farmer
en fod	fødder	feet
en ko	køer	cow

Å → Æ

en hånd	hænder	hand
en tå	tæer	toe

2.2.6.2 Vowel change + **e** (second declension)

A → Æ

en far (fader)	fædre	father

A → Ø

en datter	døtre	daughter

O → Ø

en bror (broder)	brødre	brother
en mor (moder)	mødre	mother

2.2.6.3 Vowel change + **zero** (third declension)

A → Æ

en mand	mænd	man

A → Ø

et barn	børn	child

Å → Æ

en gås	gæs	goose

2.2.7 *Plurals of nouns in -el, -en, -er (en søster – søstre)*

Nouns ending in unstressed -e + -l, -n, -r often drop the stem -e- in the plural.

2.2.7.1 **-er** plurals (first declension)

en aften	aft(e)ner	et eksempel	eksempler
evening		example	
en kartoffel	kartofler	et køkken	køk(ke)ner
potato		kitchen	

2.2.7.2 **-e** plurals (second declension)

en fa(de)r	fædre	et nummer	numre
father		number	
en søster	søstre	et register	registre
sister		register	

2.2.8 *Nouns doubling the final consonant*

Nouns ending in a short stressed vowel and single consonant double the final consonant when adding the plural ending (or end article) (see also 1.1.2):

en bus	busser	bus
en butik	butikker	shop
en hat	hatte	hat

et hotel	hoteller	hotel
en ven	venner	friend
en væg	vægge	wall
en sygdom	sygdomme	illness

2.2.9 Plurals of loanwords

2.2.9.1 Loanwords from Latin and Italian

These tend to retain the plural form from their original language:

| et faktum | fakta | fact |
| et visum | visa | visa |

Notice, however, adaptation to Danish inflections in:

et drama	dramaer	drama
en kollega	kolleg(a)er	colleague
en cello	celloer	cello
et konto	kontoer/konti	account
et gymnasium	gymnasier	upper secondary school
et museum	museer	museum
et centrum	centrummer/centrer	centre
et kursus	kursus/kurser	course

2.2.9.2 Loanwords from English

(a) Some loans retain their plural in -s, at least as an alternative to the Danish plural form:

en check – checks/check; en cowboy – cowboyer/cowboys;
en fan – fans; et foto – fotoer/fotos; en/et gag – gags;
en jumper – jumpere/jumpers; et party – partier/parties;
et show – shows/show

(b) Notice, however, adaptation to Danish inflection in the following words:

with -er: en baby – babyer; en shop – shopper; en weekend – weekender

with -e: en computer – computere; en manager – managere; en sweater – sweatere

with zero: en film – film; et job – job; et point – point

(c) Some nouns occurring in the plural only have a form in -s:

cornflakes, jeans, odds, shorts

2.2.10 Count and non-count nouns

2.2.10.1 Count nouns

Count nouns are nouns that have both a singular and a plural form. They represent individual entities and can be preceded by an indefinite article and by numerals.

en pige	to piger	en sko	to sko
a girl	two girls	a shoe	two shoes

Count nouns are often words for concrete things and creatures.

Some abstract nouns are count nouns:

en evne, ability; **et spørgsmål**, question

2.2.10.2 Non-count nouns

Non-count nouns are only found in the singular form:

kaffe (-n)	mælk (-en)	vand (-et)
coffee	milk	water

Non-count nouns are often words for materials and substances.

Most abstract nouns are non-count nouns:

kedsomhed, boredom; **lykke**, happiness

Note:

A few nouns have both a count plural and a collective plural form:

	Count plural	*Collective plural*
en mand	mænd	mand

e.g. **en gruppe på 10 mand,** a group of 10 men

	Count plural	*Collective plural*
en øl	øller (bottles/cans of beer)	øl (types of beer)

e.g. **han kom med tre øller,** he arrived with three beers

2.2.11 Nouns with no plural form

These include:

1 Verbal nouns ending in -en: **grublen**, brooding; **hensynstagen**, consideration (see also 2.1.1.2)

2 Abstract nouns: **ansvar**, responsibility; **fattigdom**, poverty

3 Substances and materials: **kød**, meat; **sne**, snow; **vand**, water

Note:
Plurals of nouns of this kind are used to indicate types or makes ('kinds of'):
teer, teas; **vine**, wines.

2.2.12 Nouns with no singular form

These include:

2.2.12.1 Articles of clothing associated with two pieces

bukser, trousers; **shorts**, shorts; **trusser**, knickers

2.2.12.2 Collectives denoting people

forældre, parents; **søskende**, brothers and sisters

Note:
The singular form, **en forælder**, a parent, is increasingly being used.

2.2.12.3 Other collectives

briller, glasses; **finanser**, finances; **klæder**, clothes; **penge**, money

2.2.13 Nouns expressing quantity

Nouns indicating the measure of quantity usually have a **zero**-plural:

fire kilo kartofler, four kilos of potatoes
tre liter mælk, three litres of milk

2.2.14 Differences in number

2.2.14.1 Singular in English, plural in Danish

kontanter, cash; **penge**, money

2.2.14.2 Singular in English, countable (singular or plural) in Danish

(et) fremskridt (plur. **fremskridt**), (an example of) progress;
(et) møbel (plur. **møbler**), (a piece of) furniture; **(en) nyhed**

35

(plur. **nyheder**), (a piece of) news; **en oplysning** (plur. **oplysninger**), (a piece of) information; **(et) referat** (plur. **referater**), (a set of) minutes; **(et) råd** (plur. **råd**), (a piece of) advice; **(en) trappe** (plur. **trapper**), (a flight of) stairs

2.2.14.3 Plural in English, singular in Danish

aske, ashes; **fåresyge**, mumps; **havre**, oats; **indhold**, contents; **løn** (plur. only **lønninger**), wages; **politik**, politics (and some others in **-ik** corresponding to '-ics' in English); **tak**, thanks; **tøj**, clothes; **umage**, pains (e.g. **gøre sig umage**, take pains)

2.2.14.4 Plural in English, countable (singular or plural) in Danish

(en) passer (plur. **passere**), (a pair of) compasses; **(en) rigdom** (plur. **rigdomme**), riches; **(en) saks** (plur. **sakse**), (a pair of) scissors

2.3 The genitive

2.3.1 Adding the genitive ending -s

The genitive ending is added to the indefinite or definite singular or to the indefinite or definite plural form:

en drengs hund	**drengens hund**
a boy's dog	the boy's dog
et barns værelse	**barnets værelse**
a child's room	the child's room
drenges hunde	**drengenes hunde**
boys' dogs	the boys' dogs
børns værelser	**børnenes værelser**
children's rooms	the children's rooms

2.3.2 Proper nouns and the genitive ending

These take the genitive -s:

Torbens kat, Torben's cat; **Grundtvigs salmer,** Grundtvig's hymns; **Danmarks hovedstad,** the capital of Denmark

2.3.3 | Nouns ending in -s, -x or -z in the singular

In these cases the genitive is marked by an apostrophe:

Jens' lejlighed	Jens' flat
Marx' bøger	Marx's books
Schweiz' hovedstad	the capital of Switzerland
Columbus' opdagelse af	Columbus' discovery of
Amerika	America

Note:

Until recently, two other ways of expressing the genitive were to be found:

1 An apostrophe + s: **Columbus's opdagelse af Amerika**
2 A colloquial form in -es: **Schweizes hovedstad.**

Frequently a prepositional phrase can be used instead:

vores hus' tag → **taget på vores hus**   the roof of our house

2.3.4 | Old genitive case endings

Some of these remain in set phrases after **til**:

til havs, by sea; **til sengs**, to bed

See also 8.2.11.

2.3.5 | The genitive -s in noun phrases

The genitive -s is placed on the last word of the noun phrase. This is known as the 'group genitive':

Herman Bangs romaner
the novels of Herman Bang

en af mine venners far
the father of one of my friends

2.3.6 | Differences in use in English and Danish

Notice the different use of the definite article in English and Danish:

the end of winter		**vinterens afslutning** (*Lit.* the winter's end)	
def.	no	def.	no
art.	art.	art.	art.

Nouns following a genitive *never* take an end article.

2.3.7 | The -s genitive

The Danish -s genitive corresponds either to the English construction with 's or s', or to the 'of-construction' as in the example in 2.3.6 (see also 8.5):

gårdens ejer	the owner of the farm
dronning Margrethes liv	the life of Queen Margrethe
Danmarks statsminister	the Prime Minister of Denmark
forårets første dag	the first day of spring
drengens far	the boy's father
drengenes far	the boys' father

2.3.8 | Special uses of the -s genitive

* in surnames:

hos Olsens	at the Olsens'
Vi køber fisk hos Hansens.	We buy our fish at Hansens'.

* as a genitive of measurement:

et fyrreminutters tv-program	a 40-minute TV programme
en 75 centiliters vinflaske	a 75 centilitre wine bottle

2.4 Articles

2.4.1 | Articles – form

The indefinite article (corresponding to English 'a(n)') is, in Danish, either **en** (common gender) or **et** (neuter). The definite (or end) article (corresponding to English 'the') is -(e)n or -(e)t in the singular and -(e)ne in the plural. The term 'end article' refers to the fact that it is added to the end of the noun, either to its dictionary form or (in the plural) to its inflected form:

Singular

Indefinite (en/et)		*Definite (End article) (-(e)n/-(e)t)*	
en mand	a man	**manden**	the man
en kvinde	a woman	**kvinden**	the woman
et hus	a house	**huset**	the house
et æble	an apple	**æblet**	the apple

Plural (both genders) (-(e)ne)

(e)r-plural

aviser	newspapers	**aviserne**	the newspapers
æbler	apples	**æblerne**	the apples

e-plural

borde	tables	**bordene**	the tables
heste	horses	**hestene**	the horses

zero-plural

mænd	men	**mændene**	the men
sko	shoes	**skoene**	the shoes

2.4.1.1 Rules for the end article singular

(a) Add -**n**, -**t** when the noun ends in unstressed -**e**:

en uge – ugen, week   **et billede – billedet**, picture

(b) When the noun ends in another vowel or stressed -**e** (é), add -**en**, -**et**:

en by – byen, town   **et strå – stråel**, straw
en café – cafeen, café   **et træ – træet**, tree

(c) When the noun ends in a consonant (but cf. (d)–(e) below), add -**en**, -**et**:

en hånd – hånden, hand   **et barn – barnet**, child

(d) When the noun ends in unstressed **e** + **l**, **n**, **r**, drop the -**e**- of the stem and add -**en**, -**et**:

en titel – titlen, title   **et teater – teatret**, theatre

But many of these nouns possess alternative definite forms with or without the vowel:

en aften – aft(e)nen, evening   **et køkken – køk(ke)net**, kitchen

(e) Nouns ending in -**um** drop the -**um** before adding the end article:

et museum – museet, museum

(f) After a short stressed vowel, the final consonant is doubled before adding the end article:

en ven – vennen, friend   **et hotel – hotellet**, hotel

2.4.1.2 Rules for the end article plural

(a) The end article plural is usually -ne:

byer – byerne, towns   **stole – stolene**, chairs
gader – gaderne, streets   **borde – bordene**, tables

But notice that nouns in -ere drop the final -e: **danskere – danskerne**, Danes

(b) If the noun has a **zero**-plural, the end article plural is -ene:

børn – børnene, children   **sko – skoene**, shoes
dyr – dyrene, animals   **år – årene**, years

2.4.2   *Article use – introduction*

2.4.2.1 Familiar/new

In most cases, the same principle applies to the use of articles in Danish as in English, namely that when a noun refers anaphorically to a previously mentioned occurrence (when it is a 'familiar idea' or has unique reference), it takes a definite (end) article, while a noun for an entity or concept not previously mentioned (non-unique reference) takes an indefinite article. In short, the first time a noun appears it is likely to be in the indefinite form; the next time it will be definite:

De havde købt *et nyt hus*. *Huset* lå ved *en sø*. *Søen* var ret lille.

           ←———   ←———

       first time   *next time*   *first time*   *next time*

They had bought a new house. The house lay by a lake. The lake was quite small.

2.4.2.2 Association

Concepts that are associated semantically with a previously mentioned noun (e.g. whole-part or type-example), and those that are obvious to everyone, use the definite form:

Han har *en cykel*, men *gearet* virker ikke.

           ←———

       first time   *associated*

He has a bike but the gear doesn't work.

Jeg købte forskellige *blomster*, men *roserne* var flottest.

              ←———

         first time   *associated*

I bought different flowers, but the roses were the nicest.

Vejret var fint. *Solen* skinnede. Så jeg vaskede *bilen*.
obvious   *obvious*   *obvious*
The weather was fine. The sun shone. So I washed the car.

2.4.2.3   Nouns without article versus nouns with indefinite article

The use of count nouns without article tends to indicate a contrast with the noun with indefinite article:

(a) No article = generality   Indefinite article = specific example

Har I bil?   **Har I en bil?**
Do you have a car?   Do you have a car?

(b) No article = generality   Indefinite article = type or sort

Bonden fandt kun sten   **Bonden fandt en sten på marken.**
på marken.
The farmer only found stone   The farmer found a stone in his field.
in his field.

(c) No article = literal   Indefinite article = figurative

Coco var klovn.   **Søren var en klovn.**
Coco was a clown.   Søren was a clown.
(i.e. by profession)   (i.e. a fool)

2.4.3   *Article use – end article in Danish, no article in English*

2.4.3.1   Abstract nouns and nouns in a generic sense

tilbage til *naturen*   back to nature
livet efter *døden*   life after death
komme i *Him(me)len*   go to Heaven

This applies especially to nouns depicting human life and thought: **arbejdet**, work; **krigen**, war; **kærligheden**, love

2.4.3.2   Proverbs

Historien gentager sig.   History repeats itself.

Sådan er *livet*.   That's life.

Livet er kort, *kunsten* er lang.   Life is short, art is long.

2.4.3.3 Idiomatic phrases for location and time

Han er i *byen*/tager til *byen*.	He's in town/going to town.

But:

Hun går i skole/på arbejde.	She goes to school/work.
om *vinteren*/*mandagen*	in winter/on Mondays
i *julen*/*påsken*	at Christmas/Easter

2.4.4 Article use – no article in Danish, definite article in English

2.4.4.1 After certain words

Samme aften kom vi hjem.	*The* same evening we arrived home.
Næste dag var vejret dejligt.	*The* next day the weather was lovely.
De bor på øverste etage.	They live on *the* top floor.

Note, however: **den næste måned,** the following month; **det næste år,** the following year.

2.4.4.2 In some idiomatic phrases

De hører radio.	They listen to *the* radio.
Bodil spiller klaver/violin.	Bodil plays *the* piano/violin.
Mor læser avis.	Mother is reading *the* paper.
Hun er datter af en præst.	She is *the* daughter of a vicar.

2.4.4.3 With proper nouns

Vi spiste frokost hos Jensens.	We had lunch at *the* Jensens'.

2.4.5 Article use – no article in Danish, indefinite article in English

2.4.5.1 With nouns denoting nationality, profession, religion or political beliefs

Marie er dansker/læge/katolik/socialist.
Marie is *a* Dane/*a* doctor/*a* Catholic/*a* Socialist.

Hun arbejder som læge./Hun læser til lærer.
She is working as *a* doctor./She is studying to become *a* teacher.

2.4.5.2   If the noun is qualified by an attributive adjective or a relative clause, the indefinite article must be added

Hun er *en* dygtig læge.
She is a skilled doctor.

Han er *en* dansker, der elsker god mad.
He is a Dane who loves good food.

2.4.6   *Article use – end article in Danish, possessive pronoun in English*

With nouns denoting parts of the body and clothing where possession is obvious, Danish prefers the end article to the possessive pronoun:

Jeg har ondt i arm*en*/ben*et*/hånd*en*/mav*en*.
I have a pain in *my* arm/leg/hand/stomach.

Erik stak hånd*en* i lomm*en*.
Erik put *his* hand in *his* pocket.

Chapter 3

Adjectives

3.1 Adjectives in outline

Adjectives inflect in Danish. In the indefinite declension, they agree with the noun in gender (singular only) and number (both attributively and predicatively). They also add inflectional endings in the definite declension. The definite forms are only used attributively.

Common gender	*Neuter*	*Plural*
Attributive		
Indefinite forms		
en stor⊗ bil	**et stort hus**	**store biler/huse**
a big car	a big house	big cars/houses
god⊗ mad	**varmt vand**	**grønne træer**
good food	hot water	green trees
Predicative		
bilen er stor⊗	**huset er stort**	**bilerne/husene er store**
the car is big	the house is big	the cars/houses are big
Definite forms		
den store bil	**det store hus**	**de store biler/huse**
the big car	the big house	the big cars/houses
min store bil	**mit store hus**	**mine store biler/huse**
my big car	my big house	my big cars/houses

3.2   Indefinite declension

3.2.1   *Indefinite form – regular*

3.2.1.1 Main rule

Adjectives agreeing with common gender nouns in the singular have no
ending ('zero' ending, marked for convenience as ⊗), those agreeing
with neuter singular nouns add -t, and those agreeing with plural nouns
add -e:

Common gender	*Neuter*	*Plural*
zero (⊗)	+t	+e
en fin⊗ have	**et fint hus**	**fine haver/huse**
a fine garden	a fine house	fine gardens/houses
en rolig⊗ by	**et roligt sted**	**rolige byer/steder**
a quiet town	a quiet place	quiet towns/places

3.2.1.2 Shortening the vowel

Note that some monosyllabic adjectives with a long vowel + consonant in
the common gender form shorten the vowel in the pronunciation of the
neuter form: **god** [goːð] – **godt** (gɔd]

Other examples of neuter forms with a shortened vowel: **dødt**, dead; **hvidt**,
white; **fedt**, fatty; **fladt**, flat; **rødt**, red; **sødt**, sweet; **vådt**, wet

3.2.1.3 Adjectives following the main rule

(a) Many monosyllabic adjectives ending in a consonant or consonant
group:

    dyb, deep; **høj**, high, tall; **kold**, cold; **mørk**, dark; **varm**, hot, warm

(b) Polysyllabic adjectives ending in –al, –bar, –el, –ig, –iv, –ær, –(i)øs:

    social, social; **dyrebar**, expensive; **kontroversiel**, controversial; **dygtig**,
    capable; **naiv**, naive; **vulgær**, vulgar; **seriøs**, serious

3.2.2 *Indefinite form – neuter same as common gender*

In the following cases, the neuter form has no special ending:

3.2.2.1 Adjectives ending in **-(i)sk**

Common gender	*Neuter*	*Plural*
en dansk⊗ forfatter	**et dansk⊗ skib**	**danske forfattere/skibe**
a Danish writer	a Danish ship	Danish writers/ships

Other examples: **automatisk**, automatic; **elektrisk**, electrical; **fynsk**, of Funen; **økonomisk**, economic; **økologisk,** ecological

This group includes most adjectives denoting nationality or geographical location: **amerikansk**, American; **engelsk**, English; **fransk**, French; **tysk**, German

In some adjectives ending in -sk, the neuter -t ending is optional: **besk(t)**, bitter; **fersk(t)**, fresh; **fjendsk(t)**, hostile

3.2.2.2 Adjectives with stems already ending in **-t**

en sort⊗ kat	**et sort⊗ hul**	**sorte katte/huller**
a black cat	a black hole	black cats/holes

Other examples: **flot**, posh; **kort**, short; **let**, light; **mæt**, replete; **smart**, smart; **tæt**, close

This group includes many polysyllabic loans ending in -t, -at, -ant, -ent: **abstrakt**, abstract; **konsekvent**, consistent; **privat**, private; **tolerant**, tolerant

3.2.2.3 Adjectives with stems ending in **-d**

A few adjectives ending in a vowel + **d** have no special neuter form:

et fremmed sprog, a foreign language

Others include: **glad**, happy; **ked**, bored; **lad**, lazy

A few adjectives ending in a consonant + **d**, where the **d** is pronounced [d], have no special neuter form:

et absurd drama, an absurd drama

Also: **lærd**, learned

3.2.3 | *Variations in plural/definite*

In the following cases, the plural form varies from the main rule given in 3.2.1.1 above (i.e. they do not simply add -e:

3.2.3.1 | Adjectives ending in **-el, -en, -er**

These drop the -e- of the stem before adding the plural or definite ending -e:

Common gender	*Neuter*	*Plural*
en gammel⊗ kone	**et gammelt hus**	**gamle koner/huse**
an old woman	an old house	old women/houses

Compare the definite forms:

den gamle kone	**det gamle hus**	**de gamle koner/huse**
the old woman	the old house	the old women/houses

This group includes:

adjectives in -el:	**simple**, simple; **ædel**, noble
adjectives in -en:	**doven**, idel; **moden**, ripe; **rusten**, rusty; **voksen**, adult; **åben**, open
adjectives in -er:	**bitter**, bitter; **lækker**, delicious; **mager**, thin; **sikker**, sure
loanwords in -abel, -ibel:	**diskutabel**, debatable; **fleksibel**, flexible

3.2.3.2 | Adjectives in **-et** change the **-t** to a **-d** before adding the plural/definite ending **-e**

en blomstret⊗ vest	**et blomstret⊗ tæppe**	**blomstrede gardiner**
a flowery waistcoat	a flowery carpet	flowery curtains

This group includes: **broget**, multicoloured, and many past participles, e.g. **elsket**, loved; **forlovet**, engaged; **malet**, painted; **pakket**, packed; **repareret**, repaired; **slukket**, extinguished; **ternet**, checked

47

3.2.4 | *Indefinite form – special cases*

3.2.4.1 | The adjective **lille**

Common gender	*Neuter*	*Plural*
en lille⊗ pige	**et lille⊗ barn**	**små piger/børn**
	(no –**t** ending)	(new stem in plural)
a small girl	a small child	small girls/children

Note also the definite forms:

den lille⊗ pige	**det lille⊗ barn**	**de små piger/børn**
the small girl	the small child	the small girls/children

3.2.4.2 | Adjectives ending in **-å**

en blå⊗ (grå⊗) skjorte	**et blåt (gråt)**	**blå (grå⊗) bukser**
	halstørklæde	(no **-e** in plural)
a blue (grey) shirt	a blue (grey) scarf	blue (grey) trousers

3.2.4.3 | Adjectives ending in **-v**

en grov⊗ stemme	**et groft brød**	**grove brædder**
	(**v → f**)	
a coarse voice	a coarse loaf	coarse boards

Also: **stiv – stift**, stiff

3.2.4.4 | Past participles of strong verbs

The past participle forms of some strong verbs – when used attributively – are usually found in the neuter form even with common gender nouns (see 6.1.6.3):

en stjålet (or stjålen) cykel, a stolen bike

en håndskrevet (or håndskreven) meddelelse, a handwritten message

The common gender form in such cases is now considered formal.

3.2.5 | Adjectives doubling the final consonant in the plural/ definite

Adjectives ending in a short stressed vowel plus a single consonant double the final consonant when adding the plural/definite ending -e:

en tom æske	**et tomt hus**	**tomme tønder**
an empty box	an empty house	empty barrels

Many adjectives do this, e.g. **flot**, posh; **grim**, ugly; **grøn**, green; **let**, easy, light; **morsom**, amusing; **mæt**, replete; **slem**, nasty; **smuk**, beautiful; **træt**, tired; **tyk**, fat; **tør**, dry.

See also 2.2.8.

3.2.6 | Indeclinable adjectives

Some adjectives add no special endings for either neuter or plural. These include the following groups:

3.2.6.1 | Adjectives ending in -e

en moderne⊗ bil	**et moderne⊗ hus**	**moderne⊗ mennesker**
a modern car	a modern house	modern people

This group includes: **bange**, afraid; **lige**, equal; **stille**, calm; **øde**, deserted; and some ordinal numbers and present participles: **tredje**, third; **fjerde**, fourth; **glimrende**, brilliant; **irriterende**, irritating; **rasende**, furious

3.2.6.2 | Many adjectives ending in a stressed vowel

en snu⊗ mand	**et snu⊗ vidne**	**snu⊗ forretningsmænd**
a wily man	a wily witness	wily businessmen

This group includes: **kry**, cocky; **sky**, shy; **tro**, faithful; **ru**, rough; **ædru**, sober

Exceptions:
fri – frit – fri(e), free; **ny – nyt – ny(e)**, new
hans ny(e) ur, his new watch; **det fri(e) ord**, the free word.

3.2.6.3	Adjectives ending in -s

en fælles⊗ sag	et fælles⊗ projekt	fælles⊗ venner
a common cause	a joint project	mutual friends

This group includes: **afsides**, remote; **ens**, identical; **gammeldags**, old-fashioned; **indbyrdes**, mutual; **stakkels**, poor; **tilfreds**, contented

Exceptions:

Adjectives ending in a long vowel or diphthong + -s: **løs – løst – løse**, loose; **nervøs – nervøst – nervøse**, nervous; **tavs – tavst – tavse**, silent.

3.2.6.4	Some other adjectives, often used only predicatively, do not inflect

Det er *forkert/slut*.	It is wrong/finished.
Det er *værd* **at lægge mærke til.**	It is worth noticing.

3.2.7	*Indefinite constructions*

The indefinite noun phrase (in this case: indefinite premodifier + adjective + noun, e.g. **en** + **ny** + **bil**) usually expresses something general and non-specific. The following indefinite constructions are found:

Common gender	*Neuter*	*Plural*
⊗**god mad**	⊗**fint vejr**	⊗**lige veje** (no premodifier)
good food	fine weather	straight roads
en ny bil	**et nyt hus**	**to nye biler/huse**
a new car	a new house	two new cars/houses
ikke nogen sjov film	**noget varmt brød**	**nogle saftige æbler**
not a funny film	some hot bread	some juicy apples
ikke nogen god idé	**ikke noget nyt forslag**	**ikke nogen gode idéer**
no good idea	no new proposal	no good ideas
en anden ung mand	**et andet ungt barn**	**andre unge kvinder**
another young man	another young child	other young women
sådan en flot jakke	**sådan et stærkt tov**	**sådan nogle store sko**
a smart jacket like that	a strong rope like that	big shoes like those
sikke(n) en kold blæst!	**sikket et fint vejr!**	**sikke nogle mørke skyer!**
what a cold wind!	what beautiful weather!	what dark clouds!

Common gender	Neuter	Plural	Indefinite declension
hvilken ung mand?	**hvilket stort slot?**	**hvilke nye møbler?**	
what young man?	what big castle?	what new furniture?	
al god mad	**alt godt tøj**	**alle unge mennesker**	
all good food	all good clothes	all young people	
–	–	**mange onde gerninger**	
		many evil deeds	

3.2.8 | Agreement and lack of agreement

3.2.8.1 | Usually adjectives agree with the noun they qualify

Common gender	Neuter	Plural
Bilen er stor⊗.	**Huset er stort.**	**Æblerne er gode.**
The car is big.	The house is big.	The apples are good.

3.2.8.2 | Some common gender nouns formed from verbs do, however, require the neuter ending on the adjective

Rygning er skadeligt. (rygning-en)   **Det er skadeligt at ryge.**
Smoking is harmful.   It is harmful to smoke.

Svømning er sjovt. (svømning-en)   **Det er sjovt at svømme.**
Swimming is fun.   It is fun to swim.

This also applies to infinitive phrases that are used as subject:

At svømme er sjovt.   Swimming is fun.

3.2.8.3 | Nouns used in a generalised sense normally require the neuter form of the adjective

Fisk er dyrt. (fisk-en)
Fish is expensive.

Frugt er sundt. (frugt-en)
Fruit is healthy.

Cf. **Det er dyrt at købe fisk.**
It is expensive to buy fish.

Det er sundt at spise frugt.
Eating fruit is healthy.

3.2.8.4 Past participle agreement

Past participles after **være/blive** usually agree with a plural subject:

Bilerne er røde/importerede.   The cars are red/imported.
ADJ/PAST PARTICIPLE

But past participles of some verbs only agree with the subject when depicting a state (adjectival use), and take the uninflected form when used to emphasise an action (verbal use), in which case they are less closely linked to the subject (see also 6.1.6.3):

State	*Action*
Stolene er malede.	**Stolene er malet.**
The chairs are painted.	The chairs have been painted.
(as opposed to 'unpainted')	(Watch out for the wet paint!)

Examples with a plural subject:

Priserne er faldet.
Prices have fallen.

De var draget bort.
They had left.

Syv dage er gået.
A week has passed.

Ti demonstranter blev arresteret.
Ten demonstrators were arrested

Alle eleverne var samlet.
All the pupils had assembled.

3.2.8.5 In a few cases the inherent sense of the subject (plural) may override the strict grammatical number (singular)

Man var uenige.
They had a difference of opinion.

Brudeparret var lykkelige/lykkeligt.
The bridal couple were happy.

3.3 Definite declension

3.3.1 Definite constructions

There are three types of definite construction of adjective + noun:

Common gender   *Neuter*   *Plural*

TYPE 1 After the front articles **den, det, de,** and the demonstratives **den, det, de** and **denne, dette, disse:**

den røde dør	**det røde tag**	**de røde vægge**
the/that red door	the/that red roof	the/those red walls
denne nye båd	**dette nye skib**	**disse nye færger**
this new boat	this new ship	these new ferries

These are the most frequent uses of the definite declension.

TYPE 2 After genitives and possessive pronouns:

Karens store gård	**familiens fattige hjem**	**barnets gamle sko**
Karen's big farm	the family's poor home	the child's old shoes
min varme jakke	**mit varme tørklæde**	**mine varme strømper**
my warm jacket	my warm scarf	my warm socks
vores grønne vase	**vores hvide spisebord**	**vores brune stole**
our green vase	our white dining table	our brown chairs

Exception:

After a genitive or possessive pronoun, the adjective **egen** is inflected according to the indefinite declension:

mors *egen* lille Niels	Mum's own little Niels
Han har købt sit *eget* store hus.	He has bought his own big house.

TYPE 3 With no word preceding the adjective + noun:

Kære ven!	**ovennævnte brev**	**omtalte forfattere**
Dear friend!	the above-mentioned letter	the aforementioned authors

Notes:

1 When an adjective is used before a noun in the definite, the end (definite) article is replaced by a front article **den, det, de:**

mande*n*	→	***den* gamle mand**
the man		the old man

53

2 The definite form of the adjective is identical with the plural form in nearly all cases (i.e. -e is added to the basic form):

en grøn skov	**grønne skove**	**den grønne skov**	**de grønne skove**
a green forest	green forests	the green forest	the green forests

3 Type 3 above is found in some names of people and places: **lille Erik, Store Kongensgade, Gamle Carlsberg, Vestre Fængsel** and in officialese.

It is also found with the words **bedste, første, sidste, forrige, næste, samme: i bedste fald,** at best; **første gang,** the first time; **sidste forestilling,** the final performance; **forrige uge,** last week; **næste fredag,** next Friday; **samme alder,** the same age.

4 With the words **hele** and **selve,** an end article is added to the noun: **hele tiden,** the whole time:

Selve lejligheden er god, men beliggenheden er dårlig.
The flat itself is fine, but its location is poor.

3.3.2 | Adjectival nouns

3.3.2.1 | There are three cases in which adjectives are used as nouns

(a) when the noun is omitted in order to avoid repetition

Han foretrækker dansk mad for fremmed (mad).
He prefers Danish food to foreign.

et stort (juletræ) og et lille juletræ
a big Christmas tree and a small one

(b) when a noun that is not mentioned is understood (these are what is usually known as adjectival nouns)

De unge forstår ikke de gamle.
Young people do not understand old people.
(**mennesker** is understood after both **unge** and **gamle**).

(c) independent use of the adjective with no noun understood

Valget stod mellem grønt og blåt.
The choice was between green and blue.

3.3.2.2 Danish uses adjectival nouns in the definite plural in the same
way as English

de arbejdsløse, the unemployed; **de fattige**, the poor; **de rige**, the rich;
de syge, the sick; **de sårede**, the wounded; **de unges verden**, the world
of the young

Notice from this last example that adjectival nouns have a (noun) genitive
in -s:

de retfærdiges søvn   the sleep of the just

3.3.2.3 Unlike English, Danish uses the common gender indefinite
singular form of the adjective as a noun to describe a
person

en fremmed, a stranger; **en gal**, a madman; **en lille**, a small child; **en lærd**,
a scholar; **en nyfødt**, a new-born baby; **en sagkyndig**, an expert; **en voksen**,
an adult

Note:
The indefinite plural is also used independently of people:
fremmede, strangers; **rejsende**, travellers.

3.3.2.4 Danish often uses the neuter definite form of the adjective
nominally

Det er det fine ved ham.   That's the good thing about him.
i det fri   in the open air
i det grønne   in nature

Note:
This also applies to the superlative:
gøre sit bedste, do one's best.

3.3.2.5 In many cases where Danish has a definite adjectival noun, English
has a common noun

den myrdede, the murder victim; **den uskyldige**, the innocent person;
de kongelige, the royals; **de overlevende**, the survivors; **de Grønne**,
the Greens; **de nygifte**, the newly-weds

3.3.2.6 Neuter adjectival nouns in Danish may correspond to abstract nouns in English

det nødvendige, the necessity; **det passende**, the suitability

3.3.2.7 In a few cases, Danish also uses the singular definite form of the adjective without an article as a noun to describe people (cf. 3.3.1, Type 3)

min elskede, my love; **undertegnede**, the undersigned

Jeg bor på fjerde (sal).   I live on the fourth (floor).

Jan går i sjette (klasse).   Jan is in the sixth class.

3.3.3 *'The English' and other nationality words*

Whereas English often employs adjectival nouns such as 'the English, the French' to express nationality, Danish prefers proper nouns (e.g. **englænderne, franskmændene**). Some frequent nationality words are listed below.

Country	Adjective	Inhabitant
Amerika (**USA, De Forenede Stater**)	**amerikansk**	**amerikaner-e**
Danmark	**dansk**	**dansker-e**
England	**engelsk**	**englænder-e**
Europa	**europæisk**	**europæer-e**
Finland	**finsk**	**finne-r**
Frankrig	**fransk**	**franskmand, -mænd**
Grækenland	**græsk**	**græker-e**
Holland	**hollandsk**	**hollænder-e**
Irland	**irsk**	**irer-e, irlænder-e**
Island	**islandsk**	**islænding-e**
Italien	**italiensk**	**italiener-e**
Japan	**japansk**	**japaner-e**
Kina	**kinesisk**	**kineser-e**
Litauen	**litauisk**	**litauer-e**

Norge	norsk	nordmand, –mænd	
Rusland	russisk	russer-e	
Spanien	spansk	spanier-e, spaniol-er	
Storbritannien	britisk	brite-r	
Sverige	svensk	svensker-e	
Tyskland	tysk	tysker-e	

3.4 Comparison

The comparative form of the adjective in -(e)re is indeclinable (i.e. the adjective has the same form for definite and indefinite). Note, however, that the superlative in -(e)st has two forms, indefinite and definite (-(e)st/ -(e)ste, see 3.3.1).

Comparison implies that

• two objects or circumstances are contrasted:

Søren er højere end Erik. Søren is taller than Erik.

• one object or circumstance is contrasted with itself at a different juncture:

Det er mere overskyet i dag. It is more overcast today.

3.4.1 Different methods of comparison

There are four different methods of comparison.

3.4.1.1 Add **-ere**, **-est** to the basic form

pæn – pænere – pænest (see 3.4.2)

3.4.1.2 Change the stem vowel of the basic form and add **-(e)re**, **-(e)st**

ung – yngre – yngst (see 3.4.3)

3.4.1.3 Irregular comparison (change of stem)

god – bedre – bedst (see 3.4.4)

57

3.4.1.4 Comparison with **mere**, **mest** and the basic form

snavset – **mere snavset** – **mest snavset** (see 3.4.5)

3.4.1.5 The particle **end** is often used with comparatives

Min bror er stærkere *end* din.
My brother is stronger than yours.

3.4.2 | *Comparison with -ere, -est*

3.4.2.1 The most common method of showing comparison is to add **-ere**
and **-est** to the adjective

Basic	*Comparative*	*Superlative*
glad⊗	**gladere**	**gladest**
happy	happier	happiest

Most adjectives compare this way, including: **dyb,** deep; **dyr,** expensive;
fin, fine; **høj,** high; **hård,** hard; **kold,** cold; **kort,** short; **lav,** low; **lys,** light;
mørk, dark; **ny,** new; **pæn,** pretty; **sjov,** fun; **tung,** heavy; **tynd,** thin

3.4.2.2 Adjectives ending in a short stressed vowel plus a consonant often
double the final consonant before adding the comparative and
superlative endings (cf. 3.2.5)

smuk	**smukkere**	**smukkest**
beautiful	more beautiful	most beautiful

See also 1.1.2, 2.2.8.

3.4.2.3 Some adjectives ending in unstressed **-el, -en, -er** drop the
-e- of the stem before adding the comparative and superlative
endings

sikker	**sikrere**	**sikrest**
safe	safer	safest

Also: **doven,** lazy; **gammel,** old; **mager,** lean; **moden,** ripe, etc.

See also nouns in -el, -en, -er in 2.2.7, 3.2.3.1.

3.4.2.4 **Nær** has deviant forms

nær	**nærmere**	**nærmest**
close	closer	closest

3.4.2.5 A few adjectives (mostly ending in **-ig** and **-som**) add **-ere** in the comparative, but **-st** (and not **-est**) in the superlative to the basic form

en kedelig film	**en kedeligere film**	**den kedeligste film**
a boring film	a more boring film	the most boring film

en morsom bog	**en morsommere bog**	**den morsomste bog**
a funny book	a funnier book	the funniest book

Others: **farlig**, dangerous; **fattig**, poor; **langsom**, slow; **voldsom**, violent

3.4.3 *Comparison with vowel change and -(e)re, -(e)st*

Only four adjectives modify the root vowel before adding the comparative or superlative ending:

Basic	*Comparative*	*Superlative*	
få	**færre**	**færrest**	few
lang	**længere**	**længst**	long
stor	**større**	**størst**	big
ung	**yngre**	**yngst**	young

3.4.4 *Irregular comparison*

3.4.4.1 A few adjectives and pronouns change their stem in the comparative and superlative

Basic	*Comparative*	*Superlative*	
dårlig, ond, slem	**værre**	**værst**	bad
gammel	**ældre**	**ældst**	old
god	**bedre**	**bedst**	good
lille	**mindre**	**mindst**	small
mange	**flere**	**flest**	many
megen, meget	**mere**	**mest**	much

| 3.4.4.2 | **Værre, værst** often indicate more of a bad quality |

Hendes dårlige ben er blevet værre, Her bad leg has got worse (i.e. it was bad to begin with), whereas **dårligere, dårligst** often indicate less of a good quality: **Kartoflerne er blevet dårligere i år,** The potatoes have got worse this year (i.e. they may have been good last year).

| 3.4.4.3 | **Flere, flest** are plural forms used with count nouns |

Vi købte flere bøger.   We bought more books.

Mere, mest are, however, singular forms used with non-count nouns:

Vil du have mere kaffe?   Would you like some more coffee?

Flere can also have an absolute (i.e. non-comparative) meaning (= several). Cf.:

Vi så flere sangfugle i går.   We saw several songbirds yesterday.

For count/non-count nouns, see 2.2.10.

| **3.4.5** | *Comparison with **mere, mest*** |

This group includes a number of different types:

| 3.4.5.1 | Present participles, past participles and most long adjectives |

Basic	*Comparative*	*Superlative*
spændende	**mere spændende**	**mest spændende**
exciting	more exciting	most exciting
velkendt	**mere velkendt**	**mest velkendt**
well-known	more well-known	most well-known

| 3.4.5.2 | Adjectives ending in **-et** |

interesseret	**mere interesseret**	**mest interesseret**
interested	more interested	most interested

Others: **forvirret,** confused; **skuffet,** disappointed; **snavset,** dirty; **tosset,** foolish

3.4.5.3 Adjectives ending in **-isk**		

praktisk	**mere praktisk**	**mest praktisk**
practical	more practical	most practical

Others: **fantastisk**, fantastic; **humoristisk**, humorous; **jordisk**, earthly; **realistisk**, realistic

Note:

Monosyllabic adjectives ending in -sk take inflectional endings:

barsk – barskere – barskest, harsh

Others include: **besk**, bitter; **fersk**, fresh; **frisk**, fresh.

3.4.5.4 Some adjectives ending in **-en**

sulten	**mere sulten**	**mest sulten**
hungry	more hungry	most hungry

Others: **voksen**, adult; **vågen**, awake; **åben**, open

3.4.5.5 Some adjectives ending in unstressed **-e** and short adjectives ending in a vowel

bange	**mere bange**	**mest bange**
afraid	more afraid	most afraid

Others: **grå**, grey; **lige**, similar; **stille**, peaceful; **ædru**, sober

3.4.5.6 Some loanwords

desperat	**mere desperat**	**mest desperat**
desperate	more desperate	most desperate

3.4.6 *Similarity, dissimilarity and reinforcement*

There are a number of ways of expressing similarity, dissimilarity and reinforcement other than by using comparison (cf. 3.4.2–3.4.5):

3.4.6.1 Similarity

lige så + adj **som**	**Hun var lige så venlig som Gerda.**
(just) as . . . as	She was (just) as friendly as Gerda.

61

samme + noun + **som**	**De taler samme dialekt som Niels.**
the same . . . as	They speak the same dialect as Niels.
ligne	**Han ligner sin far.**
be/look (just) like	He is/looks (just) like his father.

3.4.6.2 Dissimilarity

ikke så + adj + **som**	**Hun er ikke så rig som dronningen.**
not as . . . as	She isn't as rich as the Queen.

The adjectives **anden**, other, different; **anderledes**, different; and **forskellig**, different, dissimilar; also express dissimilarity:

De to søskende er meget forskellige.
The two siblings are very different.

3.4.6.3 Reinforcement

stadig comparative	**Kvaliteten blev stadig værre.**
ever	The quality got ever worse.
aller- + superlative	**Han var min allerbedste ven.**
very	He was my very best friend.

3.4.7 Inflection of the superlative

See also 3.3.1.

In the same way as other adjectives in the basic form, the superlative inflects in the definite, adding an -e:

Det er den sjoveste bog, jeg nogensinde har læst.
That is the funniest book I have ever read.

Det var en af de mest fantastiske forestillinger, jeg har set.
That was one of the most fantastic performances I've seen.

Note:
The adjectives **bedste, første, sidste** are often used without a front article, see 3.3.1, note 3.

3.4.8 | The absolute comparative and absolute superlative

3.4.8.1 | Absolute comparative

The comparative usually implies a comparison (relative comparative):

Min onkel er ældre end min mor.
My uncle is older than my mother.

When the second part of the comparative or superlative is not stated, this element of comparison may disappear. The comparative then often equates to English phrases with 'rather', 'fairly', etc. (absolute comparative):

Min onkel er en ældre mand.
My uncle is an elderly man.

Han lånte en større sum penge.
He borrowed a rather large sum of money.

Others: **en bedre middag**, a rather good dinner; **en længere samtale**, quite a long conversation

3.4.8.2 | Absolute superlative

Similarly, the absolute superlative is used to show that something has a quality to a high degree without directly comparing it to anything else:

Det er de højeste træer i haven. (relative superlative)
They are the tallest trees in the garden.

De er de bedste venner (af verden). (absolute superlative)
They are the very best of friends.

The absolute superlative often equates to English phrases with 'very', etc.:

med det venligste smil   with a very friendly smile
med største fornøjelse   with very great pleasure

Chapter 4

Numerals

4.1   Cardinal and ordinal numbers

Cardinal numbers		*Ordinal numbers*
0	nul	
1	en/et	første
2	to	anden, andet
3	tre	tredje
4	fire	fjerde
5	fem	femte
6	seks	sjette
7	syv	syvende
8	otte	ottende
9	ni	niende
10	ti	tiende
11	el(le)ve ['ɛlvə]	el(le)vte
12	tolv [tɔ'l]	tolvte
13	tretten	trettende
14	fjorten	fjortende
15	femten	femtende
16	seksten ['saisdən]	sekstende
17	sytten	syttende
18	atten	attende
19	nitten	nittende
20	tyve	tyvende
21	enogtyve	enogtyvende
22	toogtyve	toogtyvende
30	tred(i)ve	tred(i)vte
40	fyrre	fyrretyvende
50	halvtreds [hal'tres]	halvtredsindstyvende
60	tres	tresindstyvende

Cardinal numbers		Ordinal numbers
70	**halvfjerds**	**halvfjerdsindstyvende**
80	**firs**	**firsindstyvende**
90	**halvfems**	**halvfemsindstyvende**
100	**(et) hundrede**	**hundrede**
101	**(et) hundred(e) og en/et**	
125	**(et) hundred(e) og femogtyve**	
200	**to hundrede**	
1 000	**(et) tusind(e)**	**tusinde**
1 000 000	**en million**	**millionte**
1 000 000 000	**en milliard**	**milliardte**

4.1.1 | Numbers above 20

In compound numbers above 20, the units come before the tens in Danish, and numerals under 100 are written as one word, whereas those above 100 are written in several words:

seksogtyve	twenty-six
tooghalvfjerds	seventy-two
(et) hundrede og tolv	a hundred and twelve

4.1.2 | Writing thousands

The gap (or full stop) between the thousands in numbers written as figures corresponds to the English comma:

6 000 000 (6.000.000)	6,000,000

4.1.3 | Numerals 50–100

The numerals from 50 to 100 often cause confusion. They are based on a system of scores (20) and are unusual among European languages, though compare French 'quatre-vingt-dix' (ninety):

Halvtreds (originally **halvtredsindstyve**) means '2½ times 20', i.e. 50.

Tres (originally **tresindstyve**), means '3 times 20', i.e. 60.

Halvfjerds (originally **halvfjerdsindstyve**) means '3½ times 20', i.e. 70.

65

Firs (originally **firsindstyve**) means '4 times 20', i.e. 80.

Halvfems (originally **halvfemsindstyve**), means '4½ times 20', i.e. 90.

For telephone numbers, see 4.2.1.

4.1.4 | *Alternative forms*

A simpler system for writing numerals, like that used in Norway and Sweden, is used by Danes in commerce and inter-Nordic contexts:

20 **toti**, 30 **treti**, 40 **firti**, 50 **femti**, 60 **seksti**, 70 **syvti**, 80 **otti**, 90 **niti**, 25 **totifem**, etc.

4.1.5 | Én

The numeral **én** 'one' is often given an accent to distinguish it from the indefinite article **en** 'a(n)' – though an accent is never obligatory in Danish (cf. 13.3.1) – and inflects according to the gender of the following noun: **én stol**, 'one chair'; **ét bord**, 'one table'; **hundrede og ét borde**, '101 tables'. Agreement of **én** does not occur in other compound numerals: **énogtyve børn**, '21 children'; cf. **ét barn**, 'one child'.

4.1.6 | Hundrede, tusinde

The cardinal numbers **(et) hundrede, (et) tusind(e)** usually have plurals in -(e)r when used in the sense 'hundreds/thousands of', e.g. **hundreder/tusinder af mennesker**, 'hundreds/thousands of people'.

The cardinal numbers **en million, en milliard** have plurals in -**er**, e.g. **millioner/milliarder af kroner**, millions/billions of kroner'.

4.2 Major uses of cardinal and ordinal numbers

4.2.1 | *Telephone numbers*

These are given in pairs:

21 43 52 77
enogtyve – treogfyrre – tooghalvtreds – syvoghalvfjerds

4.2.2 | Dates

4.2.2.1 | Decades, centuries

in the 2000s (twenty-first century) **totusindtallet/2000-tallet**
the 21st century

Less commonly: **det enogtyvende/21. århundred(e)**

in the 1800s (nineteenth century) **i det nittende/19. århundrede
(i 1800-tallet)**

in the 1900s (twentieth century) **i det tyvende/20. århundrede
(i 1900-tallet)**

in the 1880s **i 1880'erne (i attenhundrede og
firserne)**

in the '90s **i 90'erne (i halvfemserne)**

a woman in her fifties **en kvinde i halvtredserne**

4.2.2.2 | Years

mandag den/d. 5. april or: **mandag den 5.4.**
or: **den femte i fjerde**
or: **5/4**

1993 nittenhundrede og treoghalvfems/nittentreoghalvfems
2012 totusind og tolv (tyvetolv)

4.2.3 | Temperature

Det fryser 10 grader.
Det er 10 graders frost/kulde. } It's 10 degrees below zero.
Det er minus 10 grader.

Det er 30 graders varme.
} It's 30 degrees.
Det er 30 grader varmt.

But:

Han har 40 graders feber.
} He has a temperature of 40 degrees.
Han har 40 i feber.

67

4.2.4 | Money

1,25 kr.	**en krone og femogtyve (øre)** or: **én femogtyve**
25 kr	**femogtyve kroner**
1,50 kr	**halvanden krone** (note the singular form)
2,50 kr	**to en halv (krone)** (note the singular form)
6,75 kr	**seks (kroner og) femoghalvfjerds**
25,95 kr	**femogtyve (kroner og) femoghalvfems**
165,55 kr	**(et) hundrede og femogtres (kroner og) femoghalvtreds**

en hundredkroneseddel, a 100-kroner note

en tier, a 10-kroner coin

en femmer, a 5-kroner coin

Note:

These nouns ending in -**er** (pl. -**e**) are used to indicate number generally:

Der kommer en syver.	A number seven (bus) is coming now.
Vi tager på arbejde med toeren.	We take number two (bus) to work.

4.2.5 | Stykker

The word **stykker** is often inserted after numerals used alone:

en fire-fem stykker	four or five

4.2.6 | Fractions, decimals

These are formed from ordinal numbers by adding -**del(e)**:

½	**en halv**
¼	**en fjerdedel/kvart**
⅗	**tre femtedele**
⅛	**en ottendedel**

halv inflects as an adjective: **en halv pære**, half a pear; **et halvt æble**, half an apple; **den halve tid**, half the time

Note:

1½   halvanden/halvandet or: én og en halv/ét og et halvt.

A comma is used where English has a decimal point:

0,45   **nul komma fire fem/nul komma femogfyrre**

4.2.7 | Others

et syvtal, a figure 7   **en halv snes**, 10
et par, a pair   **en snes**, 20
et dusin, a dozen   **en gang, to gange**, once, twice

4.3 | Time by the clock

4.3.1 | The time

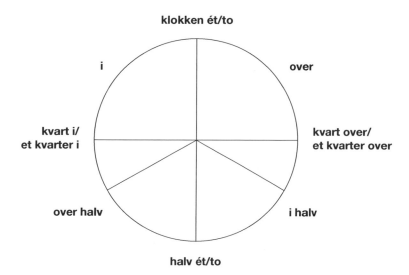

klokken ét/to

i

over

kvart i/
et kvarter i

kvart over/
et kvarter over

over halv

i halv

halv ét/to

Hvad er klokken?	What's the time?
Den/Klokken er (præcis) tolv.	It's (exactly) twelve o'clock.
Den/Klokken er ti minutter over tre.	It's ten past three.
Den/Klokken er syv minutter i fem.	It's seven minutes to five.
Den/Klokken er kvart i/over ti.	It's a quarter to/past ten.
Den/Klokken er et kvarter i/over ti.	It's a quarter to/past ten.
Den/Klokken er mange.	It's late.
Hvad tid er mødet?	What time is the meeting?
Klokken/Kl. 15.00 (femten (nul nul))	fifteen hundred, i.e. 3 p.m.
Frokosten begynder kl. 13.	The lunch starts at 1 p.m.

69

4.3.2 'Half past'

The English 'half past' an hour is always expressed **halv** ('half to' the next hour) in Danish:

Den/Klokken er halv syv.
It's half past six.

Den/Klokken er fem minutter i halv syv.
It's twenty-five past six.

Den/Klokken er fem minutter over halv syv.
It's twenty-five to seven.

Chapter 5

Pronouns

5.1 Personal and reflexive pronouns

5.1.1 *Personal and reflexive pronouns – form*

Subject pronouns		Object pronouns		Reflexive pronouns	
Singular					
1	**jeg** I	**mig**	me	**mig**	me, myself
2	**du** you	**dig**	you	**dig**	you(rself)
	De you	**Dem**	you	**Dem**	you(rself)
3	**han** he	**ham**	him	**sig**	him(self)
	hun she	**hende**	her	**sig**	her(self)
	den it	**den**	it	**sig**	it(self)
	det it	**det**	it	**sig**	it(self)
Plural					
1	**vi** we	**os**	us	**os**	us, ourselves
2	**I** you	**jer**	you	**jer**	you(rselves)
	De you	**Dem**	you	**Dem**	you(rselves)
3	**de** they	**dem**	them	**sig**	them(selves)

Notes:

1 Pronunciation: **jeg** [jai]   **De, de** [di]   **det** [de]
   mig [mai]   **dig** [dai]   **sig** [sai]

2 Unlike the English 'I', **jeg** does not have a capital letter, except at the beginning of a sentence.

3 **De** and **Dem**, the polite forms, always have capital initial letters, as does **I**.

4 **I** is the plural of **du**, the familiar form.

5.1.2 | Use of personal pronouns

5.1.2.1 | Du/De

These are used to address people. Most Danes now use the familiar **du**, notably at school, work, in the family and among friends. **De** (denoting both singular and plural) is used to address strangers, in formal situations such as in official communications, to elderly people, and usually when people are addressed by their surname:

Undskyld, hr./fru Hansen, har *De* set min kat?
Excuse me, Mr/Mrs Hansen, have you seen my cat?

Note also the following idiomatic expressions:

***Du*, kan du lige holde mit glas?**
Hey you, could you just hold my glass?

Kære *du*, vil du hjælpe mig med at fælde det træ?
My dear, would you please help me cut down that tree?

5.1.2.2 | Han/hun

These are *not* used to refer to so-called 'higher animals' (except perhaps by their owners) or countries, unlike English. Notice that countries are neuter (to agree with **et land**):

Danmark er dyrt, men dejligt.
Denmark is expensive, but lovely.

5.1.2.3 | Den/det/de

In addition to serving as personal pronouns, these words are also used as front articles (see 3.3.1) and as demonstrative pronouns (see 5.4), but **den** is never used to refer to a person. When referring to neuter nouns denoting people, such as **et barn** (a child) or **et menneske** (a human being), **han** or **hun** is used.

Examples of usage:

Knud har købt *en ny bil*.   **Den er meget stor.**
Knud has bought a new car.   It's very big.

Bente har købt *et nyt hus*.   **Det er meget stort.**
Bente has bought a new house.   It's very big.

Vi har *to hunde*.　　　　**De er meget store.**
We have two dogs.　　　　　They are very big.

5.1.2.4 The object form of personal pronouns is used as subject
complement after **være**

Hvem er det? Det er *mig*.　　Who is it? It's me.
Det er *ham*, der er den ældste.　It is he who is the eldest.

5.1.3 Uses of det

In addition to serving as a pronoun referring back to a previously mentioned
noun, **det** has a number of idiomatic uses.

5.1.3.1 As the formal subject when followed by a form of **være/blive** +
the real subject, irrespective of gender or number

Hvem er hun? *Det* er min mor.
Who's she? It's my mother.

Hvad blev det? *Det* blev en pige.
What was it? A girl. (of a birth)

Hvem er de? *Det* er mine sønner.
Who are they? They are my sons.

5.1.3.2 As the formal subject with an infinitive (phrase) as real subject

Det er sjovt at lære dansk.
It's fun to learn Danish.

Note, however, that **der** is also used as a formal subject in certain cases,
notably with a passive verb form + an indefinite real subject (see 11.9):

Der dyrkes meget rug i Danmark.
A lot of rye is grown in Denmark.

Der hænger et billede på væggen.
A painting is hanging on the wall.

Danish uses **der** + an intransitive verb in this way, while English often has
the real subject in the front position:

Der bor mange studerende her.
A lot of students live here.

5.1.3.3 As an impersonal subject

Det blæser/regner/sner.   It is windy/raining/snowing.

Det ringer/banker på døren.   There's a ring on the door bell/a knock at
                                       the door.

Det ser ud til, at han er syg.   It looks as if he's ill.

Hvordan går det? Det går fint.   How are you/things? Fine.

5.1.3.4 As an object of verbs meaning 'believe', 'fear', 'hope', 'say', 'think',
        etc. (cf. English 'so')

Fik han jobbet?   **Det håber/siger/tror de.**
Did he get the job?   They hope/say/believe so.

Note also:

Per er dansker, og det er Pia også.
Per is a Dane and so is Pia.

Hun ser glad ud, og det er hun også.
She looks happy and so she is.

5.1.3.5 In answer to questions either as subject complement of **være/
        blive** or as the object of other auxiliary verbs (there is no English
        equivalent)

Er du træt? Nej, det er jeg ikke.
Are you tired? No, I'm not.

Kan du tale dansk? Ja, det kan jeg.
Do you speak Danish? Yes, I do.

Rejser hun i dag? Ja, det gør hun.
Is she leaving today? Yes, she is.

5.1.3.6 When referring back to a whole clause

Han hævder, at han bor i Amerika, men det gør han ikke.
He claims that he lives in America, but he doesn't.

5.1.4 Reflexive pronouns

See also 6.3.4.9 for reflexive verbs.

The reflexive pronoun functions as direct/indirect object or prepositional complement when it has the same referent as the subject of the clause. Reflexive forms are identical to object forms in the first and second person, but in the third person (singular and plural) **sig** is used.

Jeg faldt og slog *mig.*	I fell and hurt myself.
Du skal lukke døren efter *dig*!	You must close the door behind you!
Hun har købt *sig* **en kjole.**	She has bought herself a dress.
Vi morede *os* **meget i aftes.**	We enjoyed ourselves a lot last night.
Skynd *jer*!	Hurry up!
De havde ingen penge på *sig.*	They had no money on them.

It is important that the reflexive forms are used correctly. There is quite a difference in meaning between **Han skød** *ham* (He shot him, i.e. someone else) and **Han skød** *sig* (He shot himself).

There is one notable exception to the main rule. After a verb followed by an object + infinitive construction, a reflexive pronoun refers to the object of the main verb (i.e. the subject of the infinitive, here: **Peter**), but a personal pronoun to the subject of the main clause (here: **Jens**); see also 5.3.1.5:

Jens (S) **bad Peter** (O) **rejse** *sig* **op.** (reflexive pronoun)
Jens asked Peter to stand up. (i.e. Peter to stand up)

Jens (S) **bad Peter** (O) **rejse** *ham* **op.** (personal pronoun)
Jens asked Peter to help him to his feet. (i.e. Jens to stand up)

The reflexive pronouns are used with a number of verbs in Danish (see 6.3.4.9) where the notion of reflexivity is absent in English:

barbere sig, shave; **gifte sig**, get married; **glæde sig**, look forward; **kede sig**, be bored; **lægge/sætte sig**, lie/sit down; **opføre sig**, behave; **rejse sig**, get/stand up; **sminke sig**, put on make-up; **ærgre sig**, be/feel annoyed; **øve sig**, practice; etc.

Reflexive pronouns are always unstressed. If emphasis is needed, for example to indicate a contrast or lack of assistance from others, the word **selv** is added to the reflexive pronoun. Note that English often uses 'own':

Kan han vaske *sig selv?*	Can he wash himself?
Hun redte *sig selv.*	She combed her own hair.
De sminkede *sig selv.*	They did their own make-up.

Selv can also function more independently, referring to nouns or pronouns. Like **sig**, it is gender-neutral and it is always stressed:

Kim skrev artiklen *selv.*
Kim wrote the article himself.

Du kan *selv* vælge menuen.
You can choose the menu yourself.

***Selv* har jeg aldrig set ham.**
I myself have never seen him.

Det var hende *selv*, der sagde det.
It was she herself who said it.

5.2   Reciprocal pronouns

Modern Danish has, in effect, only one reciprocal pronoun: **hinanden** (each other). Unlike the reflexive pronouns, which are used in connection with a simple action/state, **hinanden** implies a *mutual* action/state between two or more individuals or things. **Hinanden** refers back to a plural subject and can never itself be the subject of the clause. It has a genitive form: **hinandens**.

De elsker hinanden.	They love each other.
Vi gav hinanden hånden.	We shook hands.
Stoler I på hinanden?	Do you trust each other?
De har mødt hinandens børn.	They have met each other's children.

Until recently, **hverandre** was used to refer to more than two. It is now very formal and largely outdated.

5.3   Possessive pronouns

Possessive pronouns have the same form irrespective of position. Unlike English, there is thus no formal distinction between attributive and predicative use:

Det er *min* lampe.	It is my lamp.
Lampen er *min*.	The lamp is mine.

First and second person possessives agree in form with the noun:

Det er *din* bil, *dit* hus og *dine* penge.
Cf. **en bil, et hus, penge** (*pl.*)
It is your car, your house and your money.

Third person possessives ending in -s do *not* inflect, cf.:

Det er hans/hendes bil, hans/hendes hus og hans/hendes penge.
It is his/her car, his/her house and his/her money.

The reflexive forms **sin, sit, sine** are explained more fully in 5.3.1.

		Common gender	*Neuter*	*Plural*	
Singular					
1		**min**	**mit**	**mine**	my, mine
2	familiar	**din**	**dit**	**dine**	your, yours
	formal	**Deres**	**Deres**	**Deres**	your, yours
3	masculine	**hans/sin**	**hans/sit**	**hans/sine**	his
	feminine	**hendes/sin**	**hendes/sit**	**hendes/sine**	her, hers
	common gender	**dens/sin**	**dens/sit**	**dens/sine**	its
	neuter	**dets/sin**	**dets/sit**	**dets/sine**	its
Plural					
1		**vores (vor)**	**vores (vort)**	**vores (vore)**	our, ours
2	familiar	**jeres (jer)**	**jeres (jert)**	**jeres (jere)**	your, yours
	formal	**Deres**	**Deres**	**Deres**	your, yours
3		**deres**	**deres**	**deres**	their, theirs

Notes:

1 Possessive pronouns have possessive meaning and hence no separate genitive form:

   mine **forældres venner**   my parents' friends
   mine **venner**   my friends

2 The second person forms **din, dit, dine** correspond to **du**; **jeres** corresponds to **I**; **Deres** corresponds to **De**; but **jer, jert, jere** are now obsolete.

3 The third person plural form **deres** corresponds to **de**.

4 The form **vores** is indeclinable and used in modern everyday Danish, while **vor, vort, vore** are now only found in formal Danish and fixed expressions:

Vores børn er voksne nu.
Our children are adults now.

Vores have er dejlig om sommeren.
Our garden is lovely in summer.

But more formally:

vor dronning, vort modersmål, vore forfædre
our Queen/mother tongue/ancestors

Note also: **i vor tid/i vore dage**, in our time, nowadays; **Vor Herre, Vorherre**, Our Lord

5 **dens, dets** are used of animals and inanimate objects:

Hunden er såret, og dens ben bløder.
The dog is injured and its leg is bleeding.

Huset er gammelt, men dets tag er nyt.
The house is old but its roof is new.

6 English possessive pronouns modifying words for parts of the body or articles of clothing are usually rendered by the definite article in Danish if there is no doubt about the ownership:

| **Han har brækket armen.** | He has broken his arm. |
| **Tag skoene af!** | Take off your shoes! |

5.3.1 | Non-reflexive and reflexive possessives: hans or sin?

5.3.1.1 The reflexive forms **sin/sit/sine** modify an object or a prepositional complement and refer to the subject of the clause with which it is identical in meaning

Han elsker *sin* kone, *sit* barn og *sine* forældre.
S   ↵   ↵   ↵
He loves his wife, his child and his parents.

Note that **sin/sit/sine** *cannot* refer to a plural subject; here **deres** is used:

Børnene elsker deres mor.
The children love their mother.

De har glemt deres penge.
They have forgotten their money.

Sin/sit/sine *cannot* be used to modify the subject of the clause (i.e. it cannot be part of it); **hans** (etc.) is used instead:

Hans datter hentede ham.
        S
His daughter fetched him.

5.3.1.2 The non-reflexive forms do *not* refer back to the subject of the clause they appear in

Here, **sin/sit/sine** must be used. Compare:

Reflexive:
Svend spiste frokost med *sin* kone.
　S
Svend had lunch with his (own) wife.

Non-reflexive:
Ole er sur, fordi Jon spiste frokost med *hans* kone.
　S　　　/SC　　S
Ole is in a bad mood because Jon had lunch with his (i.e. Ole's) wife.

The non-reflexive, third person possessive pronouns **hans, hendes, dens/dets, deres** may modify the subject (S), the subject complement (Subj.Comp.), the direct object (DO), the indirect object (IO) or a prepositional complement (Prep.Comp.):

***Hans* kone er lærer.** 　　S	His wife is a teacher.
Bageren var *hendes* nabo. 　　　　　(Subj.Comp)	The baker was her neighbour.
Jeg mødte *hendes* mand i byen. 　　　　　DO	I met her husband in town.
Hun sendte *hans* sagfører et brev. 　　　　IO	She sent his lawyer a letter.
Asger leger med *hans* børn. 　　　　(Prep.Comp.)	Asger is playing with his children. (i.e. someone else's)

There are two simple ways of testing which form to use in the third person singular:

1　Draw an arrow to the *referent* of the possessive pronoun (which the pronoun must not modify). Is the referent the subject of that clause? If so, use a form of **sin/sit/sine**; if not, use a non-reflexive form.

2　Can you insert the word 'own' in English before the noun modified by the possessive pronoun? If so, use a form of **sin/sit/sine**; if not, use a non-reflexive form.

5.3.1.3 A problem arises when there is more than one clause in the sentence

Hun synes, at *hendes* søn er dejlig.
S   /SC   S
She thinks that *her* son is lovely.

Here, **hendes** is not in the same clause as **Hun** (its referent, which is the subject of the main clause), but modifies **søn** as part of the subject of the subordinate clause (**hendes søn**). Therefore, **sin** is not possible.

Compare:

Hun elsker *sin* søn.
S   O
She loves her son.

5.3.1.4 The main rule also applies when the possessive pronoun precedes the subject

Til *sin* fødselsdag fik *hun* et ur.   For her birthday she got a watch.
————————————→ S

5.3.1.5 In object + infinitive constructions, **sin/sit/sine** normally refers to the object, i.e. the subject of the infinitive (InfS); cf. 5.1.4

Lone hørte *hende* kalde på *sit* barn.
S   InfS ←——— Prep.Comp.
Lone heard her call her child. (i.e. not Lone's child)

Leif så *ham* tage *sin* cykel.
S   InfS ←——— O
Leif saw him take his bike. (i.e. not Leif's bike)

To test this, expand the ellipted clause into a full clause and apply the main rule:

Jeg så, at han tog *sin* cykel.
S   /SC S ←——— O   (**sin** now refers to the subject: **han**)

5.3.1.6 **Sin/sit/sine** may also have general reference

Det er svært at holde *sit* løfte.   It's hard to keep your promise.
At betale *sine* regninger er vigtigt. To pay one's bills is important.

5.3.1.7 Note the use of **sin/sit/sine** in abbreviated comparisons

Han er højere end *sin* far.   He is taller than his father.
Cf. **Han er højere, end *hans* far er.**   He is taller than his father is.

5.3.1.8 Note the use of **sin/sit/sine** in expressions with **hver sin**, etc., referring back to a plural subject, even in the first and second person

However, here the appropriate plural pronoun is increasingly used, i.e. hver vores/jeres/deres:

Vi fik *hver sine/vores* håndklæder.
We each got our own towels.

I kan vælge *hver sin/jeres* menu.
You may each choose your own menu.

Pigerne sov i *hver sit/deres* værelse.
The girls each slept in their own room.

Notice that **hver** is indeclinable in such phrases, and that the choice of sin/sit/sine is determined by the gender/number of the noun modified.

5.4   Demonstrative pronouns

Common gender	*Neuter*	*Plural*
'Near'		
denne (her), den her	**dette (her), det her**	**disse (her), de her**
this	this	these
'Distant'		
den (der)	**det (der)**	**de (der)**
that	that	those

5.4.1 *Proximity*

The main difference between the two sets of demonstratives (**denne/dette/ disse** versus **den/det/de**) is one of proximity to, or distance from, the speaker in space or time. This may be emphasised by the addition of **her** (nearby) or **der** (further away). Demonstratives are always stressed and often have a *deictic* (i.e. identifying or 'pointing') function:

Denne (her) vase er meget gammel.
This vase is very old.

Den (der) på bordet er ny.
That one on the table is new.

5.4.2 | Her/der *with demonstratives*

The addition of **her/der** makes the demonstrative much more colloquial, especially when preceding a noun. They are, therefore, mostly used when the noun is omitted, like 'one' in English:

Jeg mener *denne* bog, ikke *den der*.
I mean this book, not that one.

5.4.3 | *Position*

As in English, the demonstratives may be used attributively or nominally. If nominally, they take the number/gender of the 'understood' noun:

Hvad koster *de der* bananer?	What do those bananas cost?
Er de billigere end *de her*?	Are they cheaper than these?
***Dette* er noget nyt.**	This is something new.
Jeg tager *den her* fisk, ikke *den der*.	I'll take this fish, not that one.

5.4.4 | *Demonstratives with relative clause*

The demonstrative is often used in Danish to direct attention to a following restrictive relative clause (cf. 5.3.2). In such cases, it replaces the usual end article, but especially younger Danes increasingly use the end article in these cases:

Den elev, som fik de højeste karakterer, er min nevø.
(Or: **Eleven . . .**)
The pupil who got the highest marks is my nephew.

Det værelse, hun lejede, var ikke stort nok.
(Or: **Værelset . . .**)
The room she rented wasn't big enough.

If the relative clause is non-restrictive, only an end article is possible:

Træerne, som i øvrigt snart skal fældes, skygger for udsigten.
The trees, which by the way will be cut down soon, are blocking the view.

5.4.5 *The demonstrative is also used to direct attention to a following at-clause*

De traf *den* beslutning, at firmaet måtte lukke.
They took the decision that the firm had to close down.

5.4.6 *When referring to people, the genitive forms dennes, disses may be found in formal Danish*

***Dennes/Disses* forklaringer var interessante.**
This person's/These people's explanations were interesting.

5.4.7 **Dennes (ds.)** *also means 'inst.' (this month)*

Jvf. vores brev af den 10. *dennes* (ds.).
Cf. our letter of the 10th inst.

5.4.8 **Den** *is used independently of a person in proverbs, etc.*

***Den*, der ler sidst, ler bedst.**
He laughs best who laughs last.

5.4.9 *The object form of* de *(when not followed by a noun) is* dem

De sko? Nej, *dem* har jeg aldrig set før!
Those shoes! No, I've never seen those before!

5.4.10 *Coordinated idiomatic phrases*

***den* og *den* person/dato** (etc.)	such and such a person/date (etc.)
på *det* og *det* tidspunkt	at such and such a time

5.5 Relative pronouns

5.5.1 Function

Relative pronouns introduce a subordinate relative clause and usually refer back ('anaphoric reference') to a correlative (corr.) in the main clause.

Jeg har en ven, *som* er læge.   I have a friend who is a doctor.
            corr.

Relative pronouns include:

der	who, which, that
som	who(m), which, that
hvis	whose
hvem	who(m)
hvad	what, which
hvilken/hvilket/hvilke	(who(m)), which

Note that **hvor** (where) is a relative adverb.

5.5.2 Types of relative clause: restrictive and non-restrictive

A restrictive relative clause is necessary in order to identify the correlative and therefore *cannot* be omitted. In a non-restrictive (or parenthetical) relative clause the correlative is known so the relative clause merely provides extra information and can be omitted. Compare:

Restrictive:

Min kollega, *som* bor i Valby, tager bussen til arbejde.
My colleague who lives in Valby takes the bus to work. (one of several)

Non-restrictive:

Min mor, *som* er meget gammel, bor på plejehjem.
My mother, who is very old, lives in a nursing home. (identity known)

According to the comma rules, a comma before a restrictive relative clause is optional (shown here by brackets round it), but compulsory before a non-restrictive relative clause. See 14.2.2.1.

Compare the following examples:

1 **Kan du se den dreng(,) *der* leger derhenne?** (Or: **drengen . . .**)
   Can you see the boy who is playing over there?

2 **Det hus(,) *som* ligger på hjørnet, har røde mursten.**
   (Or: **Huset . . .**)
   The house that stands on the corner has red bricks.

3 **Den film(,) *(som)* vi så i går, var meget morsom.** (Or: **Filmen . . .**)
   The film (that) we saw yesterday was very funny.

4 **Vores børn, *som* I vist ikke har set, går i skole nu.**
   Our children, who(m) you haven't seen, I suppose, now go to school.

5 **Den vej(,) *(som)* hun bor på, går forbi kirken.** (Or: **Vejen . . .**)
   The road (that) she lives in goes past the church.

6 **Kirsten, *hvis* datter skal giftes, er alvorligt syg.**
   Kirsten, whose daughter is getting married, is seriously ill.

7 **Hanne kommer fra den by(,) *hvis* navn jeg ikke kan udtale.**
   Hanne comes from the town whose name I can't pronounce.

8 **Hun er den kvinde(,) med *hvem* jeg helst vil rejse til Rom.**
   She is the woman with whom I most want to go to Rome.

9 **Han spiser med fingrene, *hvad* der ikke ser pænt ud.**
   He eats with his fingers, which doesn't look very nice.

10 **Han ønsker selv reparere taget, *hvad* han ikke kan.**
   He wants to repair the roof himself, which he can't do.

11 **Gør(,) *hvad* du vil!**
   Do what you want!

12 **Det er det hus(,) i *hvilket* Per boede.**
   That is the house in which Per lived.

13 **Helle siger, at Palle ikke kan svømme, *hvilket* er noget sludder.**
   Helle says that Palle can't swim, which is nonsense.

Notes:

1 **der** is only used as subject (ex. 1). See 5.5.3.1.

2 **som** may be omitted from a non-restrictive relative clause when it is not the subject (exx. 3, 5). See 5.5.3.2.

3 A preposition *cannot* appear in the same clause directly before **som**, but may be placed at the end of the clause, whether **som** is omitted or not (ex. 5). See 5.5.3.2.

4 A preposition may preceed **hvem** and **hvilken** in formal Danish (exx. 8, 12).

5 **hvis** is found mainly in written Danish and refers to both singular and plural nouns (exx. 6, 7).

6 **hvem** can only refer to humans (ex. 8); **hvad** and (largely) **hvilken** to non-humans (exx. 9–13).

7 In a non-restrictive clause, **hvad** and **hvilken** can refer back to the whole of the previous clause (exx. 9, 10, 13).

8 When **hvad** is the subject of the relative clause, it must be followed by **der** (ex. 9).

9 **hvad** can also refer to some following information ('cataphoric reference'):

Men *hvad* han ikke fortalte os, var, at han skal opereres.
But what he didn't tell us was that he is going to have an operation.

10 Note the frequent construction: **alt hvad** (all that):

Hun gjorde alt, hvad hun kunne.
She did all that she could.

11 **hvilken** is the only relative pronoun that inflects for gender/number. It is only used in formal written language: **hvilken** (common gender, sing.); **hvilket** (neuter, sing.); **hvilke** (plural).

12 Note that **hvem, hvad, hvilken, hvis** are also interrogative pronouns. See 5.6.

5.5.3 │ Der or som?

Both words have uses other than that of a relative pronoun: **der** can function as a formal subject (***Der* sidder en fugl på min cykel**, There's a bird sitting on my bike), and as an adverb of place (**Hun står lige *der***, She is standing just there); while **som** may be a conjunction (**Svend er lige så stor *som* sin søster**, Svend is just as tall as his sister). See 7.1.1, 10.2.2, 11.9.

5.5.3.1 │ Der as *subject* in a relative clause

In this function, *either* **der** *or* **som** may be used, though **der** is more common in spoken Danish. They can introduce both restrictive and non-restrictive clauses:

Restrictive:

Så du den kamp(,) *der/som* blev vist fjernsynet i aftes?
Did you watch the match that was shown on TV last night?

Non-restrictive:

Min bedste ven, *der/som* lige har fået nyt job, har købt hus.
My best friend, who has just got a new job, has bought a house.

However, when there are two coordinated relative clauses, **der** *cannot* be used in the second one:

Det er en vin(,) *der/som* kan drikkes nu, men *som* også kan gemmes.
It's is a wine that can be drunk now, but which may also be laid down.

5.5.3.2 **Som** as *subject, direct/indirect object* or *prepositional complement* in the relative clause

When it is a prepositional complement, the preposition *cannot* precede **som**, but must come after (all forms of) the verb. **Som** *cannot* be omitted when it introduces a non-restrictive clause, as in the following examples:

Jeg har en veninde, *som* er utrolig sød.   (subject)
I have a girlfriend who is incredibly nice.

Jeg har en veninde, *som* jeg besøger hver uge.   (direct object)
I have a girlfriend whom I visit every week.

Jeg har en veninde, *som* jeg giver mange gaver.   (indirect object)
I have a girlfriend whom I give many presents.

Jeg har en veninde, *som* jeg ofte ringer til.   (Prep.Comp.)
I have a girlfriend whom I often ring.

In a restrictive relative clause, when it is *not* the subject, **som** may (optionally) be left out:

Den saks(,) (*som*) jeg købte i fredags, er blevet væk. (direct object)
The scissors (that) I bought on Friday have gone missing.

Har du set de bure(,) (*som*) de holder løver i?   (Prep.Comp.)
Have you seen the cages (which) they keep lions in?

5.6 Interrogative pronouns (hv-words)

Interrogative pronouns (**hv**-words) introduce a direct or indirect question. They include:

Common gender	Neuter	Plural	Genitive
hvem	**hvad**	**hvem**	**hvis**
who(m)	what	who(m)	whose
hvilken	**hvilket**	**hvilke**	
what/which	what/which	what/which	
hvad for en	**hvad for et**	**hvad for nogle**	
which (kind/one)	which (kind/one)	which (kinds/ones)	

Note that **hvor** (where), **hvordan** (how), **hvorfor** (why) and **hvornår** (when) are interrogative adverbs.

Examples of use:

Hvem er det?	Who is it?
Hvem talte du med?	Who(m) did you talk to?
Hun spurgte, hvem der ringede.	She asked who rang.
Hvad er klokken?	What's the time?
Kan du se, hvad Dorte laver?	Can you see what Dorte is doing?
Hvad for en ost vil De have?	Which cheese do you want?
Hvad for nogle sko har De?	What kind of shoes do you have?
Hvilken skole går Deres søn i?	Which school does your son go to?
Hvis hat er det?	Whose hat is it?
De ved ikke, hvis (hat) det er.	They don't know whose (hat) it is.

Notes:

1 **hvilken** (etc.) is mostly found in written Danish; **hvad for en** (etc.) in colloquial language.

2 **hvem** (used of humans) and **hvad** (used of non-humans) must add **der**, when they are subject in a subordinate clause (indirect question):

Jeg så ikke, hvem der gik.	I didn't see who left.
Hun spurgte, hvad der var sket.	She asked what had happened.

3 For emphasis, **hvem, hvad, hvilken** may add **som helst**:

Hvem som helst kan have gjort det.	Anyone may have done it.
Jeg kan spise hvad som helst.	I can eat anything.
Sæt annoncen i hvilken som helst avis!	Put the advert in any newspaper!

5.7 Indefinite pronouns

Indefinite pronouns include the following:

Common gender	Neuter	Plural	
al	**alt, alting**	**alle**	all, everything, everyone
		begge	both
(en)hver	**(et)hvert**		each, every(one)

Common gender	Neuter	Plural	
ingen	intet, ingenting	ingen	no, none, no one, nothing
	lidt	få	little, few
man			one, you, they
megen, meget	meget	mange	much, many
nogen	noget	nogle (nogen)	some/any, something/anything, someone/anyone

Note:

meget is also an adverb (= 'very'). See 7.1.1.

5.7.1 | Al, alt, alle

5.7.1.1 | **Al** is only used with non-count nouns

al den snak/støj   all that talk/noise

5.7.1.2 | **Alt** ('all', 'everything') is very common, while **alting** is used for emphasis

Fortæl mig *alt*!	Tell me everything!
Hvor er *alt* mit tøj?	Where are all my clothes?
***Alting/Alt* er i orden!**	Everything is in order!

Note also: **i alt**, in all; **alt i alt**, all in all; **alt for**, too; **alt hvad**, all that; **alt vel**, everything fine; **frem for alt**, above all; **trods alt**, despite everything

5.7.1.3 | **Alle** ('all', 'everyone') is plural and can appear attributively, nominally and in the genitive

***Alle* børn går i skole.**	All children go to school.
***Alle* kom til tiden.**	Everybody arrived on time.
Nu skal vi *alle* hjem og spise.	We are all going home to eat now.
Det er ikke *alles* yndlingsmusik.	It's not everyone's favourite music.

Note also: **alle og enhver**, all and sundry; **alle sammen**, one and all; **alle steder/vegne**, everywhere; **alle tiders**, fantastic, of all time; **en gang for alle**, once and for all

5.7.2 Begge

Begge is used both attributively and nominally; in nominal use it is sometimes, but not always, followed by **to** ('two'). It also has a genitive form: **begges**.

Begge forældre(ne) går på arbejde.	Both parents go to work.
Hun kan lide *begge* dele.	She likes both (things).
Jeg så *begge* forestillinger(ne).	I saw both (the) performances.
De er *begge (to)* meget venlige.	They are both very kind.
Begge (to) gav deres samtykke.	Both gave their consent.
De er voksne *begge to*.	They are both adults.
Begges cykler var væk.	The bikes of both were gone.

Note also: 'both . . . and' corresponds to **både . . . og**. See 10.4.5.

Barnet kan *både* læse *og* skrive.
The child can both read and write.

5.7.3 Hver, hvert, enhver

Hver/hvert is used both attributively and nominally; so is **enhver** (= 'any (one)', 'every(one)'), while the neuter form **ethvert** is confined to attributive use, but both forms have greater emphasis. **Enhver**, which is often preferred when used independently, has the genitive form **enhvers**:

hver time/dag/uge/måned, every hour/day/week/month; **hvert minut/år**, every minute/year; **hver anden gang**, every second time; **hver især**, each one

Hver (person) fik en gave.	Each (person) got a present.
De fik en gave *hver*.	They got a present each.
De fik *hver* en gave.	They each got a present.
Der var lidt af *hvert*.	There was a bit of everything.
Der er noget for *enhver* (smag).	There is something for everyone/ every taste.
Enhver sin lyst.	Everyone to their own.
Det kan *ethvert* barn forstå.	Any child can understand that.
alle og *enhver*	all and sundry
Det er ikke *enhvers* sag at . . .	It's not everyone who can . . .

5.7.4 | Ingen, intet, ingenting

5.7.4.1 | Ingen, intet

Ingen is used with common gender and plural nouns, **intet** with neuter nouns; both can have nominal function. **Ingen, intet** are often replaced by **ikke nogen/noget** in spoken Danish:

De har *ingen* børn/penge.	They have no children/money.
***Intet* nyt er godt nyt.**	No news is good news.
Jeg mødte *ikke nogen* (mennesker).	I didn't meet anyone/any people.
Vi har *ikke noget* at spise.	We have nothing to eat.
***Ingen* har set ham i dag.**	No one has seen him today.

5.7.4.2 | Ingenting

Ingenting is colloquial and more emphatic than **intet/ikke noget**. It is only used nominally:

Jeg hørte *ingenting*.	I heard nothing.
Der er *ingenting* i vejen.	There's nothing wrong.
Det gør *ingenting*.	It doesn't matter.

5.7.5 | Lidt, få

5.7.5.1 | Lidt

Lidt denotes a small quantity and may appear with either common gender or neuter non-count nouns, or before adjectives, but it can also be used nominally. It has positive connotations (= 'some'); it acquires negative connotations when preceded by **kun** or **meget**.

Har du *lidt* mælk?	Have you got some milk?
Jeg blev *lidt* sur.	I became a little bad-tempered.
Der er kun *lidt* tilbage i flasken.	There's only a little left in the bottle.
Hun spiser meget *lidt*.	She eats very little.
Vil du have *lidt* mere?	Do you want a little more?
Der er tre søm for *lidt*.	There are three nails too few.

Note:

Bliv/Vent lidt! Stay/Wait a little!; **lidt efter lidt**, little by little; **om lidt**, in a moment.

5.7.5.2 Få

Få denotes a small number and is used with plural nouns or nominally. On its own, **få** has negative connotations (= '(very) few'), which may be emphasised by adding **kun** or **meget**. If **nogle** precedes it, the meaning is more positive.

Der var *få* mennesker til stede.	There were few people present.
Der er kun *få* nødder i krukken.	There are only a few nuts in the jar.
Meget *få* mødte op.	Very few turned up.
Der er nogle *få* billetter tilbage.	There are a few tickets left.
Stykket er kun for de *få*.	The play is only for the few.

5.7.6 Man

Man is third-person singular and has general reference to humans (cf. French 'on' and German 'man'). There is no single English equivalent, but depending on the context 'you', 'one', 'we', 'they' or a passive construction may render it. Outside the subject case, other forms are used; like the numeral, the oblique form **en** may be given an accent (**én**) to distinguish it from the indefinite article (see 2.4, 4.1.5). Equally, an accent may differentiate the genitive form **ens** (i.e. **éns**) from the adjective **ens** (= 'identical'):

Subject	Object	Possessive	Reflexive
man	en	ens, sin/sit/sine	sig

Man kører bare ligeud.
You just drive straight on.

Man ved aldrig, hvad der kan ske.
You never know what might happen.

Man kan ikke vide alt.
One can't know everything.

I Italien spiser *man* meget pasta.
In Italy they eat a lot of pasta.

Man fangede tyven.
The thief was caught.

Kan *man* mon stole på det?
Is that reliable, I wonder?

Det giver *en/én* noget selvtillid.
It gives one some self-confidence.

***Ens/Éns* helbred er vigtigt.**
One's health is important.

***Man* må gøre sit bedste.**
One must do one's best.

***Man* kan vente sig meget af ham.**
One can expect a lot from him.

Ser *man* det!
I see!/Really!

As subject, **man** and even **en** can be used in an affected and mock-ironic way to replace **du/De** and **jeg**, respectively:

***Man* er nok i dårligt humør i dag!**
One seems rather moody today!

***En/Én* føler sig lidt utilpas.**
One feels a little unwell.

| 5.7.7 | Megen, meget, mange |

| 5.7.7.1 | **Megen** |

Megen as the common gender form with non-count nouns is now increasingly being replaced by **meget**. It is still found in formal language:

Der var megen omtale af det.
There was much talk about it.

| 5.7.7.2 | **Meget** |

Meget is the general form in the singular. It is used to modify non-count nouns, but can also have nominal function.

Er der *meget* kaffe i kanden?	Is there a lot of coffee in the pot?
Der er *meget* at gøre.	There's much to do.
Hvor *meget* koster det?	How much is it?
Det gør ikke så *meget*.	It's not that important.

Note that **meget** as an *adverb* can act as a downtoner rather than an uptoner in spoken Danish when modifying some common adjectives (e.g. **god, pæn, sød**):

Hvordan gik det? Det gik *meget* godt.
How did it go? It went all right. (but no more)

Er det ikke et pænt hus? Jo, det er *meget* pænt.
Isn't it a nice house? Yes, it is quite nice. (but . . .)

Before comparative forms, **meget** corresponds to 'much':

Deres have er *meget* større end vores.
Their garden is much bigger than ours.

Note also: **det er lige meget**, it doesn't matter; **mangt og meget**, a great many things

5.7.7.3 Mange

Mange is used with plural nouns to indicate an unspecified but substantial number. It can have attributive and nominal function.

Der var *mange* mennesker i byen.	There were a lot of people in town.
Vi hørte *mange* gode forslag.	We heard a lot of good proposals.
Har de *mange* penge?	Have they got a lot of money?
Kom der *mange* til foredraget?	Did many come to the talk?
***Mange* kan ikke lide det.**	Many (people) don't like it.

Note also: **mange gange**, many times; **klokken er mange**, it's late

5.7.8 Nogen, noget, nogle

5.7.8.1 Nogen

Nogen has both attributive and nominal function. It may appear with common gender non-count nouns in the singular and with plural nouns when it has negative (or non-assertive) connotations (= 'any(one)'). It therefore often appears with plural nouns in questions and after a negation. It has the genitive form: **nogens**.

Det tog *nogen* tid at gøre det.
It took some time to do it.

Har du *nogen* frimærker?
Have you got any stamps?

Der er ikke *nogen* hjemme.
There is no one at home.

Er der *nogen*, der vil have mere kage?
Would anyone like more cake?

Jeg har ikke talt med *nogen*.
I haven't spoken to anyone.

Er det *nogens* frakke?
Is that anybody's coat?

5.7.8.2 Noget

Noget has also attributive and nominal function and may correspond to both 'something' and 'anything'. It can modify non-count nouns (including common gender ones) and adjectives:

Har du *noget* mad? (Cf. **mad-en**)	Have you got any food?
Det skal være *noget* godt.	It must be something good.
Der er sket *noget*.	Something has happened.
Er der *noget* i vejen?	Is something the matter?
Jeg har fået *noget* i øjet.	I've got something in my eye.

Note that **ikke nogen/noget** is often used for **ingen/intet** in spoken Danish (see 5.7.4.1).

5.7.8.3 Nogle

Nogle (often pronounced like **nogen**) is largely restricted to the written language. Here, it has positive (or assertive) connotations (= 'some(one)'). It has the genitive form: **nogles**.

Her ligger *nogle* blade.
There are some magazines here.

Nogle **mennesker bliver aldrig klogere.**
Some people never get any wiser.

Nogle **af børnene kom for sent.**
Some of the children were late.

Der er *nogle*, **der snyder i skat.**
Some (people) evade taxes.

Efter *nogles* **mening er det forkert.**
In some people's view it's wrong.

Note that, in front of a plural noun, **nogen** (= 'any') often has stress, whereas **nogle** (= 'some') is unstressed:

Har du '*nogen* **'frimærker?**
Have you got any stamps? (non-assertive)

Har du *nogle* **'frimærker?**
Have you got some stamps? (assertive)

Chapter 6

Verbs

6.1 Verb forms

In modern Danish, there is only one form for all persons, singular and plural, in each of the various functions and tenses of the verb.

Danish has no continuous form of the verb (cf. 6.2.1) and, like English, employs auxiliary verbs to help form the perfect, past perfect and future tenses (cf. 6.2.3–6.2.5).

For learning purposes, it is a convenient simplification to consider the formation of the different verb forms as the addition of an inflectional *ending* to the basic part of the verb – the *stem* (see below).

There are four principal conjugations of Danish verbs. Conjugations I, II and III are *weak* conjugations, which form their past tense by means of an ending that adds another syllable to the word. Conjugation IV contains *strong verbs*, which form their past tense *either* without an ending (**zero-ending**) but often by changing the stem vowel, *or* by the ending -t, which does *not* add an extra syllable. Below is a table summarising the endings for each conjugation and verb form (note that vowel stems have no infinitive -e ending):

Conjugation	Imperative	Infinitive	Present tense	Meaning
Weak	= stem	= stem	= stem	
		+ e/zero	+ (e)r	
I	**Lev!**	**leve**	**lever**	live, be alive
	Tro!	**tro**	**tror**	believe, think
II	**Spis!**	**spise**	**spiser**	eat
III	**Læg!**	**lægge**	**lægger**	lay, put

Strong	= stem	= stem + e/zero	= stem + (e)r	
IV	**Drik!**	**drikke**	**drikker**	drink
	Løb!	**løbe**	**løber**	run
	Bed!	**bede**	**beder**	ask, pray
	Vind!	**vinde**	**vinder**	win

Conjugation	Past tense	Past participle	Present participle
Weak	stem + ede/te/de	stem + (e)t	stem + ende
I	**levede**	**levet**	**levende**
	troede	**troet**	**troende**
II	**spiste**	**spist**	**spisende**
III	**lagde**	**lagt**	**læggende**
Strong	stem (often vowel change) + zero/t	stem (often vowel change) + (e)t	
IV	**drak**	**drukket**	**drikkende**
	løb	**løbet**	**løbende**
	bad	**bedt**	**bedende**
	vandt	**vundet**	**vindende**

6.1.1 First conjugation

Infinitive + e/zero	Present + (e)r	Past + ede	Past participle + et	Meaning
arbejde	**arbejder**	**arbejdede**	**arbejdet**	work
studere	**studerer**	**studerede**	**studeret**	study
tro	**tror**	**troede**	**troet**	believe, think

6.1.1.1

More than 80 per cent of weak verbs, and all new verbs (e.g. **jobbe,** work; **lifte,** hitchhike; **printe,** print) belong to this conjugation, including those ending in -ere: **nationalisere,** nationalise; **parkere,** park.

Examples of frequent verbs in Conjugation I:

arbejde, work; **bygge,** build; **elske,** love; **forklare,** explain; **hade,** hate; **handle,** act, shop; **hente,** fetch; **huske,** remember; **lave,** do, make; **lege,** play; **lukke,** close; **pakke,** pack; **prøve,** try; **snakke,** chat, talk; **spille,** play; **vaske,** wash; **vente,** wait; **åbne,** open

6.1.1.2 Verbs ending in stressed **-e, -o, -ø, -å** in the infinitive add **-r** in the present

sne – **sner**, snow; **bo** – **bor**, live, stay; **tø** – **tør**, thaw; **nå** – **når**, reach

6.1.1.3 Verbs ending in stressed **-i, -u, -y** in the infinitive add **-(e)r** in the present tense

fri – **fri(e)r**, propose; **du** – **du(e)r**, be (any) good; **sy** – **sy(e)r**, sew

6.1.2 Second conjugation

Infinitive	Present	Past	Past participle	Meaning
+ e	+ er	+ te	+ t	
kende	**kender**	**kendte**	**kendt**	know
køre	**kører**	**kørte**	**kørt**	drive
spise	**spiser**	**spiste**	**spist**	eat

About 10 per cent of Danish weak verbs belong to Conjugation II. They include:

6.1.2.1 Some verbs with stems ending in a long vowel (or a diphthong) + **-b**, soft **-d**, soft **-g**, **-l**, **-n**, **-r**, **-s**

købe, buy; **råbe**, shout; **tabe**, lose; **bløde**, bleed; **brede**, spread; **føde**, give birth; **bruge**, use; **stege**, fry; **søge**, seek; **dele**, divide, share; **føle**, feel; **tale**, talk; **låne**, borrow, lend; **mene**, mean, think; **høre**, hear; **lære**, learn, teach; **læse**, read; **låse**, lock; **rejse**, go, travel; **vise**, show

6.1.2.2 Some verbs with a short vowel and a stem ending in **-l(d)**, **-m**, **-nd**, **-ng**

fylde, fill; **kalde**, call; **bestille**, do, order; **skille**, separate; **glemme**, forget; **ramme**, hit; **begynde**, begin; **kende**, know; **hænge**, hang; **trænge**, need, push

6.1.2.3 A few verbs with a short vowel and a stem ending in **-ls**, **-nk**

frelse, save; **hilse**, greet; **tænke**, think

6.1.2.4 Very few verbs with a vowel stem

ske, happen

6.1.2.5 A number of verbs with vowel change in the past tense

Infinitive	Present	Past	Past participle	Meaning
dølge	dølger	dulgte	dulgt	conceal
fortælle	fortæller	fortalte	fortalt	tell
følge	følger	fulgte	fulgt	follow
række	rækker	rakte	rakt	pass
smøre	smører	smurte	smurt	smear
spørge	spørger	spurgte	spurgt	ask
strække	strækker	strakte	strakt	stretch
sælge	sælger	solgte	solgt	sell
sætte	sætter	satte	sat	place
træde	træder	trådte	trådt	step
tælle	tæller	talte	talt	count
vælge	vælger	valgte	valgt	choose

The -g in -lg and -rg is dropped in the pronunciation of the past tense of the following verbs:

følge – fulgte; sælge – solgte; vælge – valgte; spørge – spurgte

6.1.2.6 Two irregular verbs

bringe	**bringer**	**bragte**	**bragt**	bring
vide	**ved**	**vidste**	**vidst**	know

6.1.2.7 Some verbs have vowel shortening in the past tense

bruger – **brugte**, use; **køber** – **købte**, buy; **træde** – **trådte**, step, tread

6.1.3 *Third conjugation*

6.1.3.1 A small group of verbs add the ending **-de** in the past tense

Infinitive	Present	Past	Past Participle	Meaning
dø	**dør**	**døde**	**død**	die
have	**har**	**havde**	**haft**	have

Note:

The past participle form **død**, dead, is now only used as an adjective (e.g. **en død fugl**, a dead bird; **fuglen er død**, the bird is dead). It therefore cannot translate 'died' in 'it has died'.

6.1.3.2 The following have both **-de** and vowel change

gøre	**gør**	**gjorde**	**gjort**	do
lægge	**lægger**	**lagde**	**lagt**	lay, put
sige	**siger**	**sagde**	**sagt**	say

6.1.3.3 Two modal verbs are included here (see 6.3.1)

burde	**bør**	**burde**	**burdet**	ought to
turde	**tør**	**turde**	**turdet**	dare

6.1.4 *Fourth conjugation*

6.1.4.1 Introduction

This conjugation includes about 120 strong verbs, i.e. those whose past tense is monosyllabic (except in compound verbs) and formed *either* by **zero**-ending and (usually) vowel change *or* (in a few verbs) by adding the ending **-t** to the stem, with or without vowel change. The vowel change often (but not always) applies to the past participle too, which may thus have (i) the stem vowel, (ii) the vowel of the past tense, or (iii) a vowel different from both the stem and the past tense.

Infinitive	*Present*	*Past*	*Past participle*	*Meaning*
+ e/zero	*+ (e)r*	*+ zero/t*	*+ (e)t*	
		(± vowel change)	*(± vowel change)*	
drikke	**drikker**	**drak**	**drukket**	drink
falde	**falder**	**faldt**	**faldet**	fall

Strong verbs are best learned individually, but many follow the same vowel change sequence. These *gradation series* are shown below in alphabetical order. Weak alternative forms are given in brackets; note that these sometimes have a different meaning.

6.1.4.2 Fourth conjugation: stem vowel **-a-**

Gradation series: a-o-a

Infinitive	Present	Past	Past participle	Meaning
drage	drager	drog	draget	drag, go
fare	farer	for	faret (farede)	hurry
jage	jager	jog	jaget (jagede)	hunt, chase
lade	lader	lod	ladet/ladt	let
		(ladede)	(ladet)	load
tage	tager	tog	taget	take

6.1.4.3 Fourth conjugation: stem vowel **-e-**

(a) Gradation series: e-a-e

Infinitive	Present	Past	Past participle	Meaning
bede	beder	bad	bedt	ask, pray

(b) Gradation series: e-o-e

Infinitive	Present	Past	Past participle	Meaning
le	ler	lo	le(e)t	laugh

(c) Gradation series: e-å-e

Infinitive	Present	Past	Past participle	Meaning
se	ser	så	set	see, look

6.1.4.4 Fourth conjugation: stem vowel **-i-**

Strong verbs with the stem vowel -i- make up the largest group. They comprise five gradation series:

(a) Gradation series: i-a-i

Infinitive	Present	Past	Past participle	Meaning
briste	brister	brast	bristet	break, burst
		(bristede)		
gide	gider	gad	gidet	feel like
give	giver	gav	givet	give
klinge	klinger	klang	klinget	ring, sound
		(klingede)		
sidde	sidder	sad	siddet	sit
stinke	stinker	stank	stinket	stink
tie	tier	tav	tiet	be silent
		(tiede)		

(b) Gradation series: **i-a-u**

Infinitive	Present	Past	Past participle	Meaning
binde	binder	bandt	bundet	bind, tie
drikke	drikker	drak	drukket	drink
finde	finder	fandt	fundet	find
rinde	rinder	randt	rundet (rindet)	pass, roll by
slippe	slipper	slap	sluppet	let go
spinde	spinder	spandt	spundet	spin, weave
springe	springer	sprang	sprunget	jump, spring
stikke	stikker	stak	stukket	prick, stick
svinde	svinder	svandt	svundet	decrease
svinge	svinger	svang (svingede)	svunget (svinget)	swing
tvinde	tvinder	tvandt	tvundet	twine, twist
tvinge	tvinger	tvang	tvunget	force
vinde	vinder	vandt	vundet	win

(c) Gradation series: **i-e-e**

Infinitive	Present	Past	Past participle	Meaning
blive	bliver	blev	blevet	be, become
drive	driver	drev	drevet	drive, idle
glide	glider	gled	gledet	glide, slide
gnide	gnider	gned	gnedet	rub
gribe	griber	greb	grebet	catch, seize
hive	hiver	hev	hevet	heave, pull
knibe	kniber	kneb	knebet	pinch
pibe	piber	peb	pebet	squeak
ride	rider	red	redet	ride
rive	river	rev	revet	scratch
skride	skrider	skred	skredet	slip, walk
skrige	skriger	skreg	skreget	cry, shout
skrive	skriver	skrev	skrevet	write
slibe	sliber	sleb	slebet	grind
snige	sniger	sneg	sneget	sneak
stige	stiger	steg	steget	rise
svide	svider	sved	svedet	burn, singe
svige	sviger	sveg	sveget	betray
vige	viger	veg	veget	retreat, yield
vride	vrider	vred	vredet	wring

(d) Gradation series: i-e-i

Infinitive	Present	Past	Past participle	Meaning
bide	bider	bed	bidt	bite
lide	lider	led	lidt	suffer
skide	skider	sked	skidt	shit
slide	slider	sled	slidt	toil, wear
smide	smider	smed	smidt	throw
stride	strider	stred	stridt	struggle

(e) Gradation series: i-å-i

Notice that the stem consonant -g- is dropped in the past tense:

Infinitive	Present	Past	Past participle	Meaning
ligge	ligger	lå	ligget	lie (position)

6.1.4.5   Fourth conjugation: stem vowel -y-

Strong verbs with the stem vowel -y- make up the second largest group. They comprise five gradation series, four of which change the vowel to -ø- in the past tense:

(a) Gradation series: y-a-u

Infinitive	Present	Past	Past participle	Meaning
synge	synger	sang	sunget	sing
synke	synker	sank	sunket	sink

(b) Gradation series: y-ø-o

Infinitive	Present	Past	Past participle	Meaning
fryse	fryser	frøs	frosset	freeze

(c) Gradation series: y-ø-u

Infinitive	Present	Past	Past participle	Meaning
bryde	bryder	brød	brudt	break
byde	byder	bød	budt	bid, offer
fortryde	fortryder	fortrød	fortrudt	regret
skyde	skyder	skød	skudt	shoot

(d) Gradation series: y-ø-y

Infinitive	Present	Past	Past participle	Meaning
betyde	betyder	betød	betydet	mean
flyde	flyder	flød	flydt	flow
gyde	gyder	gød	gydt	pour, spawn
gyse	gyser	gøs (gyste)	gyst	shiver
lyde	lyder	lød	lydt	sound
nyde	nyder	nød	nydt	enjoy
nyse	nyser	nøs (nyste)	nyst	sneeze
skryde	skryder	skrød (skrydede)	skrydet	brag, bray
snyde	snyder	snød	snydt	cheat

(e) Gradation series: y-ø-ø

Note the change of consonant in **fløj/fløjet** and **løj/løjet**:

Infinitive	Present	Past	Past participle	Meaning
flyve	flyver	fløj	fløjet	fly
fyge	fyger	føg	føget	drift, sweep
krybe	kryber	krøb	krøbet	crawl, creep
lyve	lyver	løj	løjet	tell a lie
ryge	ryger	røg	røget	smoke
smyge	smyger	smøg (smygede)	smøget (smyget)	slide, slip
stryge	stryger	strøg	strøget	cancel, iron, stroke

6.1.4.6 Fourth conjugation: stem vowel -æ-

Strong verbs with the stem vowel -æ- comprise six gradation series, but each series has very few members:

(a) Gradation series: æ-a-a

Infinitive	Present	Past	Past participle	Meaning
gælde	gælder	gjaldt	gjaldt (gældt)	apply, be valid

(b) Gradation series: æ-a-u

Infinitive	Present	Past	Past participle	Meaning
hjælpe	hjælper	hjalp	hjulpet	help
sprække	sprækker	sprak (sprækkede)	sprukket (sprækket)	crack

Infinitive	Present	Past	Past participle	Meaning
træffe	**træffer**	**traf**	**truffet**	hit, meet
trække	**trækker**	**trak**	**trukket**	draw, pull

(c) Gradation series: æ-a-æ

This gradation series has three members; note that 'intr' = intransitive, 'tr' = transitive (cf. 6.3.4). **Kvæde** is now old-fashioned and very rare. **Være** has an irregular present tense form:

Infinitive	Present	Past	Past participle	Meaning
hænge	**hænger**	**hang** (intr) **(hængte)** (tr)	**hængt**	hang
kvæde	**kvæder**	**kvad**	**kvædet**	chant, sing
være	**er**	**var**	**været**	be, exist

(d) Gradation series: æ-a-å

Infinitive	Present	Past	Past participle	Meaning
bære	**bærer**	**bar**	**båret**	bear, carry
skære	**skærer**	**skar**	**skåret**	cut, slice
stjæle	**stjæler**	**stjal**	**stjålet**	steal

(e) Gradation series: æ-o-o

Infinitive	Present	Past	Past participle	Meaning
sværge	**sværger**	**svor** **(sværgede)**	**svoret** **(sværget)**	swear

(f) Gradation series: æ-å-æ

Infinitive	Present	Past	Past participle	Meaning
æde	**æder**	**åd**	**ædt**	eat, gobble

6.1.4.7 Fourth conjugation: stem vowel -å-

Strong verbs with the stem vowel -å- comprise two gradation series, each with two members. All four verbs are vowel stems:

(a) Gradation series: å-i-å

Infinitive	Present	Past	Past participle	Meaning
få	**får**	**fik**	**fået**	get, have
gå	**går**	**gik**	**gået**	go, walk

(b) Gradation series: å-o-å

Infinitive	Present	Past	Past participle	Meaning
slå	slår	slog	slået	beat, hit
stå	står	stod	stået	stand

6.1.4.8 Fourth conjugation: verbs with the same stem vowel in all forms

Seven strong verbs have the same stem vowel in all their forms. However, they belong to the fourth conjugation since they have a monosyllabic past tense form. There are five different stem vowels and two of the verbs add -**t** in the past tense:

(a) Stem vowel -a-

Infinitive	Present	Past	Past participle	Meaning
falde	falder	faldt	faldet	fall

(b) Stem vowel -e-

Infinitive	Present	Past	Past participle	Meaning
hedde	hedder	hed	heddet	be called

(c) Stem vowel -o-

Infinitive	Present	Past	Past participle	Meaning
holde	holder	holdt	holdt	hold
komme	kommer	kom	kommet	come
sove	sover	sov	sovet	sleep

(d) Stem vowel -æ-

Infinitive	Present	Past	Past participle	Meaning
græde	græder	græd	grædt	cry, weep

(e) Stem vowel -ø-

Infinitive	Present	Past	Past participle	Meaning
løbe	løber	løb	løbet	run

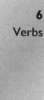

| 6.1.5 | *Infinitive* |

| 6.1.5.1 | Form |

The infinitive is formed in one of two ways:

		Stem	Infinitive	
Consonant stems:	*stem* + e	**leg**	**lege**	play
Vowel stems:	*stem* + zero	**dø**	**dø**	die

The infinitive form is usually preceded by the infinitive marker **at**, except after modal verbs, verbs of perception and the verbs **bede, lade**.

| 6.1.5.2 | Use of the infinitive *without* **at** |

(a) After the modal auxiliaries **burde, kunne, måtte, skulle, ville**:

Han kan ikke *svømme*.   He can't swim.
Jeg skal *gå* om to minutter.   I have to go in two minutes.

(b) After **bede, føle, høre, lade, se**, often in accusative + infinitive constructions:

Vi hørte ham *skrige*.   We heard him cry out.
Jeg så hende *ankomme*.   I saw her arrive.

(c) Before the second of two coordinated infinitives:

Han lovede at *komme* og *hjælpe* mig.
He promised to come and help me.

(d) In a few idiomatic expressions after **få**:

Nu får vi *se*.   We'll see about that.

(e) Colloquially in prohibition or warnings, especially to children:

Ikke *kigge/røre*!   Don't look/touch!
Ikke *pille* næse!   Don't pick your nose!

(f) After the (semi-)modals **behøve, gide, turde**, usage may vary:

Du behøver ikke (at) *gå*.   You don't have to go.
Han gider ikke (at) *rydde* op. He can't be bothered to tidy up.
Jeg tør godt (at) *springe* ned. I dare jump down.

6.1.5.3 Use of the infinitive *with* **at**

(a) In two-verb constructions (verb + **at** + infinitive) with verbs such as:

begynde, begin; **beslutte**, decide; **forstå**, understand; **forsøge**, try; **håbe**, hope; **lykkes**, succeed; **pleje**, usually do; **synes**, think; **vælge**, choose; **ønske**, want, wish

Jeg forsøgte at *åbne* døren.	I tried to open the door.
Hun valgte at *blive* hjemme.	She chose to stay at home.

(b) When the infinitive acts as subject (S), subject complement (Subj.Comp.), direct object (DO) or prepositional complement (Prep.Comp.). Note that English often uses the gerund (i.e. '-ing' form) in such cases:

At *høre* musik er afslappende.
   S
Listening to music is relaxing.

Lykken er at *spise* godt.
         Subj.Comp.
Happiness is to eat well.

Jeg lærte at *tale* dansk i skolen.
        DO
I learnt to speak Danish at school.

Han tænkte på at *gå* en tur.
        Prep.Comp.
He thought of going for a walk.

(c) When the infinitive is the complement of a noun or adjective:

Vil du have lidt te at *drikke*?
Would you like some tea to drink?

Denne bog er svær at *forstå*.
This book is difficult to understand.

(d) **for at** + infinitive indicates intention:

Hun gik ind *for at hente* en bog.	She went in to fetch a book.
Han kom *for at tale* med os.	He came to speak to us.

Note:

Danish does *not* allow a split infinitive (i.e. nothing can stand between **at** and the infinitive).

| 6.1.6 | **Past participle** |

| 6.1.6.1 | Form |

Infinitive	*Present*	*Past*	*Past participle*	*Meaning*
			-et	
I	**gro**	**gror**	**groede**	**groet**	grow
	vente	**venter**	**ventede**	**ventet**	wait
				-t	
II	**høre**	**hører**	**hørte**	**hørt**	hear
	spørge	**spørger**	**spurgte**	**spurgt**	ask
				-t (some exceptions)	
III	**lægge**	**lægger**	**lagde**	**lagt**	lay, put
				-(e)t	
IV	**hjælpe**	**hjælper**	**hjalp**	**hjulpet**	help
	vinde	**vinder**	**vandt**	**vundet**	write

Mostly -t after -d: *-t*
   flyde   **flyder**   **fløder**...

| | *-t* |
| **flyde** | **flyder** | **fløde**... |

Mostly -t after -d:				*-t*	
flyde	**flyder**	**fløde**	**flydt**	flow

Notice that in Conjugation IV (strong verbs) the vowel in the past participle may be different from that in the past tense.

When used as an attributive adjective, the past participle adds an -e in the definite and plural form. Past participles ending in -et usually end in -ede in the definite and plural form:

en ønsket gave, a desired present; **den/de ønskede gave(r)**, the desired present(s)

| 6.1.6.2 | Verbal use |

The auxiliaries **have** (**har/havde**) or **være** (**er/var**) + the past participle form composite tenses (cf. 6.2.3–6.2.5):

Susanne har *skrevet* en bog.	Susanne has written a book.
De havde *set* filmen.	They had seen the film.
Jeg er *begyndt* at lære fransk.	I have begun to learn French.
De var *taget* til Århus.	They had gone to Århus.

The past participle is also used with **blive** to form one of the passive constructions (cf. 6.4.2):

Bilen blev *standset* af politiet.
The car was stopped by the police.

6.1.6.3 Adjectival use

After the auxiliary **være** and in attributive position before a noun, the past participle may function as an adjective (cf. 3.2.4.4):

Huset er *lejet*.	The house is rented.
det *lejede* hus	the rented house
Bogen var *udvalgt*.	The book was selected.
den *udvalgte* bog	the selected book
Stillingen er *opslået*.	The position is advertised.
den *opslåede* stilling	the advertised position

When the past participle is in predicative position and has a plural subject, there can be some uncertainty about whether it should be inflected:

(a) Weak verbs – uninflected -(e)t or inflected -ede/-e?

The uninflected forms with the ending -(e)t inflect in the following ways:

Conjugation I: **+ et → -ede**, e.g. **lejet → lejede;**
                                       ventet → ventede

Conjugation II + III: **+ t → -te**, e.g. **kendt → kendte;**
                                       vedlagt → vedlagte

Both forms are found when denoting a state of affairs, but modern Danish increasingly prefers the uninflected form:

Husene er lejet (lejede).   The houses are rented.

Spillerne er kendt (kendte).   The players are (well-)known.

But usually only:

Checkene er vedlagt.   The cheques are enclosed.

When the participle is a complement after verbs other than **være**, the uninflected form is also generally preferred:

De løb forskrækket (forskrækkede) bort.
They ran away frightened.

(b) Strong verbs – uninflected -(e)t or inflected -ede/-e/-ne?
uninflected -en or inflected -ne?

In Conjugation IV, the uninflected -(e)t form is occasionally replaced with an alternative form in -en, which has the inflected form -ne (definite and plural). These -en forms are a remnant of an older stage of Danish, but are now used sparingly and are rarely the only option, except in fixed phrases, e.g. et stjål*ent* blik/stjål*ne* blikke, a stolen glance (stolen glances), where the -en is even used with a neuter ending in -t. However, this area is further complicated by certain verbs with the -et form having their inflected form in -ne.

The forms inflect in the following ways:

Singular form ending in -en: -en → -ne, e.g. stjålen → stjålne

Singular form ending in -et: -et → -ne/-ede, e.g. tvunget → tvungne;
opslået → opslåede

Singular form ending in -t: -t → -te, e.g. afbrudt → afbrudte

Here, too, both forms are sometimes possible, but in most cases with a clear preference for the uninflected form:

Bilen er stjålet (stjåle*n*).
The car is stolen.

Cf. **en stjålet (stjåle*n*) bil**   a stolen car
   den stjål*ne* bil   the stolen car

Stillingerne er opslået (opslå*ede*).
The positions are advertised.

Cf. **en opslået stilling**   an advertised position
   den opslå*ede* stilling   the advertised position

Forhandlingerne er afbrudt (afbrudte).
The negotiations are interrupted.

Cf. **en afbrudt forhandling**   an interrupted negotiation
   den afbrudte forhandling   the interrupted negotiation

(c) Only the uninflected form is used in the passive where the function is fully verbal:

Husene er blevet lejet.   The houses have been let.
Bilerne er blevet stjålet.   The cars have been stolen.
Stillingerne er blevet opslået.   The positions have been advertised.

6.1.7 | Present participle

6.1.7.1 | Form

The present participle is formed by adding -ende to the verb stem:

I	boende	II	kørende	III	døende	IV	liggende
	levende		spisende		sigende		ridende

6.1.7.2 | Verbal use

Present participles are used much less as a verbal form in Danish than is the corresponding form with '-ing' in English. They occur mainly:

(a) in verbs of motion, e.g. **cykle**, cycle; **gå**, walk; **køre**, drive; **løbe**, run; **springe**, jump; etc., or verbs of expression, e.g. **bande**, swear; **græde**, cry, weep; **le**, laugh; **råbe**, shout; **smile**, smile; etc., when they follow verbs of motion like: **gå**, walk; **komme**, come; **løbe**, run; etc.:

Han gik *bandende/smilende* bort.
He walked away swearing/smiling.

De kom *gående/kørende/løbende*.
They came walking/driving/running.

Børnene løb *grædende* hjem.
The children ran home crying.

(b) in verbs of position, e.g. **hænge**, hang; **ligge**, lie; **sidde**, sit; **stå**, stand; etc., when they follow **blive**:

Hun blev *liggende/siddende/stående*.
She remained lying/sitting/standing.

(c) in verbs of position, e.g. **hænge**, hang; **ligge**, lie; **sidde**, sit; **stå**, stand; etc., when they follow **have** + object:

Han har sin frakke *hængende* i entreen.
He has his coat hanging in the hall.

Jeg havde min cykel *stående* i skuret.
I had my bike standing in the shed.

Note that Danish has no formal equivalent to the English continuous forms (cf. 6.2.1.1):

She is reading the paper.   **Hun *læser* avisen.**
                    Or: **Hun ligger/sidder/står og læser avisen.**

6.1.7.3 Other uses

The present participle can also function as one of the following word classes:

(a) An adjective

This is by far the most frequent use of the present participle. It can occur in both attributive and predicative position:

Attributive:

Det var en *rammende* bemærkning. It was an incisive remark.
Vi står over for et *stigende* problem. We are faced with a growing problem.

Predicative:

Hun er *charmerende/irriterende*. She is charming/irritating.
Han blev efterhånden *trættende*. He gradually became tiresome.

(b) A noun (see also 3.3.2)

This is especially common when the participle denotes people characterised by some activity. Some participles can even appear with the indefinite (as well as with the definite) article, which is very rare in English, e.g. **en døende**, a dying person; **en logerende**, a lodger; **en rejsende**, a traveller, **en studerende**, a student; etc.

But there are far more examples with the definite article *both* in the singular *and* in the plural, e.g. **de(n) ankommende**, the arriving person(s); **de(n) besøgende**, the visitor(s); **de(n) dansende**, the dancer(s); **de(n) gående**, the walking person(s); **de(n) pårørende**, the relative(s); **de(n) ventende**, the waiting person(s); etc.

Den *besøgende* var en ung dame.
The visitor was a young woman.

De *pårørende* blev underrettet.
The relatives were informed.

The present participle can also appear in the genitive:

de *rejsendes* baggage the travellers' luggage

There are a few examples of neuter nouns:

et anliggende, a (business) matter; **et indestående**, a bank balance; etc.

(c) An adverb

As an adverb, the present participle usually acts as an adverb uptoner (cf. 7.6.1) for an adjective or adverb:

Hans tænder er _blændende_ hvide.	His teeth are dazzlingly white.
Det var _brændende_ varmt i solen.	It was burning hot in the sun.
Hun sang _imponerende_ godt.	She sang impressively well.

Very few present participle forms are adverbs proper, e.g. **udelukkende,** exclusively.

6.2 Tenses

Tense means the grammatical realisation of time references as shown in verbal forms. This may be done _synthetically_ through inflectional endings or _analytically_ by means of one or more auxiliary verbs plus a main verb (see 6.3.4). We shall therefore treat both kinds of realisation as verb tenses in Danish. The chief function of tense is to locate an action, an event, a situation, etc., in time relative to another temporal reference point. Below, we shall look at the five most common tenses in Danish.

6.2.1 Present tense

The present tense expresses:

6.2.1.1 What is happening here and now ('instantaneous present') (see also 6.1.7.2)

A: Hvad _laver_ du?	**B: Jeg _sidder_ og _skriver._**
A: What're you doing?	B: I'm (sitting) writing.

Danish has no exact equivalent to the English continuous forms but, apart from the present tense, certain constructions are used to indicate an ongoing state or action, e.g. **være i færd med** (+ **at** + infinitive); **være i gang med** (+ **at** + infinitive); **være ved** (+ **at** + infinitive):

Jeg _er i færd/gang med_ at male.
I'm painting.

Jeg _er ved_ at lave mad.
I'm cooking.

6.2.1.2 Statements of general facts ('timeless present')

Jorden *kredser* rundt om solen. The Earth orbits the Sun.
København *ligger* på Sjælland. Copenhagen is on Zealand.

6.2.1.3 What is often repeated ('habitual present')

Om mandagen *begynder* vi kl. 8. On Mondays we begin at 8 a.m.
Hvert år *rejser* vi til Frankrig. Every year we go to France.

6.2.1.4 Events in the (near) future

I år *rejser* vi til Polen. This year we are going to Poland.
Jeg *kommer* snart tilbage. I'll soon be back.

6.2.1.5 Events in the past that are dramatised ('historic' or 'dramatic' present)

I 1939 *udbryder* 2. verdenskrig. In 1939 World War II breaks out.

6.2.2 Past tense

The past tense expresses:

6.2.2.1 An action at a definite point in the past (without reference to 'now')

(a) Past tense only

    Vi *plantede* et træ i haven. We planted a tree in the garden.

(b) Often with a time marker

    For ti år siden *boede* de i Ribe. Ten years ago they lived in Ribe.
    Vi *kom* sent hjem i aftes. We came home late last night.

6.2.2.2 What was often repeated in the past

Dengang *gik* vi tit i teatret. We often went to the theatre then.

This meaning may also be rendered by **plejede** + (**at** + infinitive), used to:

Vi *plejede* at gå ud om lørdagen. We used to go out on Saturdays.

6.2.3 | Perfect tense

6.2.3.1 | **Have** + past participle

Transitive verbs plus intransitive verbs not expressing motion (including **have** and **være**) use **har** + the past participle to form the perfect tense (see 6.3.4):

Jeg *har slået* græsset.	I have cut the grass.
Han *har haft* mange gæster.	He has had many guests.
Vi *har været* på Madeira.	We have been to Madeira.

6.2.3.2 | **Være** + past participle

Some intransitive verbs, primarily those expressing motion or change, use **er** + the past participle:

Kufferten *er forsvundet*.	The suitcase has disappeared.
Hun *er kommet* hjem.	She has come home.
Hvad *er der sket*?	What has happened?
John *er blevet* sagfører.	John has become a lawyer.

6.2.3.3 | Intransitive verbs expressing motion may occasionally express *either* an action *or* a state of affairs

Action:	**Han *har gået* hele vejen.**	He has walked all the way.
State:	**Nu *er han gået*.**	Now he has left.
Action:	***Har* du *flyttet* sofaen?**	Have you moved the sofa?
State:	**De *er flyttet* til England.**	They have moved to England.

6.2.3.4 | The perfect tense establishes a link between the past and the present

This may take the following forms:

(a) An action at an indeterminate time in the past, but seen from the present:

Hun *har besøgt* sin bror i Kina.	She has visited her brother in China.
Han *er begyndt* at ryge igen.	He has started smoking again.

(b) An action in the past that has consequences for the present:

Det *har sneet* hele natten.	It has snowed all night. (it's still white)
Der *har været* indbrud.	There has been a burglary.
	(things are missing)

(c) An action repeated in the past, but seen from the present:

Jeg *har været* i Lund mange gange.   I have been in Lund many times.
Vi *har set* adskillige film i år.   We have seen several films this
    year.

(d) An action continuing from the past into the present; *with* a time adverbial it usually implies that this state of affairs is ongoing:

Jeg *har boet* i Birkerød i ti år (i.e. **og bor der endnu**).
I have lived in Birkerød for ten years (i.e. and still live there).

But *without* a time adverbial, there is no such implication:

Jeg *har boet* i Birkerød (i.e. **engang, men bor der ikke længere**).
I lived in Birkerød (i.e. at some stage but don't live there any longer).

(e) An action in the (near) future expressed in a subordinate clause that will be completed before the action expressed in the main clause:

Når jeg *har afsluttet* bogen, tager vi på ferie.
When I have finished the book, we'll go on holiday.

6.2.4 | Past perfect tense

6.2.4.1 | Form

The past perfect (or pluperfect) tense is formed with **havde/var** + the past participle:

Vi *havde spist*, da du ringede.
We had eaten when you phoned.

Filmen *var begyndt*, da han kom.
The film had started when he arrived.

6.2.4.2 | Use

The past perfect is used to express an action in the past that took place before another action indicated by the past tense:

Da jeg nåede frem, *var* bussen *kørt*.
When I got there, the bus had gone.

Poul sagde, at han *havde været* syg.
Poul said that he had been ill.

6.2.4.3 The past perfect may also be used to describe hypothetical events

Hvis du ikke *havde drukket* så meget, kunne du have kørt hjem.
If you hadn't drunk so much, you could have driven home. (but you had)

Hun ville have hjulpet dig, hvis du *havde bedt* hende om det.
She would have helped you if you had asked her. (but you hadn't)

6.2.5 *Future tense*

6.2.5.1 Form

Although there is no synthetic future tense form in Danish (as there is in the Romance languages, for example), the combination of **vil** + infinitive is the nearest equivalent and the most neutral way of expressing future reference:

Hvad *vil* der nu *ske?*   What will happen now?
I næste uge *vil* det *være* for sent.   Next week it'll be too late.

6.2.5.2 Other forms

The future may be expressed in other ways, too, notably the following:

(a) **skal** + infinitive implies an arrangement or a promise. A directional adverbial may replace the infinitive to denote an arrangement. Note that a promise usually has a first person subject and often includes the modal adverb **nok** as an extra assurance:

Vi *skal mødes* ved biografen.   We are meeting at the cinema.
Han *skal til Falster* på søndag.   He's going to Falster on Sunday.
Jeg *skal* nok *sende* pengene i dag.   I'll send the money today.

(b) Present tense with time adverbial:

It is more common in Danish than in English to use the present tense with future meaning. This often, but not always, refers to the near future:

Vi *tager* til Skagen i næste uge.   We are going to Skagen next week.
Om tre år *går* han på pension.   In three years he'll retire.

(c) Present tense of **blive, få, komme**, often without a time adverbial:

Tror du, det *bliver* kedeligt?
Do you think it will be boring?

Der *kommer* sikkert mange til koncerten.
A lot of people are probably coming to the concert.

6.2.6 │ *Differences in the use of tenses*

6.2.6.1 │ Present tense in Danish – past tense in English

In passive constructions when an action is completed but the result remains:

Bogen *er skrevet* i 1949.	The book was written in 1949.
Slottet *er bygget* i 1500-tallet.	The castle was built in the 16th century.
Hun *er født* i Nyborg.	She was born in Nyborg.

6.2.6.2 │ Present tense in Danish – perfect tense in English

Er det første gang, du *er* her? Is it the first time you have been here?

6.2.6.3 │ Simple present tense in Danish – present continuous form in English

A: Hvad *laver* børnene?	**B: De (*sidder* og) *ser* fjernsyn.**
A: What are the children doing?	B: They are (sitting) watching TV.

6.2.6.4 │ Past tense in Danish – present tense in English

Especially to express spontaneous feelings ('emotive past tense'):

Det *var* synd for dig!	That's a pity for you!
Det *var* pænt af dig!	That's really nice of you!
***Var* der mere?**	Is there anything else?

6.2.6.5 │ Perfect tense in Danish – past tense in English

With emphasis on the result rather than the action:

Branner *har skrevet* Rytteren.	Branner wrote *The Riding Master*.
Din mor *har ringet*.	Your mother rang.
Hvor *har* du *lært* dansk?	Where did you learn Danish?

6.3 Mood

The attitude of the speaker to the activity expressed in the verb may be indicated by:

Modal verb:	**Vi *må* løbe.**	We must run.
Imperative:	***Sov godt!***	Sleep well!
Subjunctive:	**Frederik længe *leve!***	Long live Frederik!

6.3.1 Modal verbs

6.3.1.1 Form

Modal verbs have irregular forms, in particular the present tense:

Infinitive	Present	Past	Past participle	Meaning
burde	**bør**	**burde**	**burdet**	should, ought to
kunne	**kan**	**kunne**	**kunnet**	can
måtte	**må**	**måtte**	**måttet**	may, must
skulle	**skal**	**skulle**	**skullet**	must, shall
turde	**tør**	**turde**	**turdet**	dare
ville	**vil**	**ville**	**villet**	will, want

6.3.1.2 Modal verbs also differ from other verbs in that

- Whereas other verbs only denote time/tense (past/present/future), the modals also express the speaker's own commitment or attitude to what is said.
- Modal verbs are used as auxiliary verbs in two-verb constructions with a main verb in the bare infinitive.

Jeg *kan* ikke *løbe* længere.
I can't run any further.   (ability)

Det *må være* det rigtige hus.
It must be the right house.   (logical necessity)

However, modals may also combine with a directional adverbial without an infinitive:

Nå, jeg *må hjem* nu.   Well, I'll have to go home now.

De *skal i biografen* i aften.   They are going to the cinema tonight.

6.3.1.3 Use of the modal verbs

(a) **burde**

Probability

Ordet *burde* findes i teksten.   The word ought to be in the text.

Strong recommendation

Du *bør/burde* se den forestilling.   You ought to see that performance.

Moral obligation

Man *bør* ikke lyve.   One ought not to lie.

(b) **kunne**

Possibility, probability

Hun *kan* være faret vild.   She may have got lost.
Projektet *kan* udføres.   The project can be carried out.

Permission, prohibition

Han *kan* (ikke) låne min bil.   He can/can't borrow my car.

Ability

Han *kan* ikke cykle.   He can't (i.e. is not able to) cycle.

(c) **måtte**

Logical necessity

Hun *må* have glemt tasken der.   She must have left her bag there.

Hope/wish

Må han dog snart få fred!   May he soon be at peace!

Permission, prohibition

Græsset *må* (ikke) betrædes.   You may (must not) walk on the grass.

Command

Nu *må* du altså gå!   You really must go now!

(d) **skulle**

Rumour

De *skal* være rejst til Spanien.   They are said to have gone to Spain.

Future in the past

Det *skulle* blive endnu værre.   Worse was to come.

Arrangement

Vi *skal* mødes kl. 16.   We are going to meet at 4 p.m.

Promise

Det *skal* jeg nok sørge for.   I'll see to that.

Command

Du *skal* gøre, hvad jeg siger!   You must do what I tell you!

Hypothetical

Hvis han *skulle* spørge dig . . .   If he were to ask you . . .

Uncertainty

Hvad *skal* jeg gøre?   What shall I do?

Note also:

Vi *skal* lige til at spise.   We are about to have dinner.
Tak *skal* du have.   Thank you.

(e) **turde**

Idiomatic use

Det *turde* anses for sikkert,   It may safely be assumed that . . .
    at . . .

Bravery (= dare)

Han *tør* ikke sige sandheden.   He dare not tell the truth.

(f) **ville**

Future

Han *vil* være her om en halv time.   He'll be here in half an hour.

Volition

Jeg *vil* have en is!   I want an ice-cream!
Jeg *vil* ikke bære tasken!   I won't carry the bag!

Hypothetical

En gratis billet *ville* være dejligt!   A free ticket would be nice!

Note that **vil(le) gerne** corresponds to English 'would like to', and
vil(le) hellere to 'would rather'.

123

6.3.2 │ Imperative

6.3.2.1 │ Form

The imperative has the same form as the *stem*.

	Infinitive	*Imperative*
vowel stem	**gå**	**Gå!**
consonant stem	**standse**	**Stands!**
with double consonant	**komme**	**Kom!**

6.3.2.2 │ Use

(a) The imperative is used to express a command, a request, a wish or a piece of advice:

Stop!	Stop!
Hent **avisen!**	Fetch the paper!
Hjælp **mig et øjeblik!**	Help me a moment!
Kør **hellere lidt langsommere!**	Better drive a little more slowly!
Sov **godt!**	Sleep well!

(b) All imperatives are technically second person, but the subject pronoun (**du/I** or **De**) is only occasionally made explicit, notably to express a contrast and in reflexive forms:

Sid du **der, så laver jeg kaffen.**	You sit there and I'll make the coffee.
Skynd dig/jer!	Hurry up!

(c) A command, etc., may be 'softened' by adding adverbs such as **bare**, **lige**, etc.:

Gør du bare **det!**	You just do that!
Giv **mig** *lige* **bogen!**	Just hand me the book, please!

6.3.3 │ Subjunctive

The present subjunctive form is identical to the form of the infinitive. It is rarely used nowadays and then only in a few fixed expressions:

1 Wishes:	**Gud** *velsigne* **dig!**	May God bless you!
	Ulrik *længe* **leve!**	Long live Ulrik!

2	Curses:	**Fanden _tage_ ham!**	May the Devil take him!
3	Concessions:	**takket _være_ hende**	thanks to her
		koste, hvad det vil	whatever the cost

A wish in the present may also be expressed by the use of **bare** or **gid** and the past tense of the verb:

Bare der snart _skete_ noget!   If only something would happen soon!
Gid det _var_ så vel!   If only it were like that!

Notice that the English 'were' subjunctive is often the equivalent of the Danish **var** indicative:

Hvis jeg _var_ dig ...   If I were you ...

6.3.4 | Main, auxiliary, transitive, intransitive and reflexive verbs

Verbs may be divided into different categories, e.g. _main_ and _auxiliary_ verbs, and _transitive_, _intransitive_ and _reflexive_ verbs. In this section we shall briefly summarise the chief features of these types of verb.

6.3.4.1 | Main verbs

A main verb may either be the only verb in the clause and hence be a finite form (present tense, past tense or imperative) or it may be the last in a sequence of two or more verb forms, and if so, it will appear as a non-finite verb form (infinitive or present/past participle).

Ida _læser_ en bog. (pres. t.)	Ida is reading a book.
Tim _skrev_ en artikel i går. (past t.)	Tim wrote an article yesterday.
Kør forsigtigt hjem! (imp.)	Drive home carefully!
Jeg kan ikke _vente_ længere. (inf.)	I can't wait any longer.
De gik _smilende_ bort. (pres. part.)	They went away smiling.
Huset er blevet _solgt_. (past part.)	The house has been sold.

Note that typical auxiliaries such as **blive**, **have**, **være** also function as main verbs when they constitute the only verb form:

Nu _bliver_ det snart vinter.	Now it'll soon be winter.
De _havde_ mange problemer.	They had many problems.
Det _er_ helt rigtigt.	It's quite right.

Auxiliary verbs

Auxiliary verbs mainly lend support to the main verb in the clause. The most important auxiliary verbs are **blive** (be, become), **have** (have) and **være** (be) and the modal verbs (see 6.3.1), but also **få** (get, have) in some idiomatic uses. Note that all these verbs can also function as main verbs (see 6.3.1 and 6.3.4.1). The auxiliary (or the first one if there are two or more) is always in a finite verb form.

Græsplænen *blev* slået.	The lawn was mowed.
Jeg *har* flyttet sofaen.	I've moved the sofa.
De *er/var* rejst til Norge.	They have/had gone to Norway.
Du *må* ikke ryge her.	You mustn't smoke here.
Nu *får* vi vente.	Now we shall have to wait.

6.3.4.3 Transitive verbs

Transitive verbs have a direct object (DO):

Jakob *købte* en computer.	Jakob bought a computer.
DO	

Other transitive verbs: **gribe**, catch; **huske**, remember; **sige**, say; **tage**, take; **vide**, know; etc.

6.3.4.4 Ditransitive verbs have both an indirect object (IO) and a direct object, usually in that order

Kirsten *gav* Helle en gave.	Kirsten gave Helle a present.
IO DO	

Other ditransitive verbs: **fortælle**, tell; **love**, promise; **låne**, lend; **meddele**, inform; **sende**, send; etc.

6.3.4.5 Intransitive verbs *cannot* have a direct object

Den lille *sover*.	The baby is asleep.

Other intransitive verbs: **dø**, die; **græde**, weep; **fryse**, be cold, freeze; **lyve**, tell a lie; etc.

6.3.4.6 However, some transitive verbs can be used intransitively, the direct object being 'latent'

Vi *spiser* [middag] kl. 19.	We are eating [dinner] at 7 p.m.
Spørg [X], hvis du ikke forstår det.	Ask [X] if you don't understand.

Other 'latent' transitive verbs: **drikke**, drink; **hjælpe**, help; **tabe**, lose; **vaske**, wash; **vinde**, win; etc.

6.3.4.7 Some transitive/intransitive verbs in Danish exist in pairs

Transitive	*Intransitive*
fælde, fell	**falde**, fall
lægge, lay, place	**ligge**, lie
stille, place (upright)	**stå**, stand
sænke, sink (e.g. a ship)	**synke**, sink (e.g. in the water)
sætte, set, place	**sidde**, sit

Note that in these pairs the transitive verbs are usually weak and the intransitive verbs strong. In one case both verbs are weak:

vække, wake (someone) up   **vågne**, wake up (of one's own accord)

6.3.4.8 Copula verbs

A special type of intransitive verbs are the so-called *copula verbs*. These are 'empty' verbs that require a subject complement (adjective or noun) rather than an object to complete their meaning. The subject complement is co-referential with the subject, i.e. they denote the same entity. The most common examples are **blive** and **være**:

Knud *blev* ingeniør.   Knud has become an engineer.
      Subj.Comp.

De *er* meget venlige.   They are very kind.
      Subj.Comp.

Other copulas: **forblive**, remain; **forekomme**, seem; **lyde**, sound; **se ... ud**, appear; **synes**, seem; etc.

6.3.4.9 Reflexive verbs

These consist of verb + the appropriate reflexive pronoun, where the reflexive pronoun functions as the object and agrees in form and meaning with the subject (cf. 5.1.1, 5.1.4):

Sonja *gemte sig*.   Sonja hid (herself).   (Reflexive)
Cf. **Sonja *gemte* pakken.**   Sonja hid the parcel.   (Object)

Other reflexive verbs: **barbere sig**, shave; **bevæge sig**, move; **glæde sig**, look forward; **opføre sig**, behave; **rede sig**, comb oneself; **skynde sig**, hurry; **vaske sig**, wash (oneself); **vende sig**, turn; etc.

(a) Many reflexive verbs in Danish are non-reflexive in English:

Du *har forandret dig*.	You have changed.
De *giftede sig*.	They (got) married.
Jeg *kedede mig*.	I was bored.
Hun *satte sig*.	She sat down.
Parret *viste sig* i salen.	The couple appeared in the hall.

(b) Many reflexive verbs express movement:

begive sig (til), set off (for); **bevæge sig**, move; **bøje sig**, bend (down); **lægge sig**, lie down; **rejse sig**, get up; **sætte sig**, sit down; **vende sig**, turn (round)

(c) The reflexive pronoun is usually placed directly after its verb, but when there is inverted word order (see 11.2.2, 11.16.1), the subject will come between the two elements:

John *morer sig* ofte.	John often enjoys himself.
I aftes *morede* han *sig* ikke.	Last night he didn't enjoy himself.
S	

6.4   -s verbs and the passive

6.4.1   -s forms, deponent and reciprocal verbs

6.4.1.1   Forms of -s verbs (for passive forms, see 6.4.2)

	Infinitive	*Present*	*Past*	*Past participle*	*Meaning*
I	**mindes**	**mindes**	**mindedes**	**mindedes**	recall
II	**synes**	**synes**	**syntes**	**syntes**	think
IV	**slås**	**slås**	**sloges**	**sloges**	fight

6.4.1.2   Uses of the -s form

There are three distinct uses:

- Deponent   **Det *lykkedes* ham at komme ind i huset.**
  He succeeded in getting into the house.

- Reciprocal   **Vi *mødes* ved rådhuset.**
  We'll meet at the town hall.

- Passive   **Middagen *serveres* kl. 19.**
  Dinner is served at 7 p.m.

6.4.1.3 Deponent verbs

Deponent verbs are verbs that have passive form (i.e. -s form) but active meaning. Deponent verbs do not usually have a form without -s, unlike verbs in the passive.

Deponent verbs include:

fattes, be lacking; **findes**, be, exist; **færdes**, move, travel; **længes efter**, long for, miss; **lykkes**, succeed; **mindes**, recall; **mislykkes**, fail; **omgås**, mix with; **synes**, seem; **trives**, thrive; **ældes**, age; etc.

6.4.1.4 Reciprocal verbs

Reciprocal verbs usually (but not always) have a plural subject, and the individuals denoted by the subject each carry out the action simultaneously. Reciprocal action may also be expressed by using the reciprocal pronoun **hinanden**, each other (cf. 5.2).

Vi ses i morgen.	We'll meet tomorrow.
De skiltes som gode venner.	They parted as good friends.
Han slås ofte med sin bror.	He often fights with his brother.

Reciprocal verbs include:

brydes, wrestle; **enes**, agree; **følges (ad)**, accompany (each other); **hjælpes ad**, help (each other); **mødes**, meet; **samles**, gather; **ses**, meet; **skiftes**, take turns; **skilles**, part, separate; **skændes**, quarrel; **slås**, fight; **tales ved**, talk; **træffes**, meet; **trættes**, quarrel; etc.

6.4.2 The passive

6.4.2.1 The passive transformation

Active clause	**Drengen**	**griber**	**bolden.**	The boy catches the ball.
	subject (agent)	active verb form	dir.object (patient)	

Passive clause	**Bolden**	**gribes**	**af drengen.**	The ball is caught by the boy.
	subject (patient)	passive verb form	prep. phrase (agent)	

Note that the transformation from an active to a passive clause involves three changes:

Active		Passive
object	→	subject
subject	→	(af +) complement
active verb form	→	passive verb form

However, the semantic roles of *agent* and *patient* remain unchanged, though the focus changes from the agent to the patient in the passive clause. Note that the passive transformation usually requires a transitive verb, but see 6.4.2.9.

6.4.2.2 No agent

The agent is often omitted in passive clauses when the person carrying out the action is either unknown or unimportant in the context.

Dørene *åbnes* kl. 20.	Doors open at 8 p.m.
Ordet *udtales* med stød.	The word is pronounced with a glottal stop.
Middagen *serveredes* i salen.	Dinner was served in the hall.
Mødet *blev holdt* for lukkede døre.	The meeting was held behind closed doors.
Mine nøgler *er blevet stjålet*.	My keys have been stolen.

6.4.2.3 There are two main types of passive

- -s passive: **Huset *males*.** The house is (being) painted.

- blive passive: **Huset *bliver malet*.** The house is (being) painted.

A third type also exists, however (expressing a state or result):

- være passive: **Huset *er malet*.** The house is (now) painted.

6.4.2.4 Forms of the passive for **male** (paint)

	-s passive	blive passive
Infinitive	**(at) males**	**(at) blive malet**
Present	**(kan) males**	**bliver malet**
Past	**maledes**	**blev malet**
Perfect	–	**er blevet malet**
Past perfect	–	**var blevet malet**

6.4.2.5 Form of the **-s** passive

	Infinitive	Present	Past	Past participle	Meaning
I cons	**ventes**	**ventes**	**ventedes**	–	be expected
I vowel	**ros**	**ros**	**roedes**	–	be rowed (in a boat)
II	**bruges**	**bruges**	**brugtes**	–	be used
III	**gøres**	**gøres**	**gjordes**	–	be done
IV	**ses**	**ses**	**sås**	–	be seen

Note that the -s passive does *not* normally have a past participle form; composite tenses are formed with the **blive** passive (see below).

6.4.2.6 Use of the **-s** passive

This is far less common than the **blive** passive. It is quite rare in the past tense and is virtually non-existent in the past participle. It is mainly used:

* in the infinitive with modal verbs that express notions such as obligation, permission, prohibition, volition, etc.:

Svaret bør *sendes* til kontoret.	The answer should be sent to the office.
Der må *spises* nu.	You may start eating now.
Græsset må ikke *betrædes*!	Do not walk on the grass!
Klagen skal *undersøges*.	The complaint has to be investigated.
Han vil *klippes* lige nu.	He wants to have a hair cut right now.

* in the present tense to express a habitual or repeated action (but see 6.4.2.7):

Lysene *tændes* kl. 21.	The lights go on at 9 p.m.
Varerne *bringes* ud om fredagen.	The goods are delivered on Fridays.

Some verbs can only form the passive using -s, e.g. **behøve**, need; **eje**, own; **have**, have; **skylde**, owe; **vide**, know

The -s passive of some verbs can also occur in the past tense, but this use is very limited:

De *ventedes* først hjem kl. 20.
They were not expected home till 8 p.m.

Han *sås* ofte på galopbanen.
He was often seen at the racecourse.

131

| 6.4.2.7 | The **blive** passive |

This is far more common than the -s passive and is the only option in the composite tenses. It is normally used:

- After modal verbs expressing possibility or future promise:

Per kan blive udtaget til holdet. Per may be picked for the team.
(It may happen)
Cf. **Per kan udtages til holdet.** Per can be picked for the team.
(Nothing prevents it)

Bilen skal blive vasket i dag. The car will be washed today.
(I promise it will be)
Cf. **Bilen skal vaskes i dag.** The car is to be washed today.
(It has been arranged)

Hun vil blive forfremmet. She will be promoted.
(It's certain)
Cf. **Hun vil forfremmes.** She wants to be promoted.
(It's her wish)

- To express a single action:

Min søn er blevet inviteret ud. My son has been invited out.
Cf. **Min søn inviteres tit ud.** My son is often invited out.

Nu blev lysene tændt. Now the lights came on.
Cf. **Lysene tændes hver aften.** The lights come on every evening.

Either the -s passive or the **blive** passive may be used to indicate a recurrent activity:

Der stjæles biler hver dag. / Cars are stolen every day.
Der bliver stjålet biler hver dag.

| 6.4.2.8 | The **være** passive |

(a) The participle is a verb:

Usually **være** + past participle indicates the result of an action, i.e. a state rather than an action:

Bilen er vasket. STATE/RESULT The car is washed.
Bilen er blevet vasket. ACTION The car has been washed.

In the plural, the past participle form often remains unchanged (cf. 6.1.6):

Bilerne *er vasket (vaskede)*. The cars are washed.

(b) The participle is an adjective:

The participle remains in the -t form in the singular irrespective of the gender of the noun, but inflects in the plural:

Pigen *er forelsket*.	The girl is in love.
Pigerne *er forelskede*.	The girls are in love.
Fordelen *er begrænset*.	The advantage is limited.
Fordelene *er begrænsede*.	The advantages are limited.

6.4.2.9 Impersonal passive

Impersonal passive constructions can, unlike all others, have *either* a transitive *or* an intransitive verb.

Der *spises* meget flæskekød i Danmark. (trans.)
A lot of pork is eaten in Denmark.

Der *blev talt* meget om planen. (intrans.)
They talked much about the plan.

Der *blev danset* hele natten. (intrans.)
There was dancing all night.

6.5 Compound verbs

There are two kinds of compound verb: *inseparable* and *separable*.

6.5.1 *Inseparable compound verbs*

In inseparable compound verbs, the first element forms an integral part of the verb:

Compare **tale** (speak) with **bagtale**, slander; **betale**, pay; **indtale**, record; **overtale**, persuade

| 6.5.1.1 | Inseparable compounds include verbs compounded with |

nouns	**kæderyge**, chainsmoke; **støvsuge**, vacuum-clean
adjectives	**dybfryse**, deep-freeze; **renskrive**, make a fair copy
verbs	**sultestrejke**, be on hunger-strike; **øsregne**, pour with rain
numerals	**fir(e)doble**, quadruple
unstressed prefixes	**bedømme**, judge; **forblive**, remain
stressed prefixes	**anbefale**, recommend; **undslippe**, escape

6.5.2 Separable compound verbs

| 6.5.2.1 | In separable compounds the prefix *may* separate from the verb |

Separable compounds include verbs compounded with:

stressed particles	**rejse *bort***	go away
	svare *igen*	answer back
	stige *ned*	descend
	gøre *om*	repeat
	lukke *op*	open, unlock
	arbejde *over*	work overtime
	se . . . *ud*	look

The particles are prepositions/adverbs and the stress is on the particle.

| 6.5.2.2 | Verbs with *both* the compounded *and* the separated form |

(a) With *little or no difference in meaning* between the two forms, though the compounded form tends to be more formal:

afskære – skære af	cut off
deltage – tage del	take part
fastgøre – gøre fast	secure
fremrykke – rykke frem	advance
indsende – sende ind	send in
nedrive – rive ned	demolish
opgive – give op	give up
udvælge – vælge ud	select
underskrive – skrive under	sign

(b) With a *difference in meaning* between the two forms:

Here, the compounded form often has figurative/abstract meaning and the separated form literal meaning, so the meaning of the compounded form is difficult to predict:

afsætte, remove, depose   **sætte af**, set down, take off
indse, realise   **se ind**, look into
oversætte, translate   **sætte over**, jump over, put on
udtale, pronounce   **tale ud**, finish speaking
understrege, emphasise   **strege under**, underline

Chapter 7

Adverbs

7.1 Adverbs – form

Adverbs form a heterogeneous group, but the following are the major types.

7.1.1 Simple adverbs

aldrig, never; **da**, then; **der**, there; **dog**, however; **her**, here; **ikke**, not; **jo**, you know; **just**, exactly; **kun**, only; **lidt**, somewhat, a little; **meget**, much, very; **netop**, exactly; **nok**, probably; **nu**, now; **næppe**, scarcely; **næsten**, almost; **ofte**, often; **straks**, immediately; **vel**, I suppose

7.1.2 Adverbs derived from other word classes

7.1.2.1 Many adverbs derive from adjectives by adding the ending **-t** to the common gender singular form

+ t   **dejligt, dårligt, fint, godt, højt, langt, smukt**
         delightfully, badly, nicely, well, loudly, far, beautifully

The neuter singular form of the adjective is then identical with the adverb:

Vejret er meget dårligt.   **Han tegner meget dårligt.**
The weather is very bad.   He draws very badly.
                  adjective   adverb

7.1.2.2 Other adverbs are derived from adjectives or other word classes by the addition of a suffix

There are a variety of suffixes for this purpose:

+ deles   **aldeles**, completely; **fremdeles**, still; **særdeles**, extremely

+ ledes   **ligeledes**, likewise; **således**, thus

+ mæssig(t) **forholdsmæssig(t)**, proportionately; **lovmæssig(t)**, legally; **regelmæssig(t)**, regularly

+ s   **dels**, partly; **ellers**, otherwise; **indendørs**, indoors; **udendørs**, outdoors

+ sinde   **ingensinde**, never; **nogensinde**, ever

+ steds   **andetsteds**, somewhere else; **intetsteds**, nowhere; **nogetsteds**, anywhere

+ vis   **heldigvis**, luckily; **muligvis**, possibly; **naturligvis**, naturally; **sandsynligvis**, probably

7.1.2.3 Both present and past participles (cf. 6.1.6–6.1.7) may also be used as adverbs

forbavsende/overraskende, surprisingly; **overvejende**, mainly; **begejstret**, enthusiastically; **forvirret**, confused

Notes:

1 Adverbs derived from adjectives that do not take -t in their neuter singular form (cf. 3.2.2, 3.2.4) do not add -t, nor do the adverbs listed above ending in -deles, -ledes, -s, -sinde, -steds, -vis and those derived from participles. For adverbs ending in -mæssig, the -t is optional but is normally added.

2 Adverbs derived from adjectives in -(l)ig add -t when modifying a verb (i.e. when used as adverbs of manner), but do not normally add -t when modifying other word classes (see uptoners and downtoners in 7.6).

    Hun spiller dejligt.   **Det var en dejlig varm sommer.**
    She plays delightfully.   It was a delightfully hot summer.

7.1.2.4 Compound adverbs

alligevel, nevertheless; **altid**, always; **bagefter**, afterwards; **derfor**, therefore; **efterhånden**, gradually; **endnu**, still; **hidtil**, so far; **igen**, again; **måske**, perhaps; **også**, also; **rigtignok**, certainly; **simpelthen**, simply; **stadigvæk**, still; **vistnok**, probably

7.2 Comparison of adverbs

7.2.1 Adverbs derived from adjectives

7.2.1.1 Comparison

These have the same forms in the comparative and superlative as their adjectival counterparts, whether they are regular or irregular:

Positive	Comparative	Superlative	
dårligt	dårligere/værre	dårligst/værst	badly
godt	bedre	bedst	well
langt	længere	længst	far (of distance)
sent .	senere	senest	late
tidligt	tidligere	tidligst	early

7.2.1.2 A few other common adverbs compare as follows

Positive	Comparative	Superlative	
gerne	hellere	helst	willingly
længe	længer(e)	længst	for a long time
ofte	oftere	oftest	often
tit	tiere	tiest	often
vel	bedre	bedst	well

Notes:

1 Adverbs ending in -mæssig and -vis do not normally compare.

2 Adverbs derived from present and past participles compare with **mere**, **mest**: **mere/mest overbevisende**, more/most convincingly.

7.3 Use of adverbs

7.3.1 Modification

An adverb may modify:

- a verb   **Tiden går *hurtigt*.**
  (*Lit.*) Time goes quickly (i.e. Time flies).

- an adjective **Gaden var *utrolig* lang.**
  The street was incredibly long.

- an adverb **De arbejder *forbavsende* godt sammen.**
  They work surprisingly well together.

- a clause **Der er *ofte* problemer med bilen.**
  (see 11.3.4) There are often problems with the car.

7.4 Function of adverbs

7.4.1 Adverbs and adverbials

It is important to distinguish between adverbs and adverbials (cf. 11.3.4–11.3.5). *Adverbs* constitute a word class (like nouns, verbs, etc.), whereas *adverbials* denote an element of the clause (like subjects, objects, complements, etc.). An adverbial can be an adverb, but it can also consist of a noun phrase (NP) or a prepositional phrase (PP), as in these three examples of adverbials where only the first is an adverb:

Toget kørte *hurtigt*. (adverb)   The train ran fast.
Toget kørte *hele natten*. (NP)   The train ran all night.
Toget kørte *på skinnerne*. (PP)   The train ran on the tracks.

It is therefore important to distinguish word class (adverb) from function (adverbial).

7.4.2 Adjuncts, conjuncts and disjuncts

In terms of their basic function in the clause, adverbs may be divided into three categories: adjuncts, conjuncts and disjuncts. Adjuncts usually form an integral part of the clause structure, whereas conjuncts and disjuncts are peripheral elements and therefore outside the clause structure proper.

7.4.2.1 Adjuncts

Adjuncts are often adverbs of manner, time, place or degree, cf. the following examples:

De arbejder *hårdt*.   They work hard.
De har *ofte* travlt.   They are often busy.
Hun skriver *derhjemme*.   She writes at home.
Han svømmede *temmelig* godt.   He swam fairly well.

| 7.4.2.2 | Conjuncts |

Conjuncts have a connective, or cohesive, function and establish a connection between different parts of a sentence or sequence. In the following examples, **alligevel** and **derfor** are conjuncts since they refer back to the previous clause and thus connect the two clauses:

Selvom hun havde sendt afbud, mødte hun *alligevel* op.
Even though she had sent her apologies, she turned up nevertheless.

Han var blevet syg; *derfor* gik han ikke på arbejde.
He had been taken ill; consequently he didn't go to work.

| 7.4.2.3 | Disjuncts |

Disjuncts have no connective function, but usually express the speaker's attitude or evaluation. Examples of this are **desværre** and **sandsynligvis** in:

Desværre har vi lukket.   Unfortunately we are closed.
Det var *sandsynligvis* en fejl.   It was probably an error.

7.5   Adverbs indicating motion and location

| 7.5.1 | *The distinction between location and motion* |

Danish adverbs of place show a distinction in form between motion and location, which is rarely found in English. One form (usually the shorter one) is found with verbs indicating motion towards a place or from one area to another, and another form (usually the longer one) occurs with verbs indicating location at a place or motion within a specified area.

MOTION TOWARDS
Hun cyklede *hjem*.   She cycled home.

LOCATION
Hun er *hjemme*.   She is at home.

MOTION FROM ONE AREA TO ANOTHER
Han gik *ud* i haven.   He went (out) into the garden.

LOCATION/MOTION WITHIN AN AREA
Han går *ude* i haven.   He's walking (around) in the garden.

7.5.2 | Forms of adverbs of location and motion

Below is a list of adverbs with such double forms. Note that compound adverbial forms expressing this distinction are also possible and that precise translation of these into English is often not possible.

Motion towards (Where to?) →●	Location (Where?) ●	Compounds
bort (away)	**borte** (away)	
frem (forward)	**fremme** (forward)	
hjem (/to/ home)	**hjemme** (/at/ home)	**herhjem, derhjem** (here/there/at home) **herhjemme, derhjemme**
ind (in)	**inde** (in/side/)	**herind, derind** (in here/there) **herinde, derinde**
ud (out)	**ude** (out/side/)	**herud, derud** (out here/there) **herude, derude**
op (up)	**oppe** (up)	**herop, derop** (up here/there) **heroppe, deroppe**
ned (down)	**nede** (down)	**herned, derned** (down here/there) **hernede, dernede**
hen (over)	**henne** (over)	**herhen, derhen** (over here/there) **herhenne, derhenne**
om (round)	**omme** (round)	**herom, derom** (round here/there) **heromme, deromme**
over (over)	**ovre** (over)	**herover, derover** (over here/there) **herovre, derovre**

Examples of use:

Hvornår når vi *frem* til kirken?
When will we get to the church?

Hvornår er vi *fremme* ved kirken?
When will we be at the church?

Mette gik *hen* til bordet.
Mette went over to the table.

Bogen ligger *henne* på bordet.
The book is lying on the table.

De gik *om* bag huset.
They went (round) behind the house.

Der er en sti *omme* bag huset.
There is a path behind the house.

7.6 Uptoners and downtoners

Some adverbs, especially those of degree or kind, can function as *uptoners* or *downtoners*.

7.6.1 Uptoners

7.6.1.1 Use

Uptoners (or amplifiers) are used to *amplify* or *intensify* the meaning of an adjective, an adverb or a phrase.

absolut, absolutely; **(alt) for,** (far) too; **ganske,** completely, quite; **helt,** completely, quite; **meget,** very; **ret,** rather

Det er *ganske* umuligt. (adj.)
It's completely impossible.

Han råbte *(alt) for* højt. (adv.)
He shouted (far) too loudly.

Hun er *absolut* den bedste lærer. (NP)
She's absolutely the best teacher.

Det er *helt* i orden. (PP)
It's quite all right.

7.6.1.2 Adverbs derived from adjectives

Adverbs derived from adjectives are frequently used as uptoners.

Vi så en *frygtelig* kedelig film.
It was a dreadfully boring film.

Det er en *ualmindelig* dejlig aften.
It's an unusually lovely evening.

| 7.6.1.3 | Prefixes |

Some intensifying prefixes function as uptoners. E.g. **død-, kanon-, mega-, skide-, stjerne-, super-,** etc.; this is mainly a feature of colloquial spoken language.

Den er dødsmart/kanonflot/skidegod/superdejlig!
It is [uptoner] smart/gorgeous/good/lovely!

| **7.6.2** | **Downtoners** |

By contrast, downtoners (or diminishers) are adverbs that are used to *lessen* or *weaken* the meaning of an adjective, an adverb or a phrase:

dels, partly; **lidt**, (a) little; **næsten**, almost; **rimelig**, reasonably; **slet ikke**, not at all; **temmelig**, fairly, rather

Det er *temmelig* koldt i dag. (adj.)	It's rather cold today.
Det gik *rimelig* godt. (adv.)	It went reasonably well.
Det var *slet ikke* min cykel. (NP)	It wasn't my bicycle at all.
Vi nåede *næsten* til Køge. (PP)	We almost reached Køge.

7.7 Some difficult adverbs

| 7.7.1 | **gerne, 'willingly', 'usually'** |

Jeg gør det *gerne*.	I'll willingly do it.
Jeg vil *gerne* have en kop kaffe.	I would like a cup of coffee, please.
De kommer *gerne* om søndagen.	They usually come on Sundays.
Det tror jeg *gerne*.	I'm quite prepared to believe it.

| 7.7.2 | **ikke, 'not', 'no'** |

Jeg kender *ikke* vejen.	I don't know the way.
Han er *ikke* større end Mikkel.	He's no bigger than Mikkel.

Ikke is also used, either on its own or together with **også** or **sandt**, to form 'tag questions' following positive statements:

Mødet er i dag, *ikke (også/sandt)*?	The meeting is today, isn't it?

After negative statements, **vel** is used for this purpose instead:

Toget er ikke forsinket, *vel*?	The train isn't late, is it?

7.7.3 | langt, længe

Both words derive from the adjective **lang**, but have different meanings:

langt, far

Er der _langt_ til byen?
Is it far to town?

længe, (for a) long (time)

Har I boet her _længe_?
Have you lived here long?

7.7.4 | *Modal adverbs (or discourse particles)*

da, dog, jo, lige, mon (ikke), nemlig, nok, nu, sgu, skam, vel, vist

A number of unstressed modal adverbs are used by speakers to express or 'colour' their attitude to what they are saying; hence the alternative term 'discourse particles'. These nuances can be very subtle and in most cases there is no equivalent word in English. This often makes translation into English very difficult. Notice the following examples:

Det var _da_ godt, at du ventede.
It was certainly good that you waited.

Det er _dog_ hans fridag!
It is his day off, after all!

Nej, hun er _jo_ på ferie.
No, she's holiday, of course.

Mon de nåede flyet?
I wonder if they caught the plane.

Vasen er _nemlig_ meget gammel.
The vase is very old, you see.

Det er _nok_ ikke rigtigt.
It's probably not true.

Det er _nu_ ikke min bror.
It isn't really my brother.

Han er _skam_ professor.
Yes, he really is a professor.

Det mener du _vel_ ikke?
You don't really mean that, do you?

Du har _da_ sendt brevet?
I do hope you have sent the letter?

Hvorfor gjorde han _dog_ det?
Why on earth did he do that?

Vil du _lige_ hjælpe mig?
Would you just help me, please?

Mon ikke vi kan gå nu?
I suppose we can go now?

Jeg så det _nemlig_ selv!
I actually saw it myself!

Ja, det må du _nok_ sige!
You can say that again!

Det ved jeg _sgu_ ikke!
How the hell should I know!

Hun er _vel_ på arbejde.
She's at work, I suppose.

Jeg faldt _vist_ i søvn.
I guess I fell asleep.

Chapter 8

Prepositions

8.1 Prepositions – introduction

Prepositions are indeclinable words, i.e. they always have the same form. Prepositions usually govern a *complement*, and preposition + complement is called a *prepositional phrase*.

8.1.1 Types of preposition

According to form, there are three types of preposition:

8.1.1.1 Simple prepositions

These consist of a single, indivisible word and include the most common prepositions, such as **af, efter, fra, i, med, over, på, til, under, ved**.

8.1.1.2 Compound prepositions

The preposition **i** may be prefixed to four other independent prepositions (**blandt, gennem, mellem, mod**) to form the compound prepositions: **iblandt, igennem, imellem, imod**, which are more formal variants of the simple ones and in some contexts the only option. Note that **ifølge** (according to) is composed of a preposition + a noun.

8.1.1.3 Complex prepositions

These are made up of two or more words, including at least one preposition, which form a semantic unit. There are four main types.

(a) Adverb + preposition

Together, this combination indicates different types of direction or position. Note that some of the adverbs have a short form for direction/motion, e.g. **hen, ind, ned, op, ud,** and a long form for position, e.g. **henne, inde, nede, oppe, ude** (see also 7.5). Thus:

Motion:

Tina gik *ud i* skoven.   Tina went into the wood.

Position:

Tina gik *ude i* skoven.   Tina walked (around) in the wood.

(b) Preposition + noun + preposition

As in English, there are numerous examples of this type of construction:

af frygt for, for fear of; **i stedet for,** instead of; **med hensyn til,** as regards; **på grund af,** because of; **ved hjælp af,** with the help of/by means of; etc. Thus: *på grund af* vejret . . ., due to the weather . . .; *ved hjælp af* en skruetrækker . . ., by means of a screwdriver. . .

(c) Preposition + og + preposition

These are most often opposites in meaning and thus contrastive, such as:

(stå) *af og på* (bussen), (get) on and off (the bus); *for og imod* **(forslaget),** for and against (the proposal); *til og fra* **(arbejde),** to and from (work); etc.

A few examples with **med** (with) as the second element can have a reinforcing effect:

fra og med **(torsdag),** from and including (Thursday); *til og med* **(i morgen),** up to and including (tomorrow); etc. Note also: *i og med* **at han går af . . .,** given the fact that he's retiring . . .

(d) Discontinuous prepositions

In some cases, the complement is surrounded or bracketed by two prepositions and the three elements form a prepositional phrase, i.e. the second preposition does not have a separate complement (unlike the examples in (b) above).

Examples: *ad* **(helvede)** *til,* like hell (*lit.* towards hell); *for* **(mange år)** *siden,* (many years) ago; *fra* **(nu)** *af,* from (now) onwards, etc.

8.1.2 | Types of prepositional complement

8.1.2.1 A noun (phrase)

De tog på en lang ferie med børnene.
They went on a long holiday with the children.

Vi gik rundt i den dejlige, lille by.
We walked around in the lovely, little town.

8.1.2.2 A pronoun

Jeg boede hos *dem* i en uge.
I stayed with them for a week.

Notice that after a preposition the pronoun in Danish, as in English, must be in the *object* form.

8.1.2.3 An infinitive (phrase)

Han gik uden *at sige noget*.
He left without saying anything.

Hun er bange for *at gå ud alene*.
She's afraid of going out alone.

8.1.2.4 A subordinate clause introduced by **at** or an interrogative word (an **hv-** word)

Hun er sikker på, *at hun har ret*.
She's sure that she's right.

Han er bange for, *hvad der vil ske*.
He's afraid of what will happen.

Notice that, in English, a preposition cannot govern a 'that'-clause in this way.

8.1.2.5 A prepositional phrase

Billetter kan bestilles fra *i dag* og kan afhentes indtil *på fredag*.
Tickets may be booked from today and can be collected until Friday.

8.1.3 | The position of prepositions

Prepositions may adopt three positions in relation to the complement:

8.1.3.1 | *Before* the complement, i.e. 'preposed' (the vast majority of Danish prepositions occupy this place)

fra **hans mor**	from his mother
i **stuen**	in the living-room
med **en hammer**	with a hammer
til **Danmark**	to Denmark

8.1.3.2 | *After* the complement, i.e. 'postposed' (very few prepositions are found in this position)

dagen *igennem*	throughout the day
Han blev natten *over*.	He stayed overnight/the night.

8.1.3.3 | *Bracketing* the complement ('discontinuous') (see 8.1.1.3(d))

for **ti år** *siden*	ten years ago

On rare occasions, a preposition forms a bracketing expression together with a noun:

for **din** *skyld*	for your sake
på **firmaets** *vegne*	on behalf of the firm

Note that the second, but not the first, example allows an alternative, formal construction when the genitive element is 'heavy': *på vegne* **af alle mine venner**, on behalf of all my friends.

8.1.3.4 | In Danish, as in English, the preposition may be placed as the last element in a clause ('stranded position')

(a) in **hv-** questions (see 5.6):

> *Hvad* **tænker du** *på?*
> What are you thinking of?

(b) in relative clauses (see 5.5, 11.14):

> **Det er hende,** *(som)* **jeg tænker** *på*.
> She's the one that I'm thinking of.

(c) when the prepositional complement is in the topic position (see 11.8.1):

Ham kan man ikke stole på. He's not to be relied on.
(Cf. **Man kan ikke stole på ham.**)

(d) in infinitive phrases:

en kasse at lægge vasen i	a box to put the vase in
Her er noget at stå på.	Here's something to stand on.

8.1.4 | Stressed and unstressed prepositions

8.1.4.1 | Common monosyllabic prepositions

The most common monosyllabic prepositions (**ad, af, for, fra, hos, i, med, om, på, til, ved**) are unstressed when their complement is stressed, but stressed when their complement (usually a pronoun then) is unstressed.

Stressed complement

Det var pænt af din 'ven at skrive.
It was nice of your friend to write.

Jeg har ikke hørt fra min 'tante.
I haven't heard from my aunt.

Unstressed complement

Det var pænt 'af ham at skrive.
It was nice of him to write.

Jeg har ikke hørt 'fra hende.
I haven't heard from her.

8.1.4.2 | Other prepositions

Another group of prepositions (**bag, efter, foran, forbi, før, (i)gennem, (i)mod, (i)mellem, inden, indtil, langs, omkring, over, siden, uden, under**), most of them having more than one syllable, are either stressed or unstressed when their complement is stressed, but stressed when their complement is unstressed.

Stressed complement

(')Bag 'huset stod der et træ.
Behind the house was a tree.

(')Under 'broen løb en å.
Under the bridge ran a stream.

Unstressed complement

'Bag det stod der et træ.
Behind it was a tree.

'Under den løb en å.
Under it ran a stream.

8.1.4.3 | Prepositions placed *after* the complement and coordinated prepositions are always stressed

Hun arbejdede natten i'gennem. She worked throughout the night.

'Fra og 'med i dag stiger priserne. From today prices go up.

8.1.4.4 Prepositions are stressed when their complement is omitted and they function as adverbs

Han stod 'af [bussen] på hjørnet.   He got off [the bus] at the corner.

8.2   The most common Danish prepositions

Below is a list of frequent Danish prepositions. Examples of common ways in which the 13 most frequent prepositions (asterisked) are used are given in paragraphs 8.2.1–8.2.13. The remaining prepositions are used in much the same way as their English equivalents.

ad	by, at	**(i)mellem**	between
***af**	of, with, by	***(i)mod**	to(wards), against
bag(ved)	behind	**langs**	along
blandt	among	***med**	with, by
***efter**	after, for	***om**	(a)round, about, in
***for**	before, in front of, for	**omkring**	(a)round
		***over**	over, above, across
foran	in front of	***på**	on, in, for
forbi	past	**siden**	since
for . . . siden	ago	***til**	until, to, for
***fra**	from	**trods**	in spite of
før	before	**uden**	without
hos	at (the home of)	**uden for**	outside
***i**	in, on, for	***under**	under, below, during
(i)gennem	through, by	***ved**	at, by, around

Notes:

1 ad is used:

*   together with an adverb to express direction/motion:
    De gik *hen ad* gaden.   They walked along the street.
    Børnene løb *op ad* trappen.   The children ran up the stairs.
*   with the meaning 'in that direction':
    De lo *ad* klovnen.   They laughed at the clown.
*   with the meaning 'through an opening':
    Jens kiggede *ud ad* vinduet.   Jens looked out of the window.
*   with the meaning 'towards' + time:
    Hen *ad* aften gik vi hjem.   Towards evening we went home.

Notice also: **en/to *ad* gangen**   one/two at a time

2 **forbi** means 'past' in a spatial sense:

Vi kørte *forbi* den nye bygning.   We drove past the new building.

Han smuttede *forbi* vagten.   He slipped past the guard.

3 **for . . . siden** corresponds to 'ago' and brackets the complement (cf. 8.1.1.3(d)):

Vi mødtes *for* to år *siden*.   We met two years ago.

4 **hos** often corresponds to French 'chez' and German 'bei' (= at the place/home/ work of):

Vi bor *hos* min onkel.   We're staying with my uncle.

De køber kød *hos* slagteren.   They buy meat at the butcher's.

- as part of a lifestyle or culture:

  Det er en gammel skik *hos* de indfødte.
  It's an old custom among the natives.

- in works of art:

  Det er et hyppigt tema *hos* Carl Nielsen.
  It's a frequent theme in Carl Nielsen.

5 **omkring** means 'about', '(a)round', 'circa' and is used in both a spatial and a temporal sense:

Der er en voldgrav *omkring* slottet.
There's a moat round the castle.

Vi kommer *omkring* kl. 18.
We'll be there around 6 p.m.

Der var *omkring* 50.000 tilskuere.
There were approximately 50,000 spectators.

6 **siden**, 'since' (see also **for . . . siden** in 8.1.1.3(d)):

Jeg har ikke set ham *siden* jul.   I haven't seen him since Christmas.

7 **trods**

***Trods* sin alder går hun hurtigt.**   Despite her age she walks fast.

Notice also:

***trods* alt**   after all, despite everything.

8.2.1 | Af

Af often denotes origin or source (though see also **fra** in 8.2.4) and is used to indicate the passive agent (see 6.4.2).

AGENT	MATERIAL	CAUSE	DIRECTION	MEASURE	POSSESSION
by	*of*	*from/ of/ with*	*from/ of/ off*	*of*	*of*

BY

Huset blev købt *af* Kim.	The house was bought by Kim.
en roman (skrevet) *af* Hans Kirk	a novel (written) by Hans Kirk
Rotten blev fanget *af* katten.	The rat was caught by the cat.

OF

Huset er bygget *af* træ.	The house is built (out) of wood.
Tag pungen op *af* tasken!	Take your purse out of your bag!
dø *af* sorg	die of grief
ingen/nogle/de fleste *af* dem	none/some/most of them
ejeren *af* bilen	the owner of the car

FROM

Hun led *af* høfeber.	She suffered from hay fever.
Jeg købte computeren *af* ham.	I bought the computer from him.

WITH

Hun græd *af* glæde/smerte.	She cried with joy/pain.

OFF

Han stod/sprang *af* toget.	He got/jumped off the train.

Notice also:

Pigen løb ud *af* huset.	The girl ran out of the house.
Drengen stod op *af* sengen.	The boy got out of bed.
fuld/træt *af*	full/tired of
ked *af*	bored with, sorry about

8.2.2	**Efter**

LOCATION/ DIRECTION	TIME	DESIRE	SUCCESSION	REFERENCE
after/behind	*after*	*for*	*after/by*	*according to*

AFTER

Hunden løb *efter* børnene.	The dog ran after the children.
***Efter* lang tid kom hun tilbage.**	After a long time she returned.
Kom *efter* kl. 16!	Come after 4 p.m.!
den ene *efter* den anden	one after the other

BEHIND

Luk døren *efter* dig!	Close the door behind you!
Han stod *efter* os i køen.	He was behind us in the queue.

BY

en *efter* en	one by one
spille *efter* gehør/reglerne	play by ear/the rules

FOR

Vi må ringe *efter* en taxa.	We'll have to ring for a taxi.
Damen spurgte *efter* Lise.	The lady asked for Lise.
lede/længes *efter* noget	look/long for something

ACCORDING TO

***efter* dansk lovgivning**	according to Danish law
klæde sig *efter* årstiden	dress according to the season
Det går *efter* planen.	It is going according to plan.

Notice also:

høre *efter*	listen/pay attention to
lede *efter*	look for

The most common Danish prepositions

8.2.3	**For**

For corresponds to English 'for' in a wide range of senses, but is only occasionally used with time expressions (cf. **for . . . siden** in 8.1.1.3(d)).

INTENTION/ PURPOSE	INDIRECT OBJECT	CAUSE/ MEANS	PLACE/ TIME
for	*to*	*for*	*before*

FOR

et program *for* børn	a programme for children
Jeg gjorde det *for* dig/*for* din skyld.	I did it for you/for your sake.
Tak *for* kortet!	Thank you for your card!
Han er berømt *for* det.	He is famous for that.
Vi solgte sofaen *for* 500 kr.	We sold the sofa for 500 DKr.
Hvad er det danske ord *for* "goal"?	What's Danish for 'goal'?
***for* første/anden gang**	for the first/second time

TO

beskrive/forklare noget *for* nogen	describe/explain something to someone
Hun læste brevet højt *for* mig.	She read the letter aloud to me.
Det er nyt *for* mig!	That's news to me!

BEFORE

Vi har dagen *for* os.	We have the day before us.
Sagen kom *for* retten.	The case came before the court.

Note also:

for øjeblikket	for the moment
Han er bange *for* edderkopper.	He's afraid of spiders.
Hun interesserer sig *for* musik.	She's interested in music.
år *for* år	year by year
for det første/andet, etc.	in the first/second place, etc.
chefen *for* firmaet	the manager of the firm

And the following complex prepositions expressing position:

inden/uden for døren	inside/outside the door
oven/neden for trappen	above/below the stairs

for at + infinitive expresses intention:

De tog til Norge *for at* stå på ski.	They went to Norway to go skiing.

8.2.4 | Fra

Fra is used to suggest origin of space and time, as well as distance from a point.

LOCATION	ORIGIN/SOURCE	TIME
from	*from*	*from*

FROM

Træet står en meter *fra* vejen.	The tree is a metre from the road.
toget *fra* Rødby	the train from Rødby
Hvornår flyttede du *fra* Ålborg?	When did you move from Ålborg?
Brevet er *fra* Else.	The letter is from Else.

fra september til december	from September to December
fra kl. 8 til kl. 11	from 8 till 11 a.m.

Note also:

trække gardinerne fra	draw back the curtains
bortset fra	apart from

8.2.5 I

I is the most frequent preposition and the second most frequent word in Danish, with many idiomatic uses beyond its basic meaning 'in'. With public buildings and places of work or entertainment, English 'in' is often rendered by Danish på (see 8.2.10, 8.3.2). For the uses of i with expressions of time, see 8.3.1.

LOCATION/ MATERIAL MOTION		TIME WHEN	TIME DURATION	STATE	FREQUENCY
at/ in/ into/ to	in	at/ in	for	in	a/ per

AT

Pia er i børnehave/skole.	Pia is at kindergarten/school.
Toget standser i Roskilde.	The train stops at Roskilde.
i begyndelsen/slutningen af maj	at the beginning/end of May
i fuld fart	at full speed

IN

Han arbejder i Vejle.	He's working in Vejle.
en statue i bronze	a statue in bronze
Det skete i juni/2008.	It happened in June/2008.
i bilen/båden/huset/toget	in the car/boat/house/train
være i form/tvivl	be fit/in doubt

INTO
(Motion expressed by a directional adverb + i, see 7.5, 8.1.1.3(a).)

Han gik ind i køkkenet.	He went into the kitchen.
Hun løb ud i haven.	She ran (out) into the garden.
Golfbolden trillede ned i hullet.	The golf ball rolled into the hole.

155

FOR

Vi blev der *i* fem uger.	We stayed there for five weeks.
Jeg har kendt ham *i* 30 år.	I've known him for 30 years.

TO

gå *i* biografen/teatret	go to the cinema/theatre
Klokken er fem minutter *i* ti.	It's five minutes to ten.

A/PER

en gang *i* minuttet/timen	once a minute/an hour
90 kilometer i timen	90 kilometres per hour

Notice also:

With parts of the body:

Jeg har ondt *i* hovedet/maven.	I have a headache/stomach ache.
Han vaskede sig *i* ansigtet.	He washed his face.

Others:

Hun underviser *i* dansk.	She teaches Danish.
Glasset gik *i* stykker.	The glass broke (into pieces).

8.2.6 | Med

Med may be used to render most of the meanings of English 'with'.

ACCOMPANIMENT	MANNER	MEANS	POSSESSION
with/to	*by/*	*with*	*with*
	in/		
	with		

WITH

Han rejste til Mallorca *med* Lene.	He went to Majorca with Lene.
Jeg drikker altid kaffe *med* mælk.	I always drink coffee with milk.
Hun sagde det *med* et smil.	She said it with a smile.
Spis ikke *med* fingrene!	Don't eat with your fingers!
Hvordan går det *med* dig?	How are things with you?
en mand *med* skæg/sort hår	a man with a beard/black hair

BY

De rejste *med* bus/fly/tog.	They travelled by bus/plane/train.
Vi sender en check *med* posten.	We will send a cheque by post.
Aktierne faldt/steg *med* 5 procent.	Shares fell/rose by 5 per cent.

IN

tale *med* lav stemme	speak in a low voice
Skriv titlen *med* store bogstaver!	Write the title in capital letters!

TO

Må jeg tale *med* chefen?	May I speak to/with the boss?

Note also:

Hun giftede sig *med* Anders.	She married Anders.
Lad være *med* at afbryde!	Stop interrupting!
Af *med* skoene! / Ud *med* sproget!	Off with your shoes!/Out with it!

8.2.7	Mod

DIRECTION	LOCATION	TIME	OPPOSITION	COMPARISON
to(wards)	*against*	*towards*	*against*	*against/ compared to*

TO(WARDS)

Familien kørte *mod* Esbjerg.	The family drove towards Esbjerg.
Toget *mod* Fyn er forsinket.	The train to/for Funen is delayed.
***mod* nord/syd/øst/vest**	to(wards) the north/south/east/west
***mod* jul/påske/pinse**	towards Christmas/Easter/Whitsun

AGAINST

Han stod lænet *mod* træet.	He stood leaning against the tree.
med ryggen *mod* muren	with one's back against the wall
De protesterede *mod* planen.	They protested against the plan.
Danmark skal spille *mod* Italien.	Denmark are playing against Italy.
***mod* mine principper/min vilje**	against my principles/will

(COMPARED) TO

tre heste *mod* fem køer	three horses compared to five cows
ti stemmer *mod* to	ten votes to two

157

8.2.8 | Om

Om is used in a great many idiomatic senses, perhaps most frequently in certain expressions indicating future time (see 8.3.1.2, 8.4).

LOCATION SURROUNDING	HABITUAL TIME	FUTURE TIME WHEN	SUBJECT MATTER	FREQUENCY
(a)round	*in/on*	*in*	*about/on/in*	*a/per*

(A)ROUND

Hun havde et tørklæde *om* halsen. She had a scarf round her neck.
De gik rundt *om* huset. They walked round the house.

IN

***om* morgenen/eftermiddagen/ aftenen**   in the morning(s)/afternoon(s)/ evening(s)
***om* sommeren/vinteren**   in summer/winter

De kommer *om* en uge. They're coming in a week.
***Om* to år flytter vi til Spanien.** In two years we'll move to Spain.
Der er noget *om* snakken. There is something in that.

ON

Vi spiser fisk *om* fredagen. We eat fish on Fridays.

en afhandling *om* Holberg a dissertation on Holberg

ABOUT

De snakker altid *om* tøj. They always talk about clothes.
Bogen handler *om* et mord. The book is about a murder.

A/PER

tre gange *om* dagen/ugen/året three times a/per day/week/year

In certain instances, primarily with parts of the body, **om** is used colloquially without an English equivalent (see also 2.4.6):

Han er kold/snavset *om* hænderne. His hands are cold/dirty.

Notice also:

Vi bad *om* udsættelse. We asked for an extension.

8.2.9 | Over

LOCATION	MOTION	TIME	MEASURE	LIST
above,	*across,*	*over,*	*above,*	*of*
over	*via*	*past*	*over*	

ABOVE

30 meter *over* havets overflade   30 metres above sea level
Lampen hænger over bordet.   The lamp hangs above the table.
Temperaturen er *over* frysepunktet.   The temperature is above zero.

ACROSS

De cyklede *over* broen.   They cycled across the bridge.

OVER

Helikopteren fløj *over* byen.   The helicopter flew over the town.
over en femårs periode   over a five-year period
Over 40.000 så kampen.   Over 40,000 watched the match.

PAST

Klokken er ti minutter *over* tre.   It's ten past three.
Det er *over* midnat.   It's past midnight.

OF

et kort *over* Bornholm   a map of Bornholm
en liste *over* ansøgerne   a list of the applicants

Notice also:

Toget til Århus kører *over* Sorø.   The train to Århus goes via Sorø.
bekymret/overrasket/vred over   worried about/surprised/angry at
klage/sørge/vinde over   complain about/mourn/win against

8.2.10 | På

På is used in many idiomatic senses in addition to the basic meaning of 'on (top of)'. **På** is often used to render English 'in' in connection with public buildings and places of work or entertainment (see 8.3.2). For uses of **på** with expressions of time, see 8.3.1.

LOCATION	DIRECTION	TIME	TIME	MEASURE	POSSESSION
		WHEN	DURATION		
on/	*to*	*on*	*in*	*of*	*of*
at/					
in					

ON

Avisen ligger *på* bordet/stolen.	The paper is on the table/chair.
Billedet hænger *på* væggen.	The painting hangs on the wall.

AT

Vi mødtes *på* banegården/	We met at the station/library.
biblioteket.	
Hun arbejder *på* universitetet.	She works at the university.
***på* bunden/hjørnet/toppen**	at the bottom/corner/top

IN

Festen blev holdt *på* et hotel.	The party was held in a hotel.
***på* gaden/himlen/marken**	in the street/sky/field
Man kan gøre meget *på* kort tid.	You can do a lot in a short time.

TO

Jeg skal *på* kontoret/toilettet.	I'm going to the office/toilet.

OF

et barn *på* fire (år)	a child of four
navnet *på* byen	the name of the town
prisen *på* benzin	the price of petrol

Notice also:

***på* dansk/engelsk**	in Danish/English
***på* denne måde**	in this way
tro/tænke/vente *på*	believe (in)/think of/wait for
irriteret/sur/vred *på*	irritated/annoyed/angry with
slaget *på* Rheden	the Battle of Copenhagen (1801)
	(*Lit.* on the roads of C.)

8.2.11 Til

Til often denotes motion towards a target, but it has several other uses, e.g. marking the indirect object.

MOTION	TIME WHEN	INDIRECT OBJECT	POSSESSION	'INTENDED FOR'
to	till/ until	for/ to	of	for

TO

Hun rejser snart *til* Grønland.	She's going to Greenland soon.
Vi tog *til* stranden.	We went to the seaside.
Hvad sagde han *til* de andre?	What did he say to the others?
Jeg gav blomsterne *til* mor.	I gave the flowers to mum.
***fra* ni *til* fem**	from nine to five

TILL/UNTIL

Kan du ikke blive her *til* mandag?	Can't you stay here until Monday?
Det må vente *til* næste uge.	It'll have to wait till next week.

FOR

Vi spiste fisk *til* frokost.	We had fish for lunch.
Hun købte en skjorte *til* ham.	She bought a shirt for him.
Hvad brugte du pengene *til*?	What did you use the money for?

OF

Han er forfatter *til* mange bøger.	He is the author of many books.
døren *til* soveværelset	the door of the bedroom

Remnants of old genitive endings in -s and -e are still found on nouns in some set phrases after **til**:

***til* bords**, at/to the table; ***til* fods**, on foot; ***til* sengs**, to bed; ***til* søs**, to sea; **være *til* stede**, be present

Notice also:

***til* sidst/slut**	finally
oversætte *til*	translate (in)to
vant *til*	used to

8.2.12 Under

Basically, **under** corresponds to English 'under', 'below', 'under(neath)', but it is also used to render English 'during' in certain time expressions.

LOCATION	MOTION	TIME DURATION	MEASURE	MANNER
under/ below/ beneath	under	during	below/ under	beneath/ under

UNDER

Katten ligger *under* bordet.
The cat is lying under the table.

Bilen kørte *under* broen.
The car drove under the bridge.

børn *under* femten (år)
children under 15 (years old)

***under* ingen/disse omstændigheder**
under no/these circumstances

Han gjorde det *under* protest.
He did it under protest.

BELOW

Temperaturen er *under* frysepunktet.
The temperature is below zero.

Det var et slag *under* bæltestedet.
That was a blow below the belt.

BENEATH

Det er *under* min værdighed.
It's beneath my dignity.

DURING (when used about a certain activity)

De talte *under* koncerten.
They talked during the concert.

Jeg kedede mig *under* hans tale.
I was bored during his speech.

Notice also:

Under 20 personer mødte op.
Fewer than 20 people turned up.

under forudsætning af
on condition (that)

| 8.2.13 | **Ved**

Ved suggests adjacency or proximity.

LOCATION	TIME WHEN
at/	*about/*
by/	*around/*
near	*at*

AT

De sad *ved* bordet.	They sat at the table.
***ved* brylluppet/begravelsen**	at the wedding/funeral
***ved* solopgang/solnedgang**	at sunrise/sunset
kærlighed *ved* første blik	love at first sight

BY

Vi har et sommerhus *ved* kysten.	We have a cottage by the coast.
De sidder *ved* bordet.	They are sitting by the table.

NEAR

Louisiana ligger *ved* Humlebæk.	Louisiana is near Humlebæk.

ABOUT/AROUND

***ved* syvtiden**	around seven (o'clock)

Notice also:

ved ankomsten/afrejsen
on arrival/on departure

slaget *ved* Dybbøl
the battle of Dybbøl

Der er noget mærkeligt *ved* ham.
There's something odd about him.

8.3 Common English prepositions and their Danish equivalents – summary

When translating English prepositional phrases into Danish, you may find the table below of help in choosing a suitable Danish equivalent.

	Time	Place	Manner	Subject matter	Indirect object	Agent	Measure
ABOUT	ved			om			
ABOVE		over					over
AFTER	efter	efter					
ACROSS		over					
AGAINST		mod	mod				
AROUND	om/ved						
AT	i/ til (8.3.1.1)	hos	i/ på/ ved (8.3.2)				
BEFORE	før/ inden	foran					
BENEATH		under	under				
BELOW		under					under
BY		ved (8.3.2.(3))			med		af
DURING	under						
FOR	i (8.3.1.4)				for/til		
FROM	fra	fra/ af					
IN	i (8.3.1)	i (8.3.2)	på				
INTO		ind i					
OF	8.5	8.5		8.5			af/ over/ på
ON	8.3.1.3	8.3.2		om			
OVER	over	over					over
PAST	over	forbi					
THROUGH	gennem	gennem	gennem				
TO	i	i/ til			for/ til		
UNDER		under	under				under
WITH		hos	med				

8.3.1 | Translating 'at', 'in', 'on', etc., as expressions of time

Because of the idiomatic nature of Danish prepositional expressions of time, it is impossible to formulate rules that are both concise and completely reliable. For the sake of brevity some variations have been deliberately omitted from what follows. The aim here is to present a scheme of basic conventions that applies in the majority of instances.

8.3.1.1 | 'At' + expressions of time

'At' +	Festival	Clock
past	**sidste jul**	**klokken 10 (ti)**
habitual	**i julen**	**klokken 10 (ti)**
present	**i julen**	**klokken 10 (ti)**
future	**til jul**	**klokken 10 (ti)**

Notes:

1 **Sidste jul**, *i* **julen**, and *til* **jul** render English 'last Christmas', 'this Christmas' and 'next Christmas', respectively.

2 With year date expressions, Danish has either optional i plus end article (past) or **til** without article (future):

Det begyndte (*i*) julen 2008 og slutter *til* nytår 2030.
It began at Christmas 2008 and will end at New Year 2030.

8.3.1.2 | 'In' + expressions of time

'In' +	Year	Decade/century	Month	Season
past	*i* **1964**	*i* **60'erne**/*i* **1900-tallet**	*i* **april**	*i* **foråret**
habitual	–	–	*i* **april**	**om foråret**
present	–	*i* **2010'erne**	*i* **april**	*i* **foråret**
future	**(*i*) år 2030**	*i* **(20)30'erne**	*til* **april**	*til* **foråret**

Notes:

1 The preposition **om** (Eng. 'in') answers the question 'When?' to express future action:

De rejser *om* en time/en uge/et år. They're leaving in an hour/a week/a year.

2 The preposition **på** (Eng. 'in') answers the question, 'How long does/will it take?':

De kan køre til Møn *på* en time. They can drive to Møn in an hour.
    Or: It'll take them an hour to drive to Møn.

Sidste forår renders English 'last spring'; *i* **foråret** refers to 'this past spring', i.e. of the same year; while *til* **foråret** can only mean 'next spring'.

8.3.1.3 'On' + expressions of time

'On' +	*Weekday*	*Date*
past	*i søndags*	**den 1./første juli**
habitual	*om søndagen*	**den 1. /første juli**
present	**(i dag)**	**den 1./første juli**
future	*på søndag*	**den 1./første juli**

Notes:

1 I **søndags** and **på søndag** render English 'last Sunday' and 'this/next Sunday', respectively. Note that English 'on Sunday' is ambiguous.

2 For weekday + calendar date expressions, Danish usually has the weekday without article and no preposition:

Hun ankom torsdag den 1. april og rejser igen lørdag den 8. maj.
She arrived on Thursday 1 April and will leave again on Saturday 8 May.

8.3.1.4 'For' + duration

Danish **i** + expression of time:

De har boet her *i* to år.   They've lived here for two years.
Jeg har ikke set hende *i* otte år/   I haven't seen her for eight years/
   ***i* lang tid.**   for a long time.

'During' = **under** (when the noun denotes an activity)

Han var pilot *under* krigen.   He was a pilot during the war.
Hun fortalte os det *under* middagen.   She told us during dinner.

8.3.2 | *Translating 'at', 'in', 'on', etc., as expressions of place*

Because of the idiomatic usages of **i** and **på**, translation of 'at', 'in', 'on', etc., expressing place relationships is not always straightforward. The most common instances of Danish usage (to which there are exceptions) are set out below:

På (indicating 'on a surface')   *I (indicating 'inside')*

billedet på væggen   **et hul i væggen**
the picture on the wall   a hole in the wall

dugen på bordet   **dugen i skuffen**
the cloth on the table   the cloth in the drawer

På (indicating 'on a surface')

et sår på læben
a sore on the lip

Hun sidder på en stol.
She's sitting on a(n upright) chair.

på Roskildevej

tasterne på telefonen
the keys on the telephone

knappen på radioen/
fjernsynet
the button on the radio/TV

I (indicating 'inside')

et sår i munden
a sore in the mouth

Hun sidder i en stol.
She's sitting in a(n arm)chair.

i Bredgade

tale i telefon
speak on the telephone

et program i radioen/
fjernsynet
a programme on radio/TV

Other uses of på and i to indicate location are:

rooms (dwellings)

Han er oppe på værelset.
He's up in his room.

houses

Der står nr. 12 på huset.
It says no. 12 on the house.

areas of towns

på Vesterbro

islands and small peninsulas

på Sjælland/Djursland

islands (non-independent countries)

på Færøerne/
Grønland

continents (one only)

på Antarktis

institutions

på biblioteket
på hospitalet
på universitetet

rooms (spaces)

Han kiggede ind i værelset.
He looked into the room.

houses

Der er mange døre i huset.
There are many doors in the house.

towns

i Maribo

larger peninsulas

i Jylland

countries (independent)

i Irland/
Island/
Sri Lanka

continents

i Afrika/
Amerika/
Asien/
Europa

institutions

i børnehave(n)
i kirke(n)
i skole(n)

På *(indicating 'on a surface')*   **I** *(indicating 'inside')*

places of work

på arbejde(t)	**i forretningen**
på kontoret	**i kiosken**
på værkstedet	**i laboratoriet**

places of entertainment

på diskoteket	**i biografen**
på restaurant	**i teatret**

others   *others*

på stationen	**i banken**
på toilettet	**i Brugsen/Illum** (stores)

Other Danish prepositions of location are:

hos = at someone's house, certain places of work

Hun bor *hos* sine forældre.   She lives with her parents.
***hos* bageren/tandlægen**, etc.   at the baker's/dentist's, etc.

ved = at, by

Damen sad *ved* skrivebordet/vinduet.
The woman sat at her desk/by the window.

ved = by, on (with things extending lengthwise)

Familien bor *ved* floden/kysten/Øresund.
The family live by/on the coast/river/the Sound.

ved = near

Hotellet ligger *ved* jernbanestationen.
The hotel is near the railway station.

ved = of (about battles)

slaget *ved* Isted
the battle of Isted

Prepositions in expressions of time – summary

Past	*Habitual*	*Present*	*Future*

Seasons: **Forår, sommer, efterår, vinter**

sidste forår	**om foråret**	**her i foråret**	**til foråret**
last spring	in (the) spring	now in spring	next spring

i foråret/efteråret, i sommer/vinter, last spring (etc.) (of the same year)

(Note that **forår/efterår** and **sommer/vinter** are parallel as pairs.)

Festivals: **jul, påske, pinse**

sidste jul	**i julen**	**her i julen**	**til jul**
last Xmas	at Xmas	this Xmas	next Xmas

Days: **søndag, mandag,** etc.

i går		**i dag**	**i morgen**
yesterday		today	tomorrow
i søndags	**om søndagen**	**i dag søndag**	**på/næste søndag**
last Sunday	on Sundays	today Sunday	next Sunday

Parts of the day: **morgen, formiddag, eftermiddag, aften, nat**

i morges	**om morgenen**	**her/nu til morgen**	**i morgen tidlig**
i formiddags	**om formid- dagen**	**(her) i for- middag**	**i morgen formiddag**
this (now past) morning	in the morning(s)	this morning (now)	tomorrow morning
i eftermiddags	**om efter- middag**	**her/nu i efter- middag**	**i morgen efter- middag**
this (now past) afternoon	in the afternoon(s)	now this afternoon	tomorrow afternoon
i aftes	**om aftenen**	**her/nu i aften**	**i morgen aften**
last night/evening	in the evening(s)	this evening	tomorrow evening
i nat	**om natten**	**(her) i nat**	**i morgen nat**
last night/ during the night	at night	tonight	tomorrow night

Years, months: **år, januar,** etc.

sidste år	**om året**	**i år**	**(til) næste år**
last year	per year	this year	next year
i/sidste januar	**i januar**	**her i januar**	**til januar**
last January	in January	this January	next January

8.5 Translating 'of'

The English preposition 'of' may be rendered in a great many ways in Danish. What follows is by no means a complete account, but it will provide guidance on how to translate 'of' in the most common instances.

8.5.1 Danish renderings of English 'of'

8.5.1.1 Possessive 'of'

The English possessive 'of' is commonly rendered by the Danish -s genitive (cf. 2.3):

the owner of the car	**bilens ejer**
the roof of the church	**kirkens tag**
the top of the tree	**træets top**

8.5.1.2 In many cases Danish uses a compound noun instead

the owner of the car/car owner	**bilejeren**
the roof of the church/church roof	**kirketaget**
the top of the tree/tree top	**trætoppen**

8.5.1.3 'The City of Roskilde', etc.

When English 'of' may be replaced by commas indicating apposition, it is rendered without a preposition in Danish:

The City of Roskilde	**byen Roskilde**
the kingdom of Norway	**kongeriget Norge**
the Republic of Ireland	**republikken Irland**
the month of May	**maj måned**

8.5.1.4 'A cup of tea', etc.

Expressions with 'of' denoting measure are usually rendered without a preposition in Danish:

a cup of tea	**en kop te**
a pair of shoes	**et par sko**
5 kilos of potatoes	**5 kilo kartofler**
a large number of Danes	**et stort antal danskere**

Notes:

1 half of/part of/some of/the majority of:

half/some of the books	**halvdelen/en del/nogle *af* bøgerne**
some/the majority of the voters	**nogle/flertallet *af* vælgerne**

2 Danish usually has **på** corresponding to English 'of' when it is followed by a number:

a salary of 200,000 kroner	**en løn *på* 200.000 kroner**
a woman of forty	**en kvinde *på* fyrre (år)**

8.5.1.5 Dates

Danish has no preposition for 'of' when it is used in dates:

the 1st/first of January	**den 1./første januar**
in May of 2006	**i maj 2006**

8.5.1.6 'A heart of stone', etc.

'Of' indicating material is rendered by **af** in Danish (cf. 8.2.1):

a heart of stone	**et hjerte *af* sten**
a statue of marble	**en statue *af* marmor**

8.5.1.7 'The Queen of Denmark', etc.

'Of' denoting origin or dominion may be rendered by Danish **af** or **fra**. (The sense of geographical origin is stronger with **fra**):

the Queen of Denmark	**dronningen *af* Danmark**
	(= Danmarks dronning)
a young man of Jutland	**en ung mand *fra* Jylland**
	(= en ung jyde)

Notice that where 'of' = 'in', Danish has **i**:

the mayor of Helsingør	**borgmesteren *i* Helsingør**
The Merchant of Venice	**Købmanden *i* Venedig**

8.5.1.8 'North of', etc.

'Of' with compass points = **for**:

north of Skagen	**nord *for* Skagen**

Note:

the north of England	**Nordengland**

8.5.1.9 'A map of Greenland', etc.

With maps, lists and directories, **over** is often used:

a map of Greenland	**et kort *over* Grønland**
a list of telephone numbers	**en liste *over* telefonnumre**
a survey of Danish towns	**en oversigt *over* danske byer**

8.5.1.10 'A professor of law', etc.

With job titles, **i** is normally used:

a professor of law	**en professor *i* jura**
	(= **en juraprofessor**)
a teacher of English	**en lærer *i* engelsk**
	(= **en engelsklærer**)

Chapter 9

Interjections

9.1 Interjections

9.1.1 Introduction

There are two types of interjection, both of which are overwhelmingly used
in the spoken language. They usually appear at the beginning of a sentence
and are separated from the rest of the sentence by a comma. Thus they are
not an integrated part of the clause structure. Type 1 includes exclamations
and spontaneous expressions of feelings (e.g. joy, surprise, pain, etc.) that
have no external reference, and imitations of sounds, while Type 2 consists
of formulaic words and expressions used in conventional situations (e.g.
affirmations, denials, greetings, etc.).

9.1.2 Type 1: exclamations, expressions of feelings

9.1.2.1 Positive feelings

Delight, satisfaction: **ih, næ(h),** åh

Ih, hvor er det spændende!	Oh, how exciting!
Næh, sikke en sød, lille kat!	Oh, what a sweet, little cat!
Åh, hvor er det dejligt!	Oh, how lovely it is!

Praise, joy, excitement: **bravo, hurra, juhu**

Bravo, det var flot klaret!	Bravo, well done!
Hurra, vi vandt!	Hurrah, we won!
Juhu, vi skal i Tivoli i aften!	Yippee, we are going to Tivoli tonight!

Surprise: Hovsa, ih, nej, næ(h), nå

Hovsa, jeg tabte mine briller!   Whoops, I dropped my glasses!
Ih/Næh, sikke en overraskelse!   Oh, what a surprise!
Nå, jeg troede, det var i morgen!   Really, I thought it was tomorrow.

9.1.2.2 Negative feelings

Annoyance, disappointment: øv, årh

Øv, hvorfor skal vi gå nu?   Damn, why must we go now?
Årh, nu gik det lige så godt!   Oh no, it was going so well!

Disapproval, disgust, discomfort: fy, føj, puh(a)

Fy, hvor skulle du skamme dig!   Shame on you!
Føj, hvor ulækkert!   Ugh, how disgusting!
Puh, hvor er det varmt!   Phew, it's hot!
Puha, hvor her lugter!   Pooh, it smells in here!

Fear: ih, nej, uh(a)

Ih/Nej/Uh, hvor blev jeg bange!   Oh dear, I was really scared!
Uha, hvor er her mørkt!   Gosh, isn't it dark in here?

Hesitation: øh

Øh, det kan jeg ikke huske.   Er, I don't remember.

Pain: av

Av, hvor gør det ondt!   Ow, it hurts!

9.1.2.3 Imitations of sounds (onomatopoeia)

Sounds of animals: **miav** (cat); **muh** (cow); **mæh** (sheep); **pruh** (horse); **vov** (dog); **øf** (pig)

Sounds of objects: **bang** (door, gun); **ding-dong** (bell); **plask** (into water); **tik-tak** (clock)

9.1.2.4 Commands to animals and people (a mixture of Type I and Type 2)

Animals: to dogs: **Dæk!** (down!); to horses: **Hyp! Prr!** (Gee up! Whoah!)

Commands between people: **Hys! Ssh!** (Hush! Ssh!); to soldiers: **Giv agt!** (Ready!), **Ret!** (Attention!)

9.1.3 Type 2: formulaic words and expressions

9.1.3.1 Affirmations: **ja**, **jo** and their compound forms

(a) Ja, jo (jo is used in the answer when the question contains a negation)

Har du set min nye sofa?	**Ja./Ja, det har jeg.**
Have you seen my new sofa?	Yes./Yes, I have.
Er du ikke træt?	**Jo./Jo, det er jeg.**
Aren't you tired?	Yes./Yes, I am.
Har du aldrig været i New York?	**Jo, to gange.**
Have you never been to New York?	Yes, twice.

(b) Javist, jovist (stronger affirmation, greater assurance)

Tror du, at han stadig elsker mig?	**Javist gør han det!**
Do you think he still loves me?	Of course he does!
Har du ikke vandet blomsterne?	**Jovist har jeg så!**
Haven't you watered the flowers?	Yes, I certainly have!

(c) Jamen (can express sympathy or mild protest, but may also introduce answers in a debate)

Jamen dog, har du slået dig?
Oh dear, have you hurt yourself?

De skal snart giftes.	**Jamen, de er da alt for unge!**
They are getting married soon.	But they are far too young!
Hvad er din kommentar?	**Jamen, det er da en god ide!**
What do you say to that?	Well, that's rather a good idea!

(d) Jaså (signals surprise and often disapproval)

Hun har lige skiftet arbejde.	**Jaså, det havde jeg nu ikke ventet.**
She has just got a new job.	I see, I hadn't expected that.
Jeg glemte at købe løg.	**Jaså, så må vi jo klare os uden!**
I forgot to buy onions.	Well then, we'll have to do without.

(e) Javel (denotes acceptance of a statement or an order)

Hun kan ikke komme i dag.	**Javel, det skal jeg notere.**
She can't come to today.	OK, I'll make a note of that.
Ti stille, når jeg taler!	**Javel, hr. sergeant!**
Shut up when I'm talking!	Yes, sir! (i.e. a sergeant)

9.1.3.2	Denials

(a) **Nej** (clear denial or refusal)

Kunne du lide filmen?	**Nej, jeg syntes, den var kedelig.**
Did you like the film?	No, I thought it was boring.
Har du tid et øjeblik?	**Nej./Nej, det har jeg ikke.**
Have you got a moment?	No./No, I haven't.

(b) **Næ(h)** (implies doubt or hesitation)

Skal I ikke på ferie?	**Næh, vi har ingen planer om det.**
Aren't you going on holiday?	Well, no, we have no plans.

9.1.3.3	Uncertainty: **tja(h)** (somewhere in between 'yes' and 'no')

Tror du, der er mad nok?	**Tjah, hvis de ikke er alt for sultne.**
Do you think there's enough food?	Well, if they aren't too hungry.

9.1.3.4	Greetings and exhortations

(a) On meeting (in increasing order of formality)

hej, dav(s), goddag, goddav(s), godmorgen, godaften

(b) On parting (in increasing order of formality)

hej (hej), vi ses, farvel, på gensyn

(c) Seasonal: **glædelig/god jul**, Merry Christmas; **godt nytår**, Happy New Year; **god påske**, Happy Easter; **til lykke/tillykke med fødselsdagen**, happy birthday

(d) Thanks: **(mange) tak**, (many) thanks; **tak for mad/sidst**, thanks for the food/the last time we met; **selv tak/tak i lige måde**, thank you (in return)

(e) Apologies and responses: **om forladelse**, sorry; **undskyld**, excuse me/ sorry; **åh, jeg be'r/ingen årsag/det var så lidt**, not at all/don't mention it

(f) Others: **skål**, cheers; **værsgo**, here you are

9.1.3.5 Expletives (mostly names for God, the Devil, diseases and excrement), often used for extra emphasis

fandens/helvedes/satans (også), for fanden/helvede/satan, kraftedeme, lort, pis, sateme, sgu, skid, skide- (as an uptoner, e.g. **skidegod, skidesød**, etc., cf. 7.6), **ved gud**

Euphemisms: **for katten/pokker/søren, pokkers, skam, søreme**

Chapter 10

Conjunctions

10.1 Coordinating conjunctions

10.1.1 Function

Coordinating conjunctions join clauses or clause elements of the same kind. They always appear between the words or groups of words that they link (see 11.6), but do not affect the word order within these (groups of) words.

Coordination (linking) of:

two subjects	**Hans og Grethe så et hus ude i skoven.** Hans and Grethe saw a house in the woods.
two verbs	**De *sidder* og *snakker*.** They are sitting talking.
two main clauses (straight word order)	**Han vasker op, og hun tørrer af.** He washes the dishes, and she dries them.
two main clauses (inverted word order)	**Benny kan hun godt lide, og det kan jeg også.** She likes Benny and so do I.
two subordinate clauses	**Jeg tror, at det bliver koldt, og at vi får sne.** I think it'll be cold and that we'll get snow.

10.1.2 Five coordinating conjunctions

og and	**Luk døren *og* sid ned!** Close the door and sit down!
eller or	**Vil du have kaffen i en kop *eller* et krus?** Do you want your coffee in a cup or a mug?

for	**Hun gik tidligt, *for* hun havde et møde.**
for, because	She left early for she had a meeting.
men	**Jeg spurgte ham, men han vidste det ikke.**
but	I asked him but he didn't know.
så	**Skolen var lukket, *så* eleverne gik hjem.**
so	The school was closed so the pupils went home.

10.2 Subordinating conjunctions

10.2.1 Function

These link a main clause (MC) and a subordinate clause (SC). The subordinate clause may follow or precede the main clause:

De spiser, *når* de er sultne.   They eat when they're hungry.
MC   /sub. + SC
          conj.

Når de er sultne, spiser de.   When they're hungry they eat.
sub. + SC   /MC
conj.

10.2.2 Subordinators

Subordinating conjunctions, and other subordinators (listed below) that can introduce subordinate clauses, will occupy the first position in the subordinate clause and may affect the word order in that clause (see 11.12, 11.16)

There are two main types of subordinator:

(a) General subordinators

These words introduce indirect speech (*at* = that) and indirect yes/no questions (*om* = if, whether), but carry no meaning themselves, unlike the subordinating conjunctions in (b) below. Just like 'that' in English, **at** is sometimes omitted, especially in the spoken language, but **om** never is:

at	**Hun sagde, (at) hun havde fået nyt job.**
that	She said (that) she had got a new job.
	(Cf. direct speech: **Hun sagde: 'Jeg har fået nyt job.'**)

179

om	**Jeg spurgte, om hun havde fået nyt job.**
if, whether	I asked if she had got a new job.
	(Cf. direct question: **Jeg spurgte: 'Har du fået nyt job?'**)

(b) Other subordinating conjunctions

These conjunctions introduce various kinds of adverbial clause (cf. 11.12, 11.15):

(i) Time:

when	**Når du får tid, kan du male skuret.**
	When you get the time, you can paint the shed.
when(ever)	**Når solen skinnede, gik vi ned til stranden.**
	When(ever) it was sunny we went down to the beach.
when	**Da vi kom hjem, stod døren åben.**
	When we came home, the door was open.
since	**De har købt hus, *siden* vi sidst talte sammen.**
	They've bought a house since we last spoke.
while	**Me(de)ns jeg er ude, kan du skænke kaffen.**
	While I'm out, you can pour the coffee.
before	**Inden jeg nåede stationen, var toget kørt.**
	Before I reached the station, the train had left.
until	**Hun blev oppe, *indtil* Karen kom hjem.**
	She stayed up until Karen came home.

Note:

Når (when) is used to introduce clauses that describe either present/future events or repeated actions in the past (= whenever). **Da** (when) is used about a single event or occasion in the past.

(ii) Cause:

because	**Han kommer ikke til mødet, *fordi* han er forkølet.**
	He's not coming to the meeting because he's got a cold.
because	**Eftersom det er søndag, er posthuset lukket.**
	Because it's Sunday, the post office is closed.
as	**Vi kom sent hjem, *da* toget var forsinket.**
	We got home late as the train was delayed.
since	**Siden du spørger så pænt, skal jeg fortælle dig det.**
	Since you ask so nicely, I'll tell you.

(iii) Condition:

if	***Hvis** det bliver regnvejr, må vi aflyse havefesten.*
	If we get rain, we'll have to cancel the garden party.
even if	*Jeg kommer, **om end** jeg skal gå hele vejen.*
	I'll come even if I have to walk all the way.
if (formal)	***Dersom** renten stiger, bliver alt dyrere.*
	If the bank rate goes up, everything will be more expensive.
if only	***Bare** du sidder stille, gør det ikke ondt.*
	If only you sit still, it won't hurt.

(iv) Concession:

(al)though/	**Hun frøs, *selvom* hun havde holdt frakken på.**
even though	She was cold even though she had kept her coat on.
(al)though/	**Han sagde ja tak, *skønt* han ikke kunne lide ost.**
even though	He said yes please, though he didn't like cheese.

(v) Intention:

in order that/	**De malede værelset, *for at* hun skulle føle sig**
so that	**hjemme.**
	They painted the room so that she would feel at home.
so that	**Han slog i bordet, *så (at)* vasen væltede.**
	He banged the table so that the vase fell over.

(vi) Result:

| so . . . that | **Det var *så* varmt, *at* smørret smeltede.** |
| | It was so hot that the butter melted. |

(vii) Comparison:

as . . . as . . .	**Anna er lige *så* stor *som* Tina.**
	Anna is just as big as Tina.
than	**Verner er større *end* sin bror/*end* hans bror er.**
	Verner is bigger than his brother/than his brother is.
the . . . the . . .	***Jo* flere, *jo* bedre!**
	The more, the merrier!
the . . . the . . .	***Jo* længere vi venter, *desto/jo* dyrere bliver det.**
	The longer we wait, the dearer it becomes.

181

10.3 **Other subordinators**

These are words that are not conjunctions, but nevertheless introduce subordinate clauses.

10.3.1 | *Interrogative pronouns and adverbs (hv-words)*
(cf. 5.6)

These words can introduce indirect **hv**-questions (cf. 11.2.2):

Kan du sige mig, *hvem* hun er? (pron.)
Can you tell me who she is?

Hørte du, *hvad* han sagde? (pron.)
Did you hear what he said?

Ved du, *hvordan* han har det, og *hvornår* han kommer hjem? (adverbs)
Do you know how he is and when he's coming home?

When **hvem** or **hvad** is the subject of the subordinate clause, it is followed by **der** as a subject marker:

Han vidste ikke, hvem *der* havde gjort det.
He didn't know who had done it.

Hun kunne ikke forklare, hvad *der* var sket.
She couldn't explain what had happened.

10.3.2 | *Relative pronouns and adverbs (cf. 5.5)*

These words introduce relative clauses (cf. 11.10.2), which usually form part of the correlative or (main) clause to which they refer:

Vi har fået en ny lærer, *der/som* er meget dygtig. (pron.)
We have got a teacher who's very good.

Du kan få alt, *hvad* du ønsker dig. (pron.)
You can have all that you want.

De havde glemt maden, *hvad* der var meget uheldigt. (pron.)
They had forgotten the food, which was very unfortunate.

Hun huskede pludselig, *hvor* hun havde stillet mælken. (adverb)
She suddenly remembered where she had put the milk.

10.4 Translating some difficult conjunctions

10.4.1 'After' = efter at

'After' can function as an adverb, a conjunction and a preposition in English. **Efter** can function as an adverb and a preposition but not as a conjunction (though it is increasingly being used as such in modern Danish), and therefore cannot normally introduce a subordinate clause unless it is followed by **at**:

The letter arrived after they had driven off.
Brevet kom, *efter at* de var kørt.

10.4.2 'As' = 'for' = for

He postponed the trip as he couldn't get there in time.
Han udsatte rejsen, *for* han kunne ikke nå frem i tide.

= 'while' = mens (medens):

As she was singing, it started snowing.
***Mens* hun sang, begyndte det at sne.**

= 'the moment that' = idet:

As he stood up, the door opened.
***Idet* han rejste sig, gik døren op.**

= 'because' = fordi (in the written language also da, eftersom):

He went home early because he was tired.
Han gik tidligt hjem, *fordi* han var træt.

10.4.3 'As . . . as' in comparisons = (lige) så . . . som

She is as tall as her mother/as her mother is.
Hun er *(lige) så* høj *som* sin mor/som hendes mor er.

10.4.4 'Before' = inden, før

I'd like to have the money before you leave.
Jeg vil gerne have pengene, *før/inden* du rejser.

– as a conjunction after a negative main clause = **førend**:

He had hardly got up before(/when) the phone rang.
Han var næppe stået op, *førend* telefonen ringede.

– as an adverb = 'earlier', 'previously' = **før**:

I had met her in town two days before.
Jeg havde truffet hende i byen to dage *før*.

– as a preposition = **før/inden**:

She went for a walk before the dinner.
Hun gik en tur *før* middagen.

Before long spring will be here.
***Inden* længe bliver det forår.**

10.4.5 **'Both' – as a conjunction ('both A and B') = både . . . og**

Both the husband and the wife are vegetarians.
***Både* manden *og* konen er vegetarer.**

– as a pronoun ('both Xs') = **begge (to)**:

They both studied in Odense.
De studerede *begge (to)* i Odense.

10.4.6 **'But' – as a conjunction = men**

She worked hard but she didn't earn much.
Hun arbejdede hårdt, *men* hun tjente ikke meget.

– as a preposition (= 'except') = **undtagen/uden**:

All the apples but one were rotten.
Alle æblerne *undtagen* ét var rådne.

No one but my brother has a key.
Ingen *uden* min bror har en nøgle.

10.4.7 **'If' – as a general subordinator (= 'whether', see 10.2.2(a))**
= om

I asked if she had come in a taxi.
Jeg spurgte, *om* hun var kommet med taxa.

– as a conjunction introducing a conditional clause = **hvis**:

If you give me some money, I'll go shopping.
Hvis du giver mig nogle penge, vil jeg gå ud og handle.

| **10.4.8** | *'That' – as a subordinating conjunction* = **at** *(which can often be omitted)* |

They said (that) they had had a lovely holiday.
De sagde, (at) de havde haft en dejlig ferie.

– as a relative pronoun (= 'whom', 'which', human or non-human)

when *subject* in the relative clause = either **der** or **som**:

There is nothing in the bag that can break.
Der er ikke noget i posen, *der/som* kan gå i stykker.

when *object* in the relative clause = **som** (which can often be omitted):

It was a present (that) she had wanted for a long time.
Det var en gave, (*som*) hun længe havde ønsket sig.

– in cleft sentences (see 11.14) = either **der/som** or **at**:

der/som is used when the correlative is a non-adverbial noun phrase:

It was a new novel (that) Hanne sent me last week.
Det var en ny roman, (*som*) Hanne sendte mig i sidste uge.

at is used when the correlative is an adverbial of time or place:

It was in 2000 (that) the bridge across to Sweden was opened.
Det var i 2000, (*at*) Øresundsbroen blev åbnet.

It was in Kenya (that) Karen Blixen had a coffee farm.
Det var i Kenya, (*at*) Karen Blixen havde en kaffefarm.

– in the expression 'now that' = **nu da**:

Now that he has left, I can tell you about it.
Nu da han er gået, kan jeg fortælle dig om det.

– as a demonstrative (see 5.4):

That house must be very expensive!
Det hus må være meget dyrt!

Chapter 11

Word order and sentence structure

11.1 Word classes and clause elements

Elsewhere in this book we examine word classes (or parts of speech), i.e. words classified according to their form, function and meaning, e.g. nouns, verbs, etc. In this section we examine clause elements, i.e. words and phrases and their function and position within the clause/sentence. These two levels are illustrated by the following main clause example:

	Vi	**har**	**ikke**	**set**	**solen**	**i dag.**
	We	have	not	seen	the sun	today.
Word class	pronoun	verb	adverb	verb	noun	prep.+ noun
Clause element	Subject	Finite verb	Clausal adverbial	Non-finite verb	Direct object	Other adverbial

Several clause elements (i.e. a word or group of words) can be moved to the beginning of a main clause (declarative clause or statement):

Solen har vi ikke set i dag.   The sun we haven't seen today.
I dag har vi ikke set solen.   Today we haven't seen the sun.

11.2 Clause and sentence types

A distinction is made between the terms clause and sentence. A *sentence* is the largest unit that can operate within grammatical rules and may consist of one or more clauses. In practice, it expresses a 'whole meaning' and is usually bounded by full stops. A *clause* often has the structure of a sentence and is identical with it if there is only one within the sentence. There are two types of clause: (independent) *main clause* and (dependent) *subordinate clause*. A subordinate clause is dependent on a main clause and often

constitutes an element in it, e.g. subject, object or an 'other adverbial',
just as a main clause may form part of a larger sentence. Most clauses
possess both a subject (see 11.3.1) and a finite verb (see 11.3.2).

11.2.1 FV1/FV2

In describing clauses, we often use the terms **FV1**-clause and **FV2**-clause:

- In **FV1**-clauses, the finite verb comes first in the clause.
- In **FV2**-clauses, the finite verb comes second, after some other element.

11.2.2 Sentence types

The five sentence types and the relative positions of the subject, finite verb
and other elements in Danish are shown in the table below. Under the
word order column, the designation *straight* refers to the order subject –
finite verb, and the designation *inverted* to finite verb – subject.

Position				Word order
1	2	3	4 /	
STATEMENT				
Subject	Finite verb	–	etc.	FV2, straight
De	**kommer**	–	**hjem i dag.**	
(They are coming home today.)				
Non-subject	Finite verb	Subject	etc.	FV2, inverted
I dag	**kommer**	**de**	**hjem.**	
(Today they are coming home.)				
YES/NO QUESTION				
–	Finite verb	Subject	etc.	FV1, inverted
	Kommer	**de**	**hjem i dag?**	
(Are they coming home today?)				
–	**Skal**	**de**	**ikke komme hjem idag?**	
(Aren't they coming home today?)				
HV-QUESTION				
hv-word	Finite verb	Subject	etc.	FV2, inverted
Hvorfor	**kommer**	**de**	**hjem i dag?**	
(Why are they coming home today?)				

Position				Word order
1	2	3	4 /	
hv-word/ *Subject*	*Finite verb*		*etc.*	*FV2, straight*
Hvem	**kommer**	–	**hjem i dag?**	
(Who are coming home today?)				
COMMAND				
	Finite verb		*etc.*	*FV1, no subject*
–	**Kom**	–	**hjem i dag!**	
(Come home!)				
WISH				
	Finite verb	*Subject*	*etc.*	*FV1, inverted*
–	**Måtte**	**de**	**dog komme hjem i dag!**	
(May they come home soon!)				

Notes:

1 **hv**-questions are so called because they begin with an interrogative pronoun/ adverb or **hv**-word (see 5.6).

2 Yes/no questions are so called because the answer to them is 'yes' or 'no'.

3 Notice the difference in structure between **hv**-questions (FV2) and yes/no questions (FV1).

11.3 Clause elements

The elements of the clause that occupy the positions shown in the table above and in 11.1 will now be examined in greater detail below.

11.3.1 Subjects

11.3.1.1 Types of subject

The subject may be:

• a noun (phrase):

Katten **jager mus.**	The cat chases mice.
To år **er for længe.**	Two years is too long.

Den grimme ælling blev til en svane.
The ugly duckling became a swan.

- a pronoun:

  Han skrev et brev.   He wrote a letter.

- an adjective:

  Rødt er smukt.   Red is beautiful.

- a prep. phrase:

  På mandag er fint.   (On) Monday is fine.

- an infinitive (phrase):

  At cykle er sundt.   Cycling is healthy.
  At flyve til Kastrup er let. Flying to Kastrup is easy.

- a subordinate clause:

  At vi vandt kampen var   That we won the match was unexpected.
  uventet.

11.3.1.2 Formal subject and real subject

The formal subject (FS) **der** must be inserted when there is a postponed or real subject (RS) in the form of a noun (phrase):

Der (FS) sidder en due (RS) i æbletræet.
There's a pigeon sitting in the apple tree.
(Cf. **En due sidder i æbletræet.**)

If the real subject is an infinitive (phrase), **det** is used as the formal subject instead:

Det (FS) er sjovt at lære dansk (RS).
It's fun learning Danish.

Formal subjects may also appear in questions:

Sidder der (FS) en due (RS) i æbletræet?
Er det (FS) sjovt at lære dansk (RS)?

11.3.2 Finite verbs

The finite verb is the verb form that carries the tense, i.e. which indicates present or past time. The finite forms are the present and past tense, the imperative and (in rare cases) the subjunctive (see 6.3.4.1).

Han løber hurtigt.   He runs fast.
Hun løb hurtigst.   She ran fastest.

Løb hurtigere!   Run faster!
Anna længe *leve*!   Three cheers for Anna!

In two-verb constructions, the finite verb is usually an auxiliary or modal
auxiliary verb (see 6.3.4.2):

Han *har* købt to billetter til operaen.
He has bought two tickets for the opera.

Hun *kan* svømme meget langt.
She can swim a long way.

11.3.3 Non-finite verbs

Non-finite verb forms usually occur together with a finite verb (see 6.3.4.1
and 11.3.2). Non-finite forms comprise the infinitive, the present participle
and the past participle:

Han kan ikke *huske*, hvor de bor.
He can't remember where they live.

Hun kom *spadserende* hen ad gaden.
She came walking along the street.

De har *ventet* meget længe.
They have been waiting for a long time.

11.3.4 Clausal adverbials

11.3.4.1 Modifying the clause

The clausal adverbial (sometimes called the 'sentence adverbial') usually
modifies the sense of the clause as a whole. It is often a simple adverb
(but see also 7.1, 11.4.4). For symbols (F, v, n, etc.) see 11.5.

F	v	n	a	etc.	
Vi	**rejser**	–	***aldrig***	**til Danmark i juli.**	never
			altid		always
			gerne		willingly
			ikke		not
			nok		probably
			ofte		often

Cf. the different word order in the English main clause:

<pre>
     a   v
We never (etc.)   go   to Denmark in July.
</pre>

11.3.4.2 Order of clausal adverbials

Notice the relative order when there are several clausal adverbials:

(a) Short modal adverbs: **da, jo, nok, nu, vel**

(b) Short pronominal and conjunctional **altså, derfor, dog**
adverbs:

(c) Longer modal adverbs: **egentlig, faktisk**

(d) Negations, negative adverbs: **aldrig, ikke, sjældent**

De har vel (1) derfor (2) egentlig (3) aldrig (4) været i Danmark.
Therefore, I suppose, they have actually never been to Denmark.
(*Lit.* They have, I suppose, therefore actually never been to Denmark.)

11.3.5 *Other adverbials*

The clause element called 'other adverbials' (or 'content adverbials') comprise expressions of manner, place, time, condition, cause, etc. For this reason they are called *MPT-adverbials* and, besides adverbs, they may consist of a prepositional phrase (which is an adverbial) or a subordinate clause:

Vi rejser *med toget*. **Vi rejser *til Århus*.** **Vi rejser *på torsdag*.**
   A-manner   A-place   A-time
(We're going by train   . . . to Århus . . .   on Thursday.)

  Vi rejser, *hvis vi får tid*. **Vi rejser, *fordi vi har lyst*.**
     A-condition   A-cause
(We'll go if we have time.)   (We'll go because we want to.)

Notice that the relative order of other adverbials is usually (but not always):

Vi rejser med toget (manner) **til Århus** (place) **på torsdag** (time), **hvis vi får tid** (condition) / **fordi vi har lyst** (cause).

Some simple adverbs also function as other adverbials: **Vi gik bort/ned/ud**, We went away/down/out. If not followed by a prepositional phrase, these usually come at the end of the clause. The stressed verb particle occupies the other adverbial (A) position (see also 6.5):

1	2	3	4	5	6	7
F	v	n	a	V	N	A
Jeg	**skal**	–	**jo**	**klæde**	**børnene**	**'på.**

(I have to dress the children, you know.)

| **Vi** | **måtte** | – | **endda** | **skrive** | **det hele** | **'ned.** |

(We even had to write it all down.)

11.3.6 Objects and complements

11.3.6.1 Objects

Transitive verbs (6.3.4.3) take a direct object (DO):

Niels spiser *en kage*.   Niels is eating a cake.
                DO

Intransitive verbs (6.3.4.4) take no object:

Jette sidder i sofaen.   Jette is sitting on the sofa.

The direct object – which goes in the object (N) position – may comprise:

- a noun (phrase):   **Hun har lånt *hans bil*.**
                            She has borrowed his car.

- a pronoun: **Anne har hjulpet *ham*.**
                            Anne has helped him.

- a subordinate clause: **Jeg ved, *at han er hjemme*.**
                            I know that he's at home.

For pronouns, see also 11.8.2.

Ditransitive verbs take both a direct and an indirect object (see 6.3.4.4). The indirect object (IO) is usually a person, another living creature or a thing for whose sake an action is undertaken:

Jeg gav	**Jens**	**min cykel.**		**Jeg gav**	**min cykel**	**til Jens.**
	IO	DO			DO	IO

I gave Jens my bike.   I gave my bike to Jens.

Note that the order of the objects is usually as in English, i.e. a preposition-less object precedes an object with a preposition:

Jeg gav   cyklen   til Jens.
         – prep   + prep
I gave the bike to Jens.

If neither object has a preposition, the indirect object precedes the direct object:

Jeg gav   Jens   cyklen.
          IO   DO
I gave Jens the bike.

11.3.6.2 Complements

The subject complement occupies the same position as the object (N), and is found in clauses with copula verbs such as: **blive, gøre ... til ..., hedde, kaldes, se ... ud, synes, virke, være.** The complement agrees with the subject or object:

Ole og Marie er førsteårs studerende.	*Subject complement*
Ole and Marie are first-year students.	= *noun phrase* (11.4.1)
De virker meget intelligente.	= *adjective phrase* (11.4.3)
They seem very intelligent.	
Det var *dem*, der gik nu.	= *pronoun*
It was they who left now.	

When there is an object complement, it follows the object and is co-referential with it:

Det gjorde hende meget glad.	*Object complement*
That made her very happy.	= *adjective phrase*
De kaldte deres hund *Trofast*.	= *noun phrase*
They called their dog Trofast (= loyal).	

11.3.7 The passive agent

See the passive, 6.4.2. The passive agent (preceded by the preposition **af**) usually occupies the other adverbial position (A):

F	v	n	a	V	N	A
Holdet	**bør**	–	**da**	**udtages**	–	***af træneren.***

The team should certainly be picked by the coach.

Peter	**blev**	–	–	**hentet**	–	***af sin kone.***

Peter was met by his wife.

11.4 Phrases

Phrases consist of a head word alone or with optional modifiers before (premodifiers) or after (postmodifiers) the head word (H); the whole phrase is in italics in the examples below. There are specific rules for the five different kinds of phrase (see 11.4.1–11.4.5):

små børn på gulvet
  H (Noun phrase)
(premod. + H + postmod.)
small children on the floor

meget glad for gaverne
   H (Adjective phrase)
(premod. + H + postmod.)
very pleased with the presents

Jeg *har* ofte *sagt* det til ham.
   H (Verb phrase)
(premod. + H)
I've often said it to him.

Ib kørte *meget forsigtigt*.
    H (Adverb phrase)
(premod. + H)
Ib drove very carefully.

Hun sad *på stolen*.
   H (Prepositional phrase)
(H + postmod. (Prep.Comp.)
She sat on the chair.

A clause (cf. 11.2.2) typically consists of a combination of phrases, often with the verb phrase and a noun phrase forming a *nexus* (the relationship of subject + finite verb). So, just as words make up phrases, phrases in turn make up clauses, and clauses sentences. There is, thus, an inbuilt hierarchy within a sentence. An exception to this is commands (etc.) using the imperative where there is no explicit subject: **Kom her!**, Come here!; **Stop!**, Stop!; **Vent lidt!**, Wait a little. The order of elements shows which type of clause we are dealing with (cf. the statement **Det regner**, It's raining, with the question **Regner det?**, Is it raining?. The nexus is the core of the clause.

The five types of phrase (see 11.4.1–11.4.5) are *syntactic* units that *function* as clause elements (subject, verb, object, complement, adverbial).

11.4.1 The noun phrase

11.4.1.1 Head and modifiers

A noun phrase (NP) comprises a noun or pronoun as head word (H) with possible pre- and/or postmodifiers. If the noun phrase is a pronoun, it can only have postmodification. (The head word is in italics.)

gamle *mennesker*	old people
ting, som er nyttige	things that are useful
min *cykel*	my cycle
manden på gaden	the man in the street
Poulsens *have*	Poulsen's garden

11.4.1.2 Functions of the noun phrase

The noun phrase (in italics in the following examples) is the central building block of several different constructions. The syntactic functions of the noun phrase include:

- Subject (see 11.3.1)

  Den nye bil har automatisk gearskifte.
  The new car has automatic gear change.

- Direct object (see 11.3.6)

  Britta købte en rød skjorte til ham.
  Britta bought a red shirt for him.

- Indirect object (see 11.3.6)

  Han gav sin kone blomster på bryllupsdagen.
  He gave his wife flowers for their anniversary.

- Subject complement (see 11.3.6)

  Det er den bedste hund, jeg nogensinde har haft.
  It's the best dog I've ever had.

- Object complement (see 11.3.6)

  Alle kalder ham Pingo.
  Everyone calls him Pingo.

- Other adverbial (see 11.3.5)

  Han studerede hele natten.
  He was studying all night.

- Noun attribute

  Vi købte to kilo kartofler.
  We bought two kilos of potatoes.

- Epithet

  Vi har mødt dronning Margrethe.
  We have met Queen Margrethe.

Prepositioned modifiers and attributes (premodifiers)

These come *before* the head.

Modifiers Totality	Demon- strative	Possession	Quantity	Selection	Com- parison	Adjective attribute	Head word
			en			god	bog
			to			små	børn
		fars	mange			gamle	venner
alle	disse	mine				smukke	ting
hele	denne			sidste		lange	måned
					sådanne	flotte	glas

Translations: a good book; two small children; father's many old friends; all these, my beautiful things; the whole of this last long month; such posh glasses.

Adjective attributes (see 3.2.7):

en *glad* person, a happy person; **et *stormfuldt* møde**, a stormy meeting; **den *seneste* udgave**, the latest edition; **det *gamle, faldefærdige* hus**, the old derelict house; ***smukke danske* herregårde**, beautiful Danish stately homes

den *fra fængslet flygtede* indsatte
the inmate who had escaped from prison

Instead of the adjective attribute, we may find:

- Genitive (possessive) attribute: *Lottes* taske, Lottes handbag; *skolens* rektor, the principal of the school; *deres* stolthed, their pride

- Measurement attribute: *et kilo* løg, a kilo of onions; *tre meter* gardinstof, three metres of curtain material

- Epithet: *moster* Erna, Aunt Erna; *dramatikeren* Munk, the playwright Munk

Postpositioned modifiers and attributes (postmodifiers)

These come *after* the head.

(a) General postpositioned modifiers

- Adverb   **turen *hjem***
             the trip home

- Prepositional phrase   **manden *fra Fejø***
  the man from Fejø

- Pronoun   **ejeren *selv***
  the owner him/herself

- Relative clause   **damen, *som du kender***
  the woman whom you know

- **at**-clause   **den ide, *at vi alle er lige***
  the idea that we're all equal

- Indirect question clause   **angsten for, *hvordan det* skulle gå**
  the fear of how it would go

- Comparative clause   **et lige så stort hus, *som I har***
  just as big a house as you have

- Conjunctional sub clause   **pladsen, *hvor stationen ligger***
  the square where the station is

- Infinitive phrase   **en god metode *at anvende her***
  a good method to use here

- Comparative phrase   **et lige så dyrt maleri *som hendes***
  just as expensive a painting as hers

(b) Predicative attribute

Brink, *(der var) min lærer*, er allerede gået på pension.
Brink, (who was) my teacher, has already retired.

(c) **Med**-phrase attribute

drengen *med hænderne i lommen* (= drengen, der har . . .)
the boy with his hands in his pockets (= the boy who has . . .)

| 11.4.1.5 | Definite and indefinite noun phrases (see 3.3.1, 3.2.7)

Definite noun phrases refer back to something known or familiar. Indefinite noun phrases introduce something new.

Jeg spiste *et rødt* og *et grønt* æble.
    indefinite NP
I ate a red and a green apple.

Det grønne æble smagte bedst.
definite NP
The green apple tasted best.

Nu skal jeg vise dig *en avanceret computer*.

indefinite NP

Now I will show you an advanced computer.

Only indefinite noun phrases may form the real subject (i.e. when the subject is postponed, see 11.9):

Der er sket *en ulykke* på motorvejen.
An accident has happened on the motorway.

A definite noun phrase can have a complement that agrees with it (see 3.2.8):

Æblerne er sure.   The apples are sour.

Only a definite noun phrase may be duplicated (see 11.7):

Bilen, den er på værksted.   The car, it's being repaired.

(a) Indefinite noun phrase:

> **Købte du *brød*?**   Did you buy bread?
> **Druer er meget sunde.**   Grapes are very healthy.

The indefinite noun phrase consists of a noun alone, or one preceded by:

- an indefinite article   **et vindue**, a window
- adjective attribute(s)   **hvide, danske strande**, white Danish
                                   beaches
- a measurement attribute   **en liter benzin**, a litre of petrol
- a combination of these   **mange nye ideer**, many new ideas

(b) Definite noun phrase

The definite NP consists of a proper noun (name) or a noun with end article.

> **Ida har meget travlt.**   Ida is very busy.
> **Har du glemt nøglen?**   Have you forgotten the key?

If the noun in the definite noun phrase is preceded by a definite attribute expressing quantity, possession, selection, or by a demonstrative, it has no end article:

nogle mennesker, some people; **min mobiltelefon**, my mobile phone;
i Svens værelse, in Sven's room; **den første dag**, the first day; **dette spørgsmål**, this question

11.4.2 The verb phrase

11.4.2.1 One verb form or more

The verb phrase may contain just the finite verb or a combination of two or more verbs (see 6.2.3–6.2.5, 6.3.1). As is shown in the word order rules, the verb phrase can be discontinuous, i.e. it may bracket other words (**I de seneste dage** *har* **jeg ikke rigtig** *kunnet gøre* **noget**, In recent days I haven't really been able to do anything.)

11.4.2.2 Verb forms

A narrow view of the verb phrase would include the following structures:

- finite verb alone (FV) (see 6.2.1–6.2.2)

  Hun *henter* **avisen.**
  She fetches the paper.

- FV + one or more non-finite verbs (NFV) (see 6.2.3–6.2.5, 6.3.1)

  Han *har skrevet* **nogle breve.**
  He has written some letters.

  Han *må have skrevet* **nogle breve til sin mor.**
  He must have written some letters to his mother.

- FV (+ NFV) + verb particle – phrasal verbs (see 6.5)

  Hun *har skrevet* **alle ordene** *ned.*
  She has written all the words down.

- FV (+ NFV) + preposition – prepositional verbs

  Han *havde ventet på* **hjælp.**
  He had waited for help.

- FV (+ NFV) + reflexive pronoun (see 6.3.4)

  De *har glædet sig* **i lang tid.**
  They have looked forward (to it) for a long time.

| 11.4.2.3 | Verb phrases consisting of a finite (+ non-finite) verb plus preposition or adverb |

These are of different kinds:

- Those with an unstressed preposition (except before pronouns); *prepositional verbs*:

  Vil du *sørge for* forretten?
  Will you see to the starter?

- Those with a stressed preposition without complement but where a complement may be inserted; *prepositional verbs*:

  Du *skal* bare *følge* 'med (mig)!
  You just have to follow (me)!

- Those with a stressed adverb, which, together with the verb, forms a single unit of meaning that is often idiomatic and not predictable; *phrasal verbs*. If this construction has a direct object, it comes between the verb and the adverb (see 6.5.2):

  Han *tog* frakken 'på.   He put on his coat.
         DO

- Those with an adverb (usually stressed) + preposition (+ a prepositional complement); *phrasal-prepositional verbs*:

  Han *blev* 'ved med at spise.   He kept on eating.

| 11.4.2.4 | A few verbs take both a reflexive pronoun and a preposition |

Han bryder *sig* ikke *om* krydderier.
He doesn't like spices.

| 11.4.2.5 | Copula verbs (e.g. **være**, **blive**) (see 6.3.4) |

These are devoid of real meaning and take an obligatory subject complement:

De *er* syge.	They are ill.
Han *blev* ingeniør.	He became an engineer.
Hun *hedder* Inge.	She is called Inge.

11.4.2.6 Transitive/intransitive verbs

Transitive verbs have a direct object, intransitive verbs have no object, and ditransitive verbs have both an indirect and direct object (see 6.3.4):

Jeg *lukkede* døren.	I closed the door.
Vi *sov* i ti timer.	We slept for ten hours.
Han *gav* hunden et kødben.	He gave the dog a bone.

11.4.2.7 Main verb/auxiliary verb

We also use the terms *main verb* (i.e. head in the verb phrase) and *auxiliary verbs*, which are themselves of different kinds:

- Temporal auxiliary (**have, være**, see 6.2.3):

  Vi *havde* allerede spist. — We had already eaten.
  Han *er* gået i byen. — He has gone into town.

- The passive auxiliary (**blive** in the **blive** passive, see 6.4.2.7):

  Fisken *blev* spist af Kaj. — The fish was eaten by Kaj.

- Modal auxiliary (**kunne, måtte, skulle, ville**, etc., see 6.3.1):

  Vi *må* skynde os hjem! — We have to hurry home!

11.4.3 *The adjective phrase*

11.4.3.1 Head and modifiers

The adjective phrase consists of an adjective or participle (functioning as an adjective) alone as head or with one or more adverbial modifiers (see 7.3). These modifiers are primarily adverbs.

***temmelig* stor**, rather big; ***tyve meter* høj**, twenty metres high; ***særdeles* ivrig**, extremely keen

Adjectives may also have postmodifiers:

gammel *nok*, old enough; **god *til at synge***, good at singing; **overrasket *over* resultatet**, surprised at the result

|11.4.3.2| Functions of the adjective phrase

- Predicative complement (i.e. subject or object complement) (see 3.2.7):

| **De er *virkelig søde*.** | They are really sweet. |
| **Det gjorde hende *meget glad*.** | It made her very happy. |

- Prepositioned adjective attribute to the head in a noun phrase:

et *ikke specielt godt* måltid	a not especially good meal
et *aldeles upassende* sted	a totally unfit venue
en *for børn uhyggelig* film	a for children scary film

|11.4.4| *The adverb phrase*

|11.4.4.1| Head and modifiers

The adverb phrase often consists of an adverb and any modifiers. Only adverb modifiers may be prepositioned (see 7.3), but others can also appear as postmodifiers:

Han går *meget* langsomt.	He walks very slowly.
***helt* tilfældigt**	completely by chance
tidligt *i seng*	early to bed

Directional/positional adverbs often premodify a prepositional phrase:

| **Vi var *ude* i haven.** | We were out in the garden. |
| **Han gik *op* ad trappen.** | He walked up the stairs. |

|11.4.4.2| Functions of the adverb phrase

- As clausal adverbial ('adjunct', see 11.3.4):

| **Hun kører *aldrig* med bussen.** | She never goes by bus. |
| **Han kan *faktisk ikke* gøre for det.** | He can't really help it. |

- As determiner to a nominal:

| ***Ikke kun* vi er tilfredse.** | Not only we are pleased. |

- As modifier to a verb (i.e. as other adverbial, see 11.3.5):

| ***I det hus* bor Aage.** | In that house Aage lives. |
| **Line løb *ret hurtigt*.** | Line ran quite fast. |

- As modifier to an adjective or adverb (see 7.3):

  Han blev *meget* stolt. (adj.)   He became very proud.
  De spiller *enormt* godt. (adv.) They play extremely well.

11.4.5 *The prepositional phrase*

11.4.5.1 Preposition plus complement

The prepositional phrase consists of a preposition plus a prepositional complement (see 8.1). This complement is governed by the preposition and can consist of a noun phrase (including a pronoun), an infinitive phrase or a subordinate clause:

Pigen *med den blå frakke* er min søster.
The girl with the blue coat is my sister.

Vi ventede *på dem*.
We waited for them.

De var bange *for at komme for sent*.
They were afraid of being late.

Han henviste *til, hvad han lige havde hørt*.
He referred to what he had just heard.

11.4.5.2 Functions of the prepositional phrase

- Postpositioned modifier to a noun phrase or an adjective (phrase):

træerne *i parken*	the trees in the park
vild *med dans*	crazy about dancing

- Other adverbial (manner, place, time, state, etc., see 11.3.5):

Hun valgte *med omhu*.	She chose with care.
Vi gik *langs åen*.	We walked along the river.
Vi var tilbage *inden aften*.	We were back before evening.
Han er *i dårligt humør*.	He is in a bad mood.

- Clausal adverbial (see 11.3.4):

  Det er *uden tvivl* beklageligt. It is, without doubt, regrettable.

- Verb complementation:

  Han takkede *for hjælpen*.   He said thank you for the help.

11.5 Main clause structure

Many main clauses possess other elements not detailed in 11.2. These are included in the schema below, which may be used to analyse most main clauses in Danish. Note the designations *F, v, n, a, V, N, A*, which will be used from now on for the seven positions.

1	2	3	4	5	6	7
Front position	Finite verb	(Subject)	Clausal adverbial	Non-finite verb	Object/ complement/ real subject	Other adverbial
F	v	n	a	V	N	A

STATEMENT

Han	**rejser**	–	–	–	–	**hjem i dag.**

(He is going home today.)

I morges	**havde**	**han**	**endnu ikke**	**pakket**	**sin kuffert.**	

(This morning he still hadn't packed his suitcase.)

Sin kuffert	**havde**	**han**	**endnu ikke**	**pakket**	–	**i morges.**

Så	**blev**	**de**	**natur- ligvis**	–	**vrede.**	

(Then of course they got angry.)

Der	**sidder**	–	–	–	**to klienter**	**uden for hans kontor.**

(Two clients are sitting outside his office.)

YES/NO QUESTION

–	**Flytter**	**de**	–	–	–	**til Odense?**

(Are they moving to Odense?)

–	**Vil**	**de**	**ikke**	**flytte**	–	**til Odense?**

(Don't they want to move to Odense?)

–	**Har**	**du**	**aldrig**	**villet se**	**hende**	**før?**

(Have you never wanted to see her before?)

1	2	3	4	5	6	7
Front position	Finite verb	(Subject)	Clausal adverbial	Non-finite verb	Object/complement/real subject	Other adverbial
F	v	n	a	V	N	A
–	**Gav**	**du**	–	–	**ham pengene?**	

(Did you give him the money?)

HV-QUESTION

Hvem	**kommer**	–	–	–	–	**her i aften?**

(Who is coming here tonight?)

Hvem	**gav**	**du**	–	–	**pengene**	**til?**

(Who did you give the money to?)

Hvornår	**ønsker**	**de**	–	**at rejse**	–	**til Norge?**

(When do they want to go to Norway?)

COMMAND

–	**Ring**	–	**altid**	–	–	**før kl. tolv!**

(Always ring before twelve o'clock!)

–	**Kom!**					

(Come!)

WISH

	Måtte	**der**	**aldrig**	**ske**	**dem noget!**	

(May nothing ever happen to them!)

Længe	**leve**	**dronningen!**				

(Long live the Queen!)

Notice that:

1 Main clauses always have a finite verb and usually a subject.

2 All positions except that occupied by the finite verb (*v*) may be left vacant.

3 The subject usually occupies positions 1 (*F*) or 3 (*n*).

4 The front position (*F*) is always occupied in statements and **hv**-questions, but is vacant in yes/no questions.

5 Only one clause element can usually occupy the front position (*F*) at any time.

6 There may be more than one clausal adverbial (*a*), non-finite verb (*V*), object, complement (*N*) or other adverbial (*A*).

11.6 Link position

The link position (k) is an additional position necessary before the front position (F) in order to accommodate coordinating conjunctions:

	k	F	v	n	a	V	N	A
Han kommer,	men	han	bliver	–	ikke	–	–	længe.

He is coming, but he won't stay long.

			F	v	n	a	V	N	A
			Venter	du,					
		eller	går	du	–		–	–	nu?

Are you waiting or are you going now?

11.7 Extra positions

The extra positions (X_1, X_2) are additional positions necessary both before the F-position and after the A-position to accommodate elements of various kinds outside the clause proper. These elements often duplicate elements within the clause.

	X_1	F	v	n	a	V	N	A	X_2
1	Lars,	han	er	–	jo	–	syg	i dag.	
2	Paris,	det	er	–	vel nok	–	en dejlig by!		
3	I Hillerød,	der	vil	jeg	gerne	bo.			
4	Da vi kom hjem,	lavede	vi	–	–	–	en kop kaffe.		
5		Det	er	–	ikke	–	sandt, –		at tiden læger alle sår.
6		Det	er	–	–	–	sjovt	–	at spille tennis.

Translations: 1) Lars, he's ill today, you know. 2) Paris, that's really a lovely city! 3) In Hillerød, I would like to live there. 4) When we got home, we made a cup of coffee. 5) It's not true that time heals all wounds. 6) It's fun playing tennis.

If there is also a link position (k), the order is:

k	X_1	F, etc.
men	Svend,	han er morsom . . .

but Svend, he's amusing . . .

11.8   Moving elements in the main clause

11.8.1 *Topicalisation*

11.8.1.1 Moving elements to the front

The subject usually occupies the front position (*F*), but it may be replaced by moving to the front (the 'topic' position) almost any other clause element. This is often done when one wishes to emphasise a particular clause element, or for stylistic reasons, and is known as topicalisation. When the subject is not in the *F*-position, it occupies the *n*-position, following the finite verb. In the examples below, the arrows show which element has been topicalised.

	F	v	n	a	V	N	A
Basic clause:	**Han**	**vil**	–	**alligevel**	**sælge**	**huset**	**i år.**

He'll sell the house this year anyway.

		F	v	n	a	V	N	A
1	(A to F):	**I år**	**vil**	**han**	**alligevel**	**sælge**	**huset.**	←
2	(N to F):	**Huset**	**vil**	**han**	**alligevel**	**sælge**	←	**i år.**
3	(a to F):	**Alligevel**	**vil**	**han**	←		**sælge**	**huset**	**i år.**

When the non-finite verb is moved to F, the elements governed by it will normally also be moved with it. However, this movement is more constrained:

		F	v	n	a	V	N	A
4	(V+N to F):	**Sælge huset**	**vil**	**han**	**alligevel**	←	←	**i år.**
5	(V+N+A to F):	**Sælge huset i år**	**vil**	**han**	**alligevel.**	←	←	←

Topicalisation of adverbials that usually occupy the final adverbial position (A), especially of time and place (including **her**, **der**), is by far the most frequent type:

Vi tog til Møn i juni.	→	**I juni tog vi til Møn.**
We went to Møn in June.	→	In June we went to Møn.
Peter traf Åse i Stege.	→	**I Stege traf Peter Åse.**
Peter met Åse in Stege.	→	In Stege Peter met Åse.
Hun har ikke været her/der.	→	**Her/Der har hun ikke været.**
She hasn't been here/there.	→	She hasn't been here/there.

207

In the *F*-position, it is common to find a subordinate clause that would otherwise be a final adverbial. Together the two clauses form a sentence:

Vi tog til Ærø, da vi kom hjem fra Frankrig.
We went to Ærø when we got back from France.

Da vi kom hjem fra Frankrig, tog vi til Ærø.
When we got back from France we went to Ærø.

Proper nouns and object pronouns are also commonly topicalised:

Ulf har vi ikke set længe./Ham har vi ikke set længe.
We haven't seen Ulf/him for a long time.

It is possible to topicalise direct speech:

'Fy dog!' sagde han.   'Shame on you!' he said.

The subject complement may also occasionally be topicalised:

Høflig har han nu aldrig været!
Well, he's never been polite!

[11.8.1.2] Natural topics

Most natural topics are unstressed and represent familiar information, which may link clauses/sentences together:

Vi trængte til en ferie, så *i september* kørte vi til Jylland. *Der* traf vi nogle gamle venner. *De* ejer en stor villa. *Den* har ti værelser. *Vi* boede der i 14 dage. *Så* måtte vi desværre vende hjem igen.
We needed a holiday, so in September we drove to Jutland. There we met some old friends. They own a large house. It has ten rooms. We stayed there for a fortnight. Then unfortunately we had to come home again.

[11.8.1.3] Emphatic topics

These are rarer and often represent new information. The following emphatic topics are either stylistically marked or used for contrast:

***Rart* var det nu ikke!**	But it wasn't very nice!
***En avis* købte vi også.**	A newspaper we bought too.
***Det* kan jeg ikke tro!**	That I cannot believe!
***Spille musik* kan han, men	Play music, that he can do,
***studere* vil han ikke.**	but study he won't.

11.8.2 Light elements

'Light' elements are short, unstressed clause elements, e.g. object pronouns and reflexive pronouns. In clauses *without a non-finite verb* (i.e. the V-position is empty), they move leftwards into the subject position (*n*) after the finite verb. An indirect object (IO) with no preposition will nevertheless always precede the direct object (DO). Note also the position of the reflexive pronoun **sig**.

F	v	n	a	V	N	A
Jeg	**kender**	**ham**	**ikke.**			
		(light DO)				
Jeg	**har**	–	**aldrig**	**kendt**	**ham.**	
Jeg	**kender**	–	**ikke**	–	*ham.*	
					(stressed DO)	
Hun	**gav**	**mig**	**ikke**	–	**bogen.**	
		(light IO)				
Hun	**har**	–	–	**givet**	**mig bogen.**	
					(IO + DO)	
Hun	**gav**	**mig den ikke.**				
		(light IO + DO)				
Hun	**gav**	–	**ikke**	–	*mig* **den.**	
					(stressed IO)	
Henrik	**viste**	**sig**	**ikke.**			
Henrik	**har**	–	**ikke**	**vist sig**		**i dag.**

Translations: I don't know him/I have never known him/I don't know *him*. She didn't give me the book/She has given me the book/She didn't give me it/She didn't give *me* it. Henrik didn't turn up/Henrik hasn't turned up today.

Similarly, the adverbs **her** (here) and **der** (there) move leftwards to occupy the *n*-position when they are unstressed and the V-position is vacant:

Hun var *her/der* ikke. (= unstressed)
Hun var ikke *her/der*. (= stressed)

But with the V-position filled:

Hun har ikke været *her/der*.
She has not been here/there.

| **11.8.3** | *Position of* ikke *and negative elements* |

The position of **ikke** (not) and other negative adverbials, e.g. **aldrig** (never), etc., can vary. When they negate the entire clause, they occupy the clausal adverbial *a*-position immediately *after* the *n*-position (see 11.5):

Frans kommer *ikke* i dag.	Frans isn't coming today.
I dag kommer Frans *ikke*.	Today Frans isn't coming.
I dag er Frans *ikke* kommet.	Today Frans hasn't come.
Frans vil *aldrig* gøre det.	Frans will never do it.

Occasionally, for contrast, the negative may come between the finite verb and the subject in inverted statements:

I dag kommer *ikke* kun Frans, men også hans familie.
Today it's not only Frans who is coming but also his family.

Pronominal or noun phrase objects containing a negation are also attracted to the *a*-position:

| **Jeg havde *ikke* gjort noget.** | I hadn't done anything. |

But:

| **Jeg havde *ingenting* gjort.** | I had done nothing. |
| **Katten har *ikke* fået noget mad i dag.** | The cat hasn't had any food today. |

But:

| **Katten har *ingen* mad fået i dag.** | The cat has had no food today. |
| **Jim har *ikke* ramt noget.** | Jim hasn't hit anything. |

But:

| **Jim har *intet* ramt.** | Jim has hit nothing. |

For the position of negative elements in subordinate clauses, see 11.12.

| **11.8.4** | *Passive transformation* |

When the active verb is transformed into a passive form, some of the other elements change position within the clause (see 6.4.2):

Active verb   **Andersen** (= subject, agent) **ejer hele huset** (= object, patient).
Andersen owns the whole house.

Passive verb   **Hele huset** (= subject, patient) **ejes af Andersen**
(= Prep.Comp., agent).
The whole house is owned by Andersen.

Passive transformation can be used in either main or subordinate clauses.
For the position of elements in the passive see 11.3.7.

11.9   Existential sentences

If we do not wish to introduce a subject at the beginning of a clause, we
can postpone it (i.e. move it to the right), but must then fill the front position
(F) with a *formal subject* (FS) or place-holder subject; the postponed
subject is known as the *real subject* (RS) (cf. 5.1.3, 11.3.1.2):

En lærer sidder ofte inde i køkkenet.
Subject
A teacher is often sitting in the kitchen.
→

Der sidder ofte en lærer inde i køkkenet.
FS   *RS*
There's often a teacher sitting in the kitchen.

At holde op med at ryge er svært.
Subject
Stopping smoking is hard.
→

Det er svært at holde op med at ryge.
FS   *RS*
It's hard to stop smoking.

The real subject may be of two types:

Type 1: When the real subject is an indefinite noun phrase (such as **en
lærer**), it occupies the N-position and the formal subject is **der**:

F	v	n	a	V	N		A
Der	**findes**	–	–	–	**ingen bjerge**		**i Danmark.**
Der	**sidder**	–	**ofte**	–	**en lærer**		**inde i køkkenet.**
–	**Sidder**	**der**	**ofte**	–	**en lærer**		**inde i køkkenet?**

Translations: There are no mountains in Denmark. There's often a teacher sitting
in the kitchen. Is there often a teacher sitting in the kitchen?

The verb in Danish existential sentences is always intransitive, and usually expresses:

- existence: **findes, være**
- non-existence: **mangle, savne**
- location: **ligge, sidde, stå, være**
- motion: **gå, komme**

In English the only corresponding constructions are: 'there is (are) –ing'. Note that, in this case, the formal subject is **der** = 'there'.

Type 2: When the real subject is an infinitive phrase (like **at holde op med at ryge**), it occupies the X_2 position (see also 5.1.3, 11.7, 11.10.1, 11.11) and the formal subject is **det**:

F	v	n	a	V	N	A	X_2
Det	**er**	–	–	–	**svært**	–	**at holde op med at ryge.**
Det	**er**	–	–	–	**dejligt**	–	**at svømme.**

Translations: It's hard to stop smoking. It's lovely to swim.

11.10 Subordinate clause as an element in the main clause sentence

11.10.1 Function of subordinate clause in the sentence

Subordinate clauses usually constitute the subject, object or other adverbial in a main clause sentence. As such, they may occupy several different positions:

F	v	n	a	V	N	A	X_2
Subject clause:							
At du er rask,	**glæder**	**mig**	–	–	–	**meget.**	
Det	**glæder**	**mig**	–	–	–	**meget,**	*at du er rask.*
Object clause:							
Han	**sagde**	–	**ikke**	–	–	**i går,**	*at han skal giftes på lørdag.*
At han skal giftes på lørdag,	**sagde**	**han**	**ikke**	–	–	**i går.**	

F	v	n	a	V	N	A	X₂

Adverbial clause:

F	v	n	a	V	N	A	X₂
Vi	**går,**	–	–	–	–		**når han kommer.**
Når han kommer,	**går**	**vi.**					

Translations: That you are well makes me very glad. I am very glad that you are well. He didn't say yesterday that he was getting married on Saturday. That he was getting married on Saturday he did not say yesterday. We will go when he comes. When he comes we will go.

Notice that:

- Subject and object clauses occupy the *F* or *X₂* positions.

- Most adverbial clauses (time, place, condition, cause) occupy the *F* or *A* positions.

- Some adverbial clauses (intention, result) can only occupy the *A* position:

F	v	n	a	V	N	A
Vi	**må**	–	–	**støtte**	**ham,**	*for at han ikke skal falde.*
Jeg	**blev**	–	–	–	**så sur,**	*at jeg straks gik hjem.*

Translations: We have to support him so that he doesn't fall. I got so fed up that I went home right away.

11.10.2 Relative clause

A *relative clause* usually functions as an attribute to its correlative, usually a noun phrase:

Han kiggede på de fugle (corr.)**, *der sad på græsset.***
He looked at the birds that were sitting on the grass.

Den film (corr.)**, (*som*) *vi så i går,* var fantastisk.**
The film we saw yesterday was fantastic.

11.11 Main clause structure – an extended positional schema

The table below gives a schema with examples.

		1	2	3	4	5	6	7	
	k	X₁	F	v	n	a	V	N	A	X₂
1			Han	havde	–	ikke	pakket	kufferten	i går.	
2			I går	havde	han	ikke	pakket	kufferten.		
3			Vi	giver	–	–	–	Ole en gave	i aften.	
4			Senere	blev	de	desværre	–	syge.		
5			Det	gjorde	–	–	–	ham glad.		
6			Der	er	–	allerede	kommet	to pakker.		
7	Og	–	det	er	–	da	–	sjovt	–	at spille tennis.
8			Ruth	ville	–	jo altid	drille	os,	–	Marie og mig.
9	Men	Bo,	han	er	–	nu ikke	–	så dum.		
10			Bilen	blev	–	–	repareret	–	i går.	
11			Jeg	blev	–	–	hentet	–	af Lise på skolen i dag.	
12			Katten	er	–	–	løbet	–	bort.	
13			Jeg	skal	–	jo	klæde	børnene	på.	
14			Hun	kan	–	–	læse	–	meget hurtigt.	
15			I går	kedede	han sig	bestemt ikke.				
16			De	har	–	aldrig	giftet	sig.		
17			Vi	kender	ham	ikke.				
18			Sælge huset	vil	han	alligevel ikke	–	–	i år.	
19				Kom!						

Translations: 1) He had not packed the case yesterday. 2) Yesterday he had not packed his case. 3) We are giving Ole a present this evening. 4) Later unfortunately they became ill. 5) It made him happy. 6) Two parcels have already come. 7) And it's fun of course playing tennis. 8) Ruth always wanted to tease us, you know, Marie and me. 9) But Bo, he's not so stupid, as a matter of fact. 10) The car was repaired yesterday. 11) I was met by Lise at school today. 12) The cat has run away. 13) I have to dress the children, you know. 14) She can read very quickly. 15) Yesterday he was certainly not bored. 16) They have never got married. 17) We don't know him. 18) He won't sell the house this year, anyway. 19) Come!

KEY to the schema			For details, see paragraph:
k =	link position (conjunction)		11.6
X_1 =	extra position	– duplicates elements in the clause	11.7
F =	front position	– any clause element except the finite verb. Normally there is only one element in this position	11.8, 11.11
v =	finite verb	– present or past tense or imperative	11.3.2
n =	nominals	– subject (if not in F), reflexive pronoun, unstressed pronominal object, ('light') elements	11.3.1, 11.4.2.2, 11.8.2
a =	clausal adverb(ial)	– short modal adverb, short conjunctional/ pronominal adverb, longer modal adverb, negation	11.3.4, 11.4.2
V =	non-finite verb	– infinitive, present or past participle	11.3.3
N =	nominals	– real subject, subject complement, indirect object, direct object, object complement	11.3.6, 11.9
A =	other adverbial	– verb particle, passive agent, manner adverbial, place adverbial, time adverbial, long adverbials	11.3.5, 11.3.7
X_2 =	extra position	– duplicates elements in the sentence, subject and object clauses	11.7

11.12 Subordinate clause structure

Subordinate clauses (which, as we have seen above, may simply be considered as elements in main clauses) also possess an internal structure of their own, which differs from that of main clauses in the following way.

Context	1 Conjunc-tion	2 Subject	3 Clausal adverbial	4 Finite verb	5 Non-finite verb	6 Object/ comp.	7 Other adverbial
	k	n	a	v	V	N	A
Vi starter,	når	han	–	kommer.			
Vi spurgte,	om	han	ikke	havde	pakket	kufferten.	
–	Da	de	ikke	havde	sagt	et ord, –	vidste vi intet.
Hun sagde,	(at)	det	ikke	var	–	sjovt	længere.
Hvis vi er stille,	og hvis	vi	ikke	er	–	trætte,	må vi se TV i aften.

Translations: We will start when he comes. We asked if he hadn't packed the case. As they hadn't said a word we knew nothing. She said it wasn't funny any more. If we're quiet and we're not tired, we'll be allowed to watch TV tonight.

Notice the following characteristics of the subordinate clause.

11.12.1 No F-position

There is no *F*-position in the subordinate clause; the order is always:

conjunction – subject – clausal adverbial – finite verb

- The clause always begins with a subordinating conjunction or other subordinator (see 10.2–10.3).
- The clausal adverbial comes immediately before the finite verb.
- The word order is straight, i.e. the subject comes before the finite verb.

11.12.2 The subject position

The subject position (*n*) is always occupied. If there is both a formal and a real subject, the latter is postponed to the object position (*N*).

11.12.3 The conjunction

The conjunction **at** (that) may sometimes be omitted:

Frederik lovede, (at) han ikke ville sige noget.
Frederik promised (that) he wouldn't say anything.

Jeg håber, (at) jeg snart kan træffe dig igen.
I hope (that) I can meet you again soon.

11.12.4 Rules for subordinate clause order

The guidelines and rules concerning main clause word order outlined earlier apply equally to subordinate clauses, with the exception of the following.

11.12.4.1 Light pronouns

'Light' or unstressed pronouns, whether as direct or indirect objects, do not move leftwards to the *n*-position but remain in the *N*-position:

. . . selvom han ikke gav mig det.
. . . although he didn't give me it.

11.12.4.2 No extra position at front

There is no initial extra position in subordinate clauses; any other elements will appear at the end of the clause in the same way as in main clauses:

. . . fordi han var enormt irriterende, den fyr.
. . . because he was extremely irritating, that chap.

11.12.4.3 No topicalisation in subordinate clauses

The subject will appear first in most subordinate clauses so that topicalisation of other elements cannot normally happen (cf. 11.15).

The *k*-position

The *k*-position is used to indicate a subordinating conjunction; should there also be a coordinating conjunction introducing the subordinate clause, this is placed in the same position immediately preceding the subordinating conjunction, e.g.: ..., **og fordi** ... (..., and because ...).

11.13 Independent clauses

An *independent clause* is a subordinate clause that stands alone as a sentence and does not therefore form part of a larger sentence. It is usually an exclamation or a wish, and has the same structure as other subordinate clauses:

k	n	a	v	V	N	A
Hvis	**du**	**bare**	**kendte**	–	**sandheden!**	

If you only knew the truth!

At	**I**	**ikke**	**bliver**	–	**trætte!**	

That you don't get tired!

Clauses beginning with the words **bare, blot, gid, mon** have subordinate clause word order:

Gid hun ikke var så syg!
If only she weren't so ill!

Mon han nogensinde finder sig et arbejde?
I wonder if he'll ever find a job.

11.14 Cleft sentences

In order to emphasise an element together with the action of the verb, that element (X) may be extracted from the sentence and inserted into the construction:

Det er/var X, som/der/at ...
It is/was X who/that ...

The remainder of the original sentence is downgraded and relegated to a subordinate clause added onto the end. Notice that **som** and **der** are used to refer to a non-adverbial noun phrase or pronoun, and **at** (unless omitted) is used to refer to a time or place adverbial:

Cf. **Klaus sendte mig en bog i sidste uge.**
Klaus sent me a book last week.

→ **Det var *en bog*, (*som*) Klaus sendte mig i sidste uge.**
It was a book that Klaus . . .

→ **Det var *Klaus*, *der* sendte mig en bog i sidste uge.**
It was Klaus who . . .

→ **Det var *i sidste uge*, (*at*) Klaus sendte mig en bog.**
It was last week that Klaus . . .

The cleft sentence is also very common in questions:

Var det oppositionen, der kritiserede regeringen?
Was it the opposition who criticized the government?
(Cf. **Kritiserede oppositionen regeringen?**)

Er det *dig*, *der* bestemmer her?
Is it you who decides here?

Er det *kaffe*, han drikker?
Is it coffee he drinks?

11.15 Three types of subordinate clause with main clause structure

These are all exceptions, in different ways, to 11.12 above, in that the subordinate clause forms part of a sentence (cf. 11.10), but has a word order structure that can be the same as that of the main clause (see 11.5, 11.11).

11.15.1 At-clauses with a 'topic'

Subordinate clauses that represent reported speech usually have subordinate clause word order, yet, in spoken and informal written language, it is increasingly common for an element to follow the conjunction as a kind of topic. When a non-subject comes immediately after the conjunction **at**, the finite verb and subject are inverted (i.e. main clause word order):

Kristian sagde, at *i går* var hele familien i Tivoli.
Kristian said that yesterday the whole family went to Tivoli.

219

At-clauses with a finite verb – clausal adverb order

In some cases the clausal adverbial adopts the same position as in the main clause, i.e. *after* the finite verb, rather than its usual subordinate clause position *before* the finite verb:

Kristian sagde, at han *skulle ikke* på arbejde i dag.
Kristian said that he wasn't going to work today.

This is only found in spoken Danish and should never be written. Write:

Kristian sagde, at han *ikke skulle* på arbejde i dag.

An explanation for this order is that the **at**-clause is regarded as a statement in direct speech, i.e. as a main clause, cf.:

Kristian sagde: 'Jeg *skal ikke* på arbejde i dag.'
Kristian said: 'I'm not going to work today.'

The conjunction **at**, therefore, almost has the function of a colon.

| 11.15.3 | **Conditional clauses with yes/no question order**

Conditional clauses are usually introduced by **hvis**:

Hvis du ikke ringer til mor, bliver hun ked af det.
If you don't ring Mother she'll feel sad.

But conditional clauses may have no subordinating conjunction, and rely on inverted word order (finite verb – subject) to indicate condition:

(Conditional)
Ringer du ikke til mor, bliver hun ked af det.
If you don't ring mother, she'll feel sad.

Cf. (Yes/no question)
Ringer du ikke til mor?
Won't you ring mother?

Clauses of this type also occur in English:

Had I known you were arriving, I would have waited.
Were you to agree to this, it would be disastrous.

Major word
order and
sentence
structure
problems –
summary

11.16 Major word order and sentence structure problems – summary

A number of aspects of word order are similar in Danish and English. This summary concentrates only on some of the major differences.

Key:	S	=	subject
	O	=	object
	V	=	finite verb
	Advl	=	clausal adverbial
	T	=	clause element (non-subject) which may come first in the clause

11.16.1 Main clause – inversion (see 11.2, 11.5, 11.8.1, 11.11)

In Danish, non-subjects often come first in the main clause, and this causes inversion of subject and finite verb. In English, the order is always subject – verb.

Danish	*English*
S – V – T	S – V – T
Han sover nu.	He is asleep now.
T – V – S	T – S – V
Nu sover han.	Now he is asleep.

11.16.2 Main clause – adverb(ial)s (e.g. ikke, aldrig) (11.3.4, 11.4.4, 11.11)

In main clauses in Danish, the clausal adverbial (adverb) usually comes immediately *after* the finite verb. In English, it usually comes immediately *before* the finite verb.

Danish	*English*
S – V – Advl	S – Advl – V
De leger aldrig.	They never play.

11.16.3	*Subordinate clause – adverb(ial)s (e.g. ikke, aldrig)*
	(11.12, 11.15)

In subordinate clauses in Danish, the clausal adverbial (adverb) always comes immediately *before* the finite verb.

Danish   English

S – Advl – V   S – V – Advl
De sagde, at de *ikke* havde   They said that they had not written.
skrevet.

S – Advl – V
De ved, at jeg *aldrig* løber.   They know that I never run.

Remember: Subject – **ikke** – Verb in Danish. In English, the order varies.

11.16.4	*Objects, etc., with and without stress (11.3.6, 11.8.1)*

When object pronouns lose their stress in Danish, they move left in the sentence. In English, there is no difference in word order.

Danish   English

S – V – Advl – O   S – V – Advl – O
Jeg kender ikke *ham*. (stressed)   I don't know *him*.

S – V – O – Advl
Jeg kender ham ikke. (unstressed)   I don't know him.

Chapter 12

Word formation

12.1 Introduction

The vocabulary of Danish is constantly being altered by five main processes.

12.1.1 Borrowing from other languages

From English:	'a strike'	→	**en strejke**
From French:	'un café théâtre'	→	**et caféteater**
From German:	'ein Gastarbeiter'	→	**en gæstearbejder**

12.1.2 Compounding existing stems

en cykel + en hjelm → **en cykel|hjelm** cycle helmet

12.1.3 Affixation

u- + ven → **uven** (lit. 'un-friend') enemy

12.1.4 Abbreviation

præventiv-pille → **p-pille** contraceptive pill

12.1.5 Change of form, meaning or word class

et veto (noun) → **at vetoe** (verb) veto

Borrowing from other languages normally involves the eventual assimilation of a loanword into the Danish system of orthography, pronunciation and inflection.

12.2 Compounding

12.2.1 First element/second element

The first element (FE) of a compound may be a noun, adjective, verb, pronoun, numeral, adverb, preposition or word group, while the second element (SE) is usually a noun, adjective or verb.

Some examples:

Noun + noun:	**sommer|ferie**	summer holiday
Noun + adjective:	**kul|sort**	black as coal
Noun + verb:	**kæde|ryge**	chain smoke
Verb + noun:	**skrive|bord**	writing desk
Verb + adjective:	**køre|klar**	ready to drive away
Verb + verb:	**øs|regne**	rain cats and dogs
Adjective + noun:	**central|varme**	central heating
Adjective + adjective:	**høj|effektiv**	extremely efficient
Adjective + verb:	**dyb|fryse**	deep freeze

For separable and inseparable compound verbs, see 6.5.

12.2.1.1 Inflection

Notice that the second element in compounds determines the gender and inflection of the compound as in the compound noun:

en skole + et køkken → **et skole\|køkken**, a school kitchen

12.2.2 Compound nouns

12.2.2.1 Compound nouns may have a large number of word classes as FE

Noun:	**møbel|firma**	furniture company
Adjective:	**fjern|syn**	television
Pronoun:	**selv|hjælp**	self-help
Numeral:	**ti|år**	decade
Verb:	**gå|gade**	pedestrianised street
Preposition:	**over|klasse**	upper class
Adverb:	**frem|tid**	future

These may be formed by three main methods:

- Noun + noun: **pige|skole**   girls' school
- Noun + link -e- + noun: **jul|e|dag**   Christmas Day
- Noun + link -s- + noun: **forsikring|s|præmie** insurance premium

12.2.2.2 The -s- and -e- link

Whether or not -s- is used as a link between nouns depends to some
extent on the form of the elements. Generally speaking:

(a) An -s- link is usual in nouns that:

- have an FE ending in -**dom**, -**else**, -**hed**, -**(n)ing**, -**sel**, -**skab**:

  **kristendom|s|undervisning, ledelse|s|struktur, sundhed|s|farlig,
  landing|s|bane, fødsel|s|kontrol, redskab|s|skur**

- have an FE ending in one of the borrowed Romance suffixes -**ion**,
  -**tion**, -**tet**, -**um**:

  **opinion|s|måling, navigation|s|skole, pietet|s|følelse,
  petroleum|s|kamin**

- have an FE which is itself a compound:

  rød|vin|s|glas   cf. **vin|glas**
  skrive|bord|s|skuffe   cf. **bord|skuffe**

(b) An -e- link is found in some compound nouns that derive from an
original genitive (**natt|e|leje**), but it also occurs in the following cases:

- when the FE ends in a consonant and the SE begins with a consonant:

  invalid|e|vogn, ost|e|mad, sogn|e|præst

- when the FE is a word for a living being and ends in the affix -**ing**:

  viking|e|flåde, yngling|e|alder

12.2.2.3 First element forms

(a) When they are FE, nouns are usually found in their singular (uninflected)
form: **bil|sæde**; but when they denote a plural concept, this may be
reflected in a plural FE form: **blomster|bed, børne|have, engle|skare**.

225

(b) When they are FE, adjectives are found in their basic form: **gråt vejr** → **grå|vejr**.

Exceptions: **nyt|år, små|børn**

(c) When they are FE, verbs are found in their infinitive form: **skrive|maskine, spille|mand.**

Exceptions: Verb stems occasionally form the FE: **brus|hane, byg|mester.**

12.2.3 Compound adjectives

Compound adjectives have as their FE a number of different word classes:

Noun:	**gryde|klar**	oven-ready
Adjective:	**mørke|blond**	fair
Verb:	**stryge|fri**	non-iron
Pronoun:	**selv|optaget**	self-obsessed
Adverb:	**vel|smagende**	tasty
Preposition:	**under|jordisk**	underground

12.3 Affixation

12.3.1 Prefix and suffix

Affixes in Danish are either *prefixes* or *suffixes* and affixation involves adding a *prefix* to the *beginning* or a *suffix* to the end of a *stem*. While prefixes do not alter the word class or inflection of the stem, suffixes are often employed precisely to form words of a different class:

Prefix

cf. **u-**	+	**ven**	→	**uven**
negative		*noun*		*noun*
prefix				
		'friend'		'enemy'

Suffix

venlig	+	**-hed**	→	**venlighed**
adjective		*noun*		*noun*
		suffix		
'friendly'				'friendliness'

tank	+	-e	→	tanke	Affixation
noun		*verb*		*verb*
stem		*suffix*		
'tank'				'to fill up the tank'

12.3.2 Affixes and meaning

The same basic meaning may be expressed by several different prefixes, e.g. the words *dis*harmoni, *ikke*-vold, *in*tolerant, *non*konformisme and *u*lykkelig all have negative prefixes. The same is true of some suffixes: udvandr*er*, emigr*ant*, inspekt*or* and inspekt*ør* all have suffixes meaning 'a person carrying out a specific task'. Generally speaking, prefixes and suffixes are much vaguer in meaning than the stems they modify.

12.3.3 Productive and non-productive affixes

Productive affixes are those still being used to form derivatives whose meaning can be predicted from the form:

-agtig = 'like', as in: **en Google-agtig søgning**, a Google-like search

-bar = 'possible to', as in: **bærbar**, 'possible to carry', 'portable'

Non-productive affixes are those no longer used to form derivatives:

-dom in: **fattigdom, sygdom, ungdom**, etc.

Non-productive affixes may have been borrowed in many loanwords but have never been used to form any new indigenous derivatives, e.g.: Latin **kon-: konflikt, konsonant.**

12.3.4 Prefixes

The table that follows contains a list of some frequent examples.

Prefix	Meaning	Examples	Translation

NEGATIVE and PEJORATIVE

Prefix	Meaning	Examples	Translation
u-	not, opposite of	**ukonventionel, uven**	unconventional, enemy
	bad	**uvane**	bad habit
il-	not, opposite of	**illegal**	illegal
im-	not, opposite of	**immobil**	immobile
in-	not, opposite of	**intolerant**	intolerant
ir-	not, opposite of	**irrelevant**	irrelevant
non-	not, opposite of	**nonkonformisme**	non-conformism
mis-	wrongly	**misbruger**	addict
	bad	**mislyd**	dissonance
van-	wrongly	**vanskabt**	misshapen
	bad	**vanrøgte**	neglect

ATTITUDE

Prefix	Meaning	Examples	Translation
ko-	together with	**koordinere**	coordinate
kol-	together with	**kollaboratør**	collaborator
kom-	together with	**kompagnon**	partner
kon-	together with	**kongenial**	congenial
kor-	together with	**korrespondere**	correspond
sam-	together with	**samboer**	partner, cohabitee
sær-	separate from	**særtilfælde**	special case
anti-	against	**antikommunist**	anti-communist
kontra-	against	**kontrarevolution**	counter-revolution
pro-	favourable towards	**provestlig**	pro-western

LOCATION or DIRECTION

Prefix	Meaning	Examples	Translation
eks-	from	**ekskludere**	exclude
trans-	across	**transplantation**	transplantation

DIRECTION (time or place)

Prefix	Meaning	Examples	Translation
an-	to, towards	**ankomme**	arrive
for-	away from	**fordrive**	expel
und-	away from	**undslippe**	escape
gen-	back, again	**genfinde**	rediscover
re-	back, again	**reetablere**	re-establish
fort-	further	**fortsætte**	continue
videre-	further	**videreuddannelse**	further education

NUMBER

Prefix	Meaning	Examples	Translation
mono-	one	**monogami**	monogamy
bi-	two	**bilateral**	bilateral
tve-	two	**tvekamp**	duel
pan-	all	**panamerikansk**	pan-American

CONVERSION VERB TO VERB

Prefix	Meaning	Examples		Translation
an-	transitivising	**råbe**, call	→	**anråbe**, shout
be-	transitivising	**bo**, live	→	**bebo**, inhabit

CONVERSION ADJECTIVE TO VERB

Prefix	Meaning	Examples		Translation
be-	make into X	**fri**, free	→	**befri**, liberate
for-	make into X	**ny**, new	→	**forny**, renew

12.3.5 Suffixes

The table that follows contains a list of some frequent examples.

Suffix	Deriving from	Meaning	Examples	Translation
NOUN-FORMING				
PEOPLE				
-ant	N-ik	performer of	**musikant**	musician
-ent	V-ere	occupation	**assistent**	assistant
-at	N	person	**demokrat**	democrat
-er	V-ere	occupation	**snedker**	carpenter
-er	V-e	occupation	**bager**	baker
-er	N	origin	**belgier**	Belgian
-iner	N	origin	**filipiner**	Phillipino
-ing	N	origin	**islænding**	Icelander
-ling	N	origin	**ætling**	descendant
-ning	V-e	agent of an action	**flygtning**	refugee
-iker	N-ik	occupation	**politiker**	politican
-ist	V-ere, N	hobby	**motionist**	jogger
-ør	V-ere	occupation	**inspektør**	inspector
FEMININE				
-inde	N	wife of	**værtinde**	hostess
-esse	N	title	**prinsesse**	princess
-ske	V-e, N-er	occupation	**plejerske**	nurse
-trice	N-ør	occupation	**direktrice**	(female) director
-øse	V-ere, N-ør	occupation	**massøse**	masseuse
ACTIVITY				
-ende	V-e	activity	**forehavende**	project
-else	V-e	sense	**følelse**	feeling
-(n)ing	V-e	activity	**skrivning**	writing
	V-e	activity	**udvikling**	development
-sel	V-e	activity	**indførsel**	importation
-sion	V-ere	result	**eksplosion**	explosion
-(i)tion	V-ere	product	**komposition**	composition
-(a)tion	V-ere	service	**information**	information
-tion	V-ere	activity	**funktion**	function
Zero-suffix	V-e	result	**duft**	fragrance
	V-e	result	**sult**	hunger
ABSTRACTIONS				
-ance	A		**elegance**	elegance
-ence	A		**kompetence**	competence
-ens			**frekvens**	frequency
-dom	A		**sygdom**	illness
-else	V-e		**fristelse**	temptation
-ende	Adv, V-e		**velbefindende**	well-being

Suffix	Deriving from	Meaning	Examples	Translation
-hed	Prep, V-e		medlidenhed	compassion
-ing	V-e		afmagring	slimming
-isme	A		socialisme	socialism
-itet	A		popularitet	popularity
-sel	V-e		glemsel	oblivion
-skab	A		ondskab	evil

ADJECTIVE-FORMING

FROM VERBS

-abel	V-ere	possible	diskutabel	debatable
-ibel	V-ere	possible	disponibel	disposable
-at	V-ere	different	separat	separate
-bar	V-e	possible	vaskbar	washable
-et	V-e	state	nystartet	recently launched
-et	V-ere	state	indstuderet	rehearsed
-lig	V-e	possible	læselig	readable
-ig	V-e	inclination	syndig	sinful
-siv	V-ere	different	eksklusiv	exclusive
-sk	V-e	inclination	indbildsk	conceited
-som	V-e	inclination	arbejdsom	hard-working
-tiv	V-ere	inclination	demonstrativ	demonstrative

FROM NOUNS

-agtig	N	characteristic of	barnagtig	childish
-ant	N	who has X	elegant	elegant
-el	N	belonging to	kulturel	cultural
-(e)lig	N	belonging to	kristelig	Christian
-en	N	which consists of X	ulden	woolen
-ent	N	who has X	intelligent	intelligent
-et	N	who has X	enarmet	one-armed
-ig	N	who has X	listig	sly
		characteristic of	søsterlig	sisterly
-(i)sk	N	origin	britisk	British
	N	origin	hollandsk	Dutch
-iv	N	who/which has X	aktiv	active
-mæssig	N	in accordance with	kontraktmæssig	contractual
-ær	N	belonging to	litterær	literary
-øs	N	who has X	nervøs	nervous

FROM ADJECTIVES

-agtig	A	like	blødagtig	soft
-artet	A	with the property of	godartet	benign

VERB-FORMING

FROM NOUNS

delete -r	N	remove X	støvsuge	hoover
-e	N	activity	cykle, vaske	cycle, wash

Suffix	Deriving from	Meaning	Examples	Translation
	N	(with prefix)	**forklare**	explain
-ere	N	add/provide with	**adressere**	address
	N	place in	**logere**	lodge
	N	perform X	**kritisere**	criticise
	N	act as	**vikariere**	stand in
	N	make like X	**amerikanisere**	Americanise
FROM ADJECTIVES				
-e	A	make X	**varme, tørre**	heat, dry
	A	(with prefix)	**bemyndige**	authorise
	A	(with prefix)	**forbitre**	embitter
-ne	A	become X	**gulne, mørkne**	go yellow, go darker

12.4 Abbreviation

Abbreviation involves the loss of a morpheme or part of a morpheme. Abbreviations may arise from three different processes.

12.4.1 Clipping

This implies reduction at the beginning or end of a word:

	Whole morpheme lost:	Part morpheme lost:
Initial reduction:	**(bi)cykel** bicycle	**(frika)delle** meatball
Final reduction:	**kilo(gram)** kilogramme	**el(ektricitet)** electricity

12.4.2 Blend (or telescope reduction)

This implies the removal of the middle of a word:

m(erværdi)oms(ætningsafgift)
value added tax

| 12.4.3 | Acronym |

This implies that only an initial letter or letters remain after reduction. Acronyms are of three kinds.

12.4.3.1 Alphabetisms

These are acronyms where the initials are pronounced as letters of the alphabet:

LO ['el'o], Danish Trades Union Congress; **bh** ['be'hå], bra(ssiere)

12.4.3.2 Acronyms pronounced as words

Nato ['naːto], **Saab** [saːb]

12.4.3.3 Hybrid forms

p-plads (parkeringsplads), car park
u-båd (undervandsbåd), submarine

12.5 List of common abbreviations

What follows is not a full list. However, a number of dictionaries of abbreviations are currently available.

AB	**andelsboligforening**	**AMU**	**arbejdsmarkeds-**
adb	**automatisk**		**uddannelse**
	databehandling	**ang.**	**angående**
adr.	**adresse**	**ank.**	**ankomst**
ADSL	**asymmetric digital**	**anm.**	1 **anmeldelse**
	number line		2 **anmærkning**
AF	**arbejdsformidlingen**	**apr.**	**april**
afd.	1 **afdeling**	**ApS**	**anpartsselskab**
	2 **afdøde**	**art.**	1 **artikel**
afg.	**afgang**		2 **artium, e.g. mag.art.**
afs.	**afsender**	**A/S, a/s**	**aktieselskab**
alm.	**almindelig**	**ass.**	**assistent**
a.m.b.a.	**andelsselskab med**	**ATP**	**arbejdsmarkedets**
	begrænset ansvar		**tillægspension**
AMBI	**arbejdsmarkedsbidrag**	**aug.**	**august**

att.	attention (til)	edb	elektronisk
aut.	1 automatisk		databehandling
	2 autoriseret	eftf.	efterfølger
bd.	bind	EF	Europæiske
bh	brystholder		Fællesskaber
bio.	billion	eftm.	eftermiddag
BK	boldklub	egl.	egentlig
BNP	bruttonationalprodukt	e.Kr.	efter Kristus
bl.a.	blandt andet/andre	eks.	eksempel
C	Celsius	ekskl.	eksklusive
c.	cent	ekspl.	eksemplar
ca.	cirka	el	elektricitet
cand.	candidatus	el.	eller
c.c.	carbon copy (kopi til)	e.l.	eller lignende
cf.	confer (jævnfør)	enk.	enkelt
civiling.	civilingeniør	EM	europamesterskab
Co.	kompagni	em.	eftermiddag
CPR-nr	nummer i Det Centrale	etc.	etcetera
	Personregister	evt.	eventuel (-t, -le)
CVR-nr	nummer i Det Centrale	F	fahrenheit
	Virksomhedsregister	f.	1 femininum
d.	1 den		2 for
	2 død		3 født
dat.	dateret		4 følgende (side)
dav.	daværende	feb.	februar
d.d.	dags dato	ff.	følgende (sider)
d.e.	det er (det vil sige)	fa.	firma(et)
dec.	december	fakt.	faktura
dir.	1 direkte	f.eks.	for eksempel
	2 direktorat	fhv.	forhenværende
	3 direktør	fk.	fælleskøn
	4 dirigent	f.Kr.	før Kristus
div.	1 diverse	fl.	flaske
	2 division	flg.	følgende
DM	danmarksmesterskab	flt.	flertal
d.m.	denne måned	fm.	1 formiddag
do.	ditto		2 fuldmægtig
dr.	1 doctor, e.g. dr.phil.	f.m.	foregående måned
	2 doktor	fmd.	formand
	3 drenge	f.o.m.	fra og med
d.s.	1 den/det/de samme	forb.	1 forbindelse
	2 dennes		2 forbud
d.s.s.	det samme som	foreg.	foregående
dvs.	det vil sige	forf.	forfatter
d.y.	den yngre	fork.	forkortelse, forkortet
d.æ.	den ældre	forsk.	forskellig
d.å.	dette år	forts.	fortsættelse, fortsættes

FOU	forskning og udvikling	**iht.**	**i henhold til**
FSA	folkeskolens	**ib., indb.**	**indbundet**
	afgangsprøve	**IK**	**1 idrætsklub**
FP	førtidspension		**2 intelligenskvotient**
fr.	**1 fredag**	**ing.**	**ingeniør**
	2 fru, frøken	**inkl.**	**inklusive**
FSU	folkeskolens udvidede	**instr.**	**1 instruktion,**
	afgangsprøve		**instruktør**
frk.	**frøken**		**2 instrument**
f.t.	**for tiden**	**I/S, i/s**	**interessentselskab**
f.v.t.	**før vor tidsregning**	**isl.**	**islandsk**
fx	**for eksempel**	**istf.,**	**i stedet for**
f.å.	**foregående år**	**i st. for**	
g	**1 gram**	**itk.**	**intetkøn**
	2 gymnasieklasse	**jan.**	**januar**
g., gg.	**gang(e)**	**jf., jvf.**	**jævnfør**
gl.	**1 gammel**	**j. nr., jnr.**	**journalnummer**
	2 glas	**kap.**	**kapitel**
g.m.	**gift med**	**kat.**	**1 katalog**
gn., gnsn.	**gennemsnit**		**2 katolsk**
gr.	**1 grad**	**kbh.**	**københavnsk**
	2 gruppe	**kgl.**	**kongelig**
grdl	**grundlagt**	**kl.**	**1 klasse**
G/S, g/s	**gensidigt selskab**		**2 klokken**
GT	**Gamle Testamente**	**kld.**	**kælder**
ha	**hektar**	**km/t.**	**kilometer i timen**
hd	**herred**	**Kr.**	**1 Kirke** (in place names)
henv.	**1 henvendelse**		**2 Kristi**
	2 henvisning	**kr.**	**krone(r)**
Hf.	**højere forberedelsesek-**	**K/S, k/s**	**kommanditselskab**
	samen	**kt.**	**konto**
hft.	**hæftet**	**kv.**	**kvinde(lig)**
HH	**højere handelseksamen**	**kvt.**	**kvartal**
hhv.	**henholdsvis**	**l**	**liter**
HIV	**human immuno-**	**l.**	**linie, linje**
	deficiency virus	**lb.nr.**	**løbenummer**
hk	**hestekraft**	**lejl.**	**lejlighed**
HKH	**Hans/Hendes Kongelige**	**lign.**	**lignende**
	Højhed	**Ll.**	**Lille** (in place names)
hpl.	**holdeplads**	**LO**	**Landsorganisation**
hr.	**herr**	**lok.**	**1 lokal(nummer)**
HU	**højere uddannelse**		**2 lokale**
i alm.	**i almindelighed**	**lø.**	**lørdag**
ib.	**indbundet**	**m.**	**med**
if.	**ifølge**	**ma.**	**mandag**
ift.	**i forhold til**	**m.a.o.**	**med andre ord**
i henh. til	**i henhold til**	**maks.**	**maksimum**

mc	1 motorcykel	off.	1 offentlig
	2 musikkassette		2 officiel
md.	måned	ofl., o.fl.	og flere
mdl.	1 mandlig	og lign.	og lignende
	2 månedlig	okt.	oktober
mdtl.	mundligt	OL	Olympiske Lege
medd.	meddelelse	o.l.	og lignende
medflg.	medfølgende	OM	Olympisk Mesterskab
medl.	medlem	o/m	omdrejninger per minut
MF	Medlem af Folketinget	o.m.a.	og mange andre,
mfl., m.fl.	med flere		og meget andet
mgl.	mangler, manglende	omg.	1 omgang
mhp.,	med henblik på		2 omgående
m.h.p.		omkr.	omkring
mht.,	med hensyn til	omr.	område
m.h.t.		omtr.	omtrent
mia.	milliard(er)	ons.	onsdag
mio.	million(er)	opg.	opgang
m/k	mand(lig)/kvinde(lig)	opl.	1 oplag
ml.	mellem		2 oplysning
m.m.	med mere	opr.	1 oprettet
modsv.	modsvarende		2 oprindelig
modt.	modtager	OSS	ofte stillede spørgsmål
MS	motorskib	ovenn.	ovennævnte
m/s	meter per sekund	ovenst.	ovenstående
mv., m.v.	med videre	overs.	oversat, oversættelse,
mvh.,	med venlig hilsen		oversætter
m.v.h.		ovf.	ovenfor
N	nord	p-	parkerings-,
n.	neutrum		præventiv(pille)
ndf.	nedenfor	par.	paragraf
ned.	nederst	p.b.v.	på bestyrelsens vegne
nedenst.	nedenstående	pct.	procent
NM	nordisk mesterskab	pga.	på grund af
NN	nomen nescio (= I do not	pk.	pakke
	know the name)	pkt.	punkt
nord.	nordisk	Pl.	Plads (in place names)
nov.	november	pl., plur.	pluralis
Nr.	Nørre (in place names)	PM	promemoria
nr.	nummer	PPS	postpostscriptum
NT	Ny Testamente	PS	postscriptum
nto.	netto	P&T	post- og telegrafvæsenet
nuv.	nuværende	pr.	per
o.	omkring	pt.	patient
o.a.	og andet/andre	p.t.	pro tempore (for the
obl.	obligatorisk		time being)
obs!	observer!	p . . . v.	på . . . s vegne

på gr. af	på grund af	tdl.	tønde(r) land
R	rekommanderet	t.eks.	til eksempel
	(letters)	th., t.h.	til højre
rad.	radikal	tidl.	tidligere
red.	redaktion, redaktør,	tilh.	tilhørende
	redigeret (af)	tilsv.	tilsvarende
regn.	regning	tirs.	tirsdag
rep.	republik	tlf.	telefon
repr.	repræsentant	to., tors.	torsdag
resp.	respektive	t.o.m.	til og med
S	1 syd	t/r	tur-retur
	2 small	tsk.	teskefuld
s	sekund	tv., t.v.	til venstre
s.	side	u.	1 uden
sa.	samme		2 under
s.d.	se denne (dette, disse)	uafh.	uafhængig
Sdr.	Sønder, Søndre	udb.,	udbetaling
	(in place names)	udbet.	
sek.	1 sekund(er)	udg.	udgave, udgivet (af)
	2 sektion	uds.	udsendelse
sept.	september	ug.	udmærket godt
s/h	sort-hvid	ugtl.	ugentlig
sg., sing.	singularis	undt.	undtagen
Skt.	Sankt	u.p.	1 uden for partierne
s.m.	samme måned		2 uden portefølje
s.m.b.a.	selskab med begrænset	u.å.	uden år
	ansvar	V	vest
sml.	sammenlign	V.	Vestre (in place names)
sn	sogn	v.	ved
spec.	specielt	vedk.	vedkommende
spm.	spørgsmål	vedr.	vedrørende
spsk.	spiseskefuld	vejl.	vejledning
St.	Store (in place names)	vh.	venlig hilsen
st.	1 station	VM	verdensmesterskab
	2 stuen (etage)	vvs	'varme, ventilation,
	3 størrelse		sanitet'
stk.	styk(ke)	vær.	værelse
s.u.	svar udbedes	Ø	øst
søn.	søndag	Ø.	Østre (in place names)
sædv.	sædvanlig(vis)	ø-	økologisk
s.å.	samme år	øv.	øverst
t	ton	øvr.	øvrige
t.	time	årg.	årgang
TAP	teknisk og administrativt	årh.	århundrede
	personal	årl.	årlig

Chapter 13

Orthography

13.1 The alphabet

The Danish alphabet contains the same letters as the English alphabet, but after z come three additional letters: æ/Æ, ø/Ø and å/Å in that order. The letters c, q, w, x and z are less commonly used in Danish, and are usually found only in loanwords.

13.2 AA, Å, aa, å

In 1948, Denmark officially replaced the spelling **AA** and **aa** with the letters **Å** and **å** in most words, and words such as **aaben** and **paastaa** became **åben** (open) and **påstå** (claim). This change in spelling did not affect the pronunciation of such words.

This reform brought Danish spelling into line with spelling in Norway and Sweden. There was initially resistance on the part of some towns, institutions and individuals, so that spellings such as **Aabenraa, Grenaa, Aalborg** or **Aage Skovgaard** are still found. Individuals may retain the older spelling, but have to be consistent, while local authorities legally have to use the new ones. Strangely, the position of this new letter in the alphabet was not officially determined until 1955. In fact, it moved from the beginning to the end of the Danish alphabet (which begins with **A** and now ends with **Å**), causing a lot of work for lexicographers and others.

13.3 Other diacritics

13.3.1 Acute accent: é

This is no longer obligatory, but is found optionally in 70 or more words, many loaned from French, including:

allé (alle), avenue; **café (cafe)**, café; **entré (entre)**, admission

The acute accent is occasionally useful to distinguish the unstressed indefinite article **en** from the stressed numeral **én**.

13.3.2 Grave accent: à

This is quite rare, but may be found in:

à la carte officially **a la carte**
vis-à-vis officially **vis-a-vis**

13.4 Small or capital letters?

13.4.1 Small initial letter

Where English has a capital letter at the beginning of words, in many cases Danish has a small letter, such as:

• Days of the week, months and festivals:
  tirsdag, Tuesday; **juni**, June; **påske**, Easter

• Nationality words (both nouns and adjectives):
  dansk, Danish; **engelsk**, English; **finsk**, Finnish; **en amerikaner**, an American; **en franskmand**, a Frenchman; **en tysker**, a German

13.4.2 Simple proper nouns

Proper nouns (names) constituting a single word have a capital letter:

Var Diderichsen dansker?   Was Diderichsen a Dane?

13.4.3 Capitals in compound names

In compound names, the first element of the compound has a capital letter, but the second element loses its capital:

Stor|københavn, Greater Copenhagen
cf. **København**, Copenhagen

Note that, in some compounds that have become fixed expressions, the first element may lose its capital letter:

et danmark|s|kort, a map of Denmark
cf. **Danmark**, Denmark

13.4.4 Phrases

In phrases, the first and other significant words tend to have capital letters:

Forenede Nationer, the United Nations; **Gorm den Gamle**, King Gorm the Old; **Dansk Kirke i Udlandet**, the Danish Church in Foreign Ports

If the name is introduced by a definite article, the article has a capital letter:

Det Kongelige Teater, The Royal Theatre; **De Kanariske Øer**, The Canary Islands; except with an addition: **det nye Kongelige Bibliotek**, The new Royal Library

13.5 Word division

Sometimes it is necessary to divide words at the end of lines, and this word division (or hyphenation) in Danish follows some basic principles.

13.5.1 Division by elements

Compounds are divided into their separate elements:

møbel–fabrik, gå–gade, halv–år

| 13.5.2 | **Division by affix** |

Derivatives may be divided according to prefix of suffix:

u–vane, af–folke, musik–ant, arbejd–som

| 13.5.3 | **Division by inflectional ending** |

Inflectional endings that constitute a syllable can be divided from the stem:

huse–ne, lav–ere, nævne–de

| 13.5.4 | **One vowel on each line** |

As there must be a vowel on each line, a one-syllable word cannot be divided:

blomst, mindst, strengt

| 13.5.5 | **Division by number of syllables** |

Words that are neither compounds nor derivatives divide according to the number of consonants involved.

| 13.5.5.1 | One consonant or two identical ones – one consonant goes on the new line |

bo–gen, bus–sen

| 13.5.5.2 | A consonant group may move to the new line if it can begin a Danish word |

bis–pen or **bi–spen, tas–ke** or **ta–ske**

| 13.5.5.3 | Consonants in different syllables cannot move together |

knog–le   NOT   **kno–gle**
tek–nik   NOT   **te–knik**

Chapter 14

Punctuation

14.1 Punctuation marks

The names of the principle punctuation marks (**skilletegn**) used in Danish are:

.	**punktum**
,	**komma**
:	**kolon**
;	**semikolon**
?	**spørgsmålstegn**
!	**udråbstegn**
/	**skråstreg**
-	**bindestreg**
—	**tankestreg**
'	**apostrof**
...	**prikker**
( )	**parentes**
[ ]	**firkantet parentes**
{ }	**klammer**
" " „ " ' ' » «	**anførselstegn**

14.2 The comma

For Danes, the 'correct' position of commas is a very serious matter indeed. In the last two decades, in particular, an intense debate has been conducted and it only recently seems to have reached its conclusion. Only time will tell how permanent this present solution turns out to be.

For a long time in the twentieth century, Danish employed two different systems for using the comma. One system, known as *grammatisk komma* ('grammatical comma'), was clause-based and was applied mechanically to the text. Thus, where there were two consecutive clauses, whether main or subordinate, a comma was placed between them, and commas were also found on either side of inserted clauses, for example relative clauses. The other system, known as *pausekomma* ('pause comma'), used the comma to indicate natural pauses in the text, though the interpretation of where such pauses occurred was highly subjective. This latter system is closer to English practice.

After an earlier attempt had been made to conflate the two systems under the term *enhedskomma* ('unitary comma'), *Dansk Sprognævn* (the Danish National Language Council) decided, in 1996, to solve the problem officially by creating a system called *nyt komma* ('new comma'), which was closer to the previous 'pause comma'. At the same time, however, they allowed the grammatical comma to be preserved, but now under the name *traditionelt komma* ('traditional comma'), although they strongly recommended the use of the 'new comma'.

Over the following years, it turned out that there was reluctance, in some quarters even fierce resistance, to using the 'new comma', including from a number of official bodies and the press in general. This prompted *Dansk Sprognævn* to abandon the 'new comma' in 2004 and adopt a system that was virtually identical with the 'traditional comma'. Even so, there was still an element of choice in the system, in so far as it became voluntary whether to use a so-called *startkomma* ('start – or initial – comma'), i.e. to have a comma in front of one or more subordinate clauses when they follow a main clause. To leave out a comma in such cases (as is usual in English) is a remnant of the 'new comma', and this practice is recommended by *Dansk Sprognævn*, though they stress that whatever one's choice is in this regard, usage should be *consistent* within the same text. The option not to use the *startkomma* is thus the main deviation from a total acceptance of the 'traditional comma'. The present book makes use of *startkomma* in all the relevant examples.

14.2.1 Obligatory use of the comma

The comma *should* be used in the following cases:

14.2.1.1 Between two main clauses

Det er koldt, og det sner.
It's cold and it's snowing.

Du må ikke drille mig, for så går jeg hjem.
You mustn't tease me because then I'll go home.

|14.2.1.2| Between subordinate clause and main clause

This is sometimes known as the 'end comma' ('*slutkomma*'), as it marks the end of the subordinate clause:

Da jeg var færdig, tog jeg et brusebad.
When I had finished, I had a shower.

Hvis du kommer i morgen, kan vi spise middag sammen.
If you come tomorrow, we can have dinner together.

|14.2.1.3| Between two coordinated subordinate clauses

Plant træet(,) hvor jorden er god, og hvor der er sol.
Plant the tree where the soil is good and where there is sun.

|14.2.1.4| To mark a parenthetical (i.e. non-restrictive) clause or
        expression

Jeg kendte hendes far, som døde for to år siden.
I knew her father, who died two years ago.

Den nye Lillebæltsbro blev indviet for længe siden, nemlig i 1970.
The new bridge across 'Lillebælt' was inaugurated long ago, viz. in 1970.

|14.2.1.5| To mark parenthetical (non-restrictive) apposition

Danmarks østligste punkt, Østerskær, ligger i Østersøen.
Denmark's most easterly point, Østerskær, is in the Baltic Sea.

Min søster, Rikke Svendsen, er turistguide.
My sister, Rikke Svendsen, is a tourist guide.

|14.2.1.6| To mark elements in extra positions (see 11.7)

Ulla, hvor har du parkeret bilen?
Ulla, where have you parked the car?

Han har vundet i lotteriet, den heldige fyr.
He has won the lottery, the lucky chap.

|14.2.1.7| To mark off interjections

Av, min finger!	Ow, my finger!
Hold nu op, for satan!	Now stop it, damn you!

14.2.1.8 In enumerations, though not before the last one

Søren, Mads, Maren og Mette går i samme skole.
Søren, Mads, Maren and Mette go to the same school.

Vi købte øl, vin, vand, juice og mælk.
We bought beer, wine, water, juice and milk.

14.2.1.9 To indicate an 'afterthought'

Køb lige en pose kartofler, og noget fløde til desserten!
Go and buy a bag of potatoes, and some cream for the dessert!

14.2.1.10 Before **men**

Ferien var dyr, men dejlig.
The holiday was expensive but lovely.

14.2.2 *Optional use of the comma*

The comma is *optional* in the following cases:

14.2.2.1 Between main clause and subordinate clause

This is knows as the 'start comma', as it is used to mark the beginning of the subordinate clause.

Hun sagde(,) at hun ikke kunne finde sin mobiltelefon.
She said that she couldn't find her mobile phone.

Jeg ved(,) at han arbejder på posthuset.
I know he works in the post office.

Kender du pigen(,) der står derovre i hjørnet?
Do you know the girl standing over there in the corner?

14.2.2.2 Between two non-coordinated subordinate clauses

This applies to the second comma position in the following examples:

De opdagede(,) at det var naboen(,) der havde klippet hækken.
They discovered that it was the neighbour who had cut the hedge.

Vi forventer(,) at han kommer hjem(,) når han får fri.
We expect him to come home when work is over.

Note:

The Danish National Language Council recommends not using a *startkomma*, i.e. a comma before subordinate clauses, in practice before conjunctions such as **at**, **der**, **som**, **når**, **da**, **hvis**, etc., where this is optional.

14.3 The full stop

14.3.1 At the end of a sentence

Vi stillede bordet midt i spisestuen.
We placed the table in the middle of the dining-room.

14.3.2 In some abbreviations (cf. 12.4)

bl.a., inter alia; **f.eks.**, e.g.; **m.m.**, etc.

14.3.3 In mathematical expressions (cf. 4.2)

1.000.000 kr	1,000,000 kroner
kl. 07.45	7.45 am
2.4. 2010 (den 2. april 2010)	2 April 2010

Note that Danish uses a decimal comma, where English has a decimal point (cf. 4.2.6):

7,5 l	7.5 l

14.4 The colon

14.4.1 Before direct speech

The colon is used before a quotation, dialogue in a play or thoughts in direct speech after a reporting verb (e.g. **sige**, say; **spørge**, ask; **tænke**, think; etc.). The word immediately following the colon has a capital letter.

Anders: "Vil du lave en kop kaffe?"
Anders: 'Will you make a cup of coffee?'

245

Jette: "Ja, hvis du rydder op imens."
Jette: 'Yes, if you tidy up in the meantime.'

Hun sagde: "Nu vil jeg læse avisen!"
She said, 'Now I want to read the paper!'

Jeg tænkte: "Bare det bliver solskin i morgen!"
I thought, 'If only tomorrow will be sunny!'

14.4.2 *Before lists, examples, explanations and summaries*

Køb disse ting i supermarkedet: brød, smør, ost, æg . . .
Buy these things at the supermarket: bread, butter, cheese, eggs . . .

14.5 The exclamation mark

The exclamation mark is used when addressing people directly, and after commands, exclamations, rhetorical questions, etc.:

Mine damer og herrer!	Ladies and gentlemen!
Hej!	Hi!
Sid ned!	Sit down!
Er du blevet vanvittig!	Have you gone mad!

14.6 Direct speech

Several different typographical conventions are used to indicate dialogue:

14.6.1 *Dash (tankestreg)*

— Hvad hedder du? spurgte han.
'What's your name?' he asked.

14.6.2 *Inverted commas*

Danish uses „. . ." or ". . .", unlike English ". . ." or '. . .'

„Hvad er der sket?" spurgte hun.
'What has happened?' she asked.

14.6.3 Guillemet

»Det ved jeg ikke«, svarede han.
'I don't know,' he answered.

14.7 The apostrophe

14.7.1 Not used for possessor

Unlike English, the apostrophe is *not* normally used to indicate a possessor
(i.e. to mark a genitive):

kattens hale	the cat's tail
Gretes onkel	Grete's uncle

14.7.2 Indicating genitive after -s, -x, -z

However, the apostrophe is found marking the genitive after nouns ending
in -s, -x, -z (see also 2.3.3):

Lars' kusiner	Lars's (female) cousins
Marx' skrifter	Marx's writings
den tidlige jazz' historie	the history of early jazz

14.7.3 Indicating an inflectional ending

The apostrophe is sometimes used to mark an inflectional ending:

In abbreviations without a full stop:

pc'en, the PC (personal computer); **tv'et**, the TV set; **wc'er**, toilets.

After numerals to indicate decades: **2010'erne**, the 2010s.

14.8 The hyphen

14.8.1 As a replacement for og

dansk-svensk samarbejde	Danish-Swedish cooperation
en engelsk-dansk ordbog	an English-Danish dictionary

247

14.8.2 **Between figures or names of places to indicate period,**
extent, distance, etc.

A hyphen often indicates the meaning 'from . . . to' or 'between . . . and':

Butikken er åben 9-18.	The shop is open 9 to 6.
en billet Køge-Ringsted	a ticket between Køge and Ringsted
årene 1939-45	the years 1939 to 1945
side 9-11	pages 9 to 11

14.8.3 **To avoid repetition of the first or second element**

haveborde og -stole	garden tables and (garden) chairs
syv- til otteårige børn	seven- to eight-year-old children

14.8.4 **Where one of the elements is an abbreviation or a number**

p-plads, parking place; **NATO-øvelse**, NATO exercise; **fodbold-VM**, the World Cup in football; **2000-tallet**, the 21st century

14.9 The dash

The dash (double the length of the hyphen) is used in the following circumstances.

14.9.1 **To indicate a pause before an unexpected conclusion to a**
statement

Han ønskede sig en Jaguar, men fik – en Lada.
He wanted a Jaguar but got – a Lada.

Pludselig – et skrig og lyden af et skud.
Suddenly – a cry and the sound of a shot.

14.9.2 *As brackets around a parenthetical phrase, before additional information, etc.*

Hvis De siger ja – og det håber jeg da! – kan vi underskrive kontrakten i dag.
If you accept – and I do hope so! – we can sign the contract today.

Vi fik tordenvejr – sådan som vejrudsigten havde lovet.
We had a thunderstorm – just as the weather forecast had predicted.

14.9.3 *To indicate that something is unfinished*

Gør, hvad jeg siger, ellers –
Do what I say, otherwise . . .

Linguistic terms

This list comprises terms that may not be familiar to a student of language, as well as those that are not already explained in the text. Users should also consult the index for references in the text.

ABSTRACT NOUNS refer to unobservable notions, e.g. **musik, påstand, vanskelighed** (music, assertion, difficulty).

ABSTRACT SENSE is when the literal sense is no longer transparent. Compare the meaning of the verb in: **Hun satte kartoflerne over**, She put the potatoes on (literal sense) with: **Hun oversatte bogen**, She translated the book (abstract sense) (cf. FIGURATIVE SENSE).

ADJECTIVE PHRASES consist of an adjective or a participle with one or more modifiers, e.g. **Han er *utrolig energisk***, He is incredibly energetic.

ADVERB PHRASES consist of an adverb with one or more modifiers, e.g. **Han kørte *temmelig hurtigt***, He drove quite fast.

ADVERBIALS (see CLAUSAL ADVERBS) are words, phrases or clauses that function as adverbs. Adverbs, noun phrases, prepositional phrases and subordinate clauses can all be adverbials of different kinds (manner, place, time, condition, etc.), e.g. **Hun sang *smukt*** (adverb, manner), She sang beautifully; **Hun sang *hele aftenen*** (noun phrase, time), She sang the whole evening; **Hun sang *i Det Kongelige Teater*** (prep. phrase, place), She sang in the Royal Theatre; **Hun sang kun, *hvis hun havde lyst*** (sub. clause, condition), She only sang when she felt like it.

AFFIX is a prefix added to the beginning or a suffix added to the end of a word, e.g. ***u*lykkelig**, unhappy; **god*hed***, goodness.

AGENT is the person or thing carrying out the action in both active and passive constructions, e.g. ***Pigen* spiser kagen**, The girl eats the cake; **Kagen spises *af pigen***, The cake is eaten by the girl.

AGREEMENT is a way of showing that two grammatical units have a certain feature in common, e.g. **mine hunde**, my dogs; **slottet er stort**, the castle is big.

APPOSITION is where two consecutive noun phrases, separated only by a comma, denote the same entity and thus have the same referent, e.g. **Per, min bror, er rig**, Per, my brother, is rich.

ATTRIBUTIVE is used to describe adjectives or pronouns that precede a noun and modify it, e.g. et **stort** hus, a big house; **min** taske, my bag.

BLENDS are new words formed by omitting part of an existing word, e.g. m(erværdi)oms(ætningsafgift) → *moms*, VAT.

CLAUSAL ADVERBS are adverbs that modify the sense of the clause as a whole, e.g. **Han er *ikke* dum**, He's not stupid; **De er *altid* ude**, They are always out.

CLAUSE is a syntactic unit that usually consists of at least a finite verb and a subject (though the subject may be understood, as in most imperative clauses, e.g. **Hent lige avisen!** Do fetch the paper, please!). There are two major types of clause: main clauses (MC) and subordinate clauses (SC), e.g. **Middagen stod på bordet** (MC), **da jeg kom hjem** (SC), The dinner was on the table when I got home (cf. SENTENCE).

CLIPPINGS are new words formed by omitting the beginning or end of a word, e.g. **automobil** → *bil*, car; **biograf** → *bio*, cinema.

COLLECTIVE NOUNS are nouns whose singular form denotes a group, e.g. **familie**, family; **hold**, team; **kvæg**, cattle.

COMMON NOUNS are all nouns that are not PROPER NOUNS, e.g. **en hund**, a dog; **to borde**, two tables.

COMPLEMENTS express a meaning that adds to (or complements) that of the subject or object. They can be either an ADJECTIVE (PHRASE) or a NOUN (PHRASE), e.g. **Dorthe og Sven er *intelligente*. De er *gode venner*** (Subj.Comp.), Dorthe and Sven are intelligent. They are good friends; **De slog ham *bevidstløs*** (Obj.Comp.), They knocked him unconscious. (For 'prepositional complement', see PREPOSITIONAL PHRASE.)

COMPLEX VERBS have two or more parts: **Jeg *har prøvet at spise* snegle**, I have tried eating snails; **Cyklen *er blevet stjålet***, The bike has been stolen.

COMPOUND VERBS are verbs consisting of a STEM and a prefix or particle, which may be inseparable or separable from the stem, e.g. *be*tale, pay; but *del*tage/tage *del*, take part.

251

CONJUGATION denotes the way a verb is inflected, i.e. its pattern of endings, and the grouping of verbs according to their endings, e.g. past tense forms in: Conj. I leve – levede, live; Conj. II spise – spiste, eat.

COPULAS are verbs linking a subject complement to the subject, e.g. Pia *er* dansker, Pia is a Dane; Søren *blev* sur, Søren became bad-tempered.

CORRELATIVE is the word or phrase that a pronoun replaces or refers to, e.g. Den tale is replaced by som in: Den tale, som han holdt, var kedelig, The speech that he made was boring.

COUNT NOUNS are nouns that denote individual countable entities and therefore usually have a plural form (including zero-ending), e.g. bog – bøger, book-s; dreng – drenge, boy-s; æg – æg, egg-s.

DECLENSION denotes the different ways of INFLECTING count nouns in the plural, e.g. bil*er*, krig*e*, flag, cars, wars, flags. It also denotes adjective inflection, e.g. en rød bil, a red car; et rød*t* hus, a red house; den rød*e* bil, the red car.

DEFINITE refers to a specified entity, cf. *Tyven* har stjålet cyklen, The thief has stolen the bike. Indefinite refers to a non-specified entity, e.g. *En tyv* har stjålet cyklen, A thief has stolen the bike.

DERIVATIVE refers to a word derived from a STEM, usually by the addition of an AFFIX, e.g. angå (concern), foregå (take place), and overgå (surpass) are all derivatives of the verb gå (go).

DIRECT OBJECT denotes a noun phrase, a pronoun or a clause governed by a (transitive) verb, e.g. Drengen hentede *bolden/den*, The boy fetched the ball/it; Hun sagde, *at hun var træt*, She said that she was tired.

DUPLICATION involves the repetition of a subject, object or adverbial, usually in the form of a pronoun or adverb, e.g. *Jens, han* er kvik, Jens, he is bright.

ELLIPSIS involves the omission of a word or word group in the sentence, e.g. Må jeg få en is? Nej, du må ikke /*få en is*/, Can I have an ice-cream? No, you can't /have an ice-cream/.

FIGURATIVE SENSE is when the literal sense has been extended but is still somehow transparent, e.g. Han fulgte i sin faders fodspor, He followed in his father's footsteps (cf. ABSTRACT SENSE).

FINITE VERB is a verb form, which in itself shows tense (and sometimes mood and/or voice). There are three finite verb forms in Danish: the present tense, the past tense and the imperative, e.g. Jeg venter; Jeg ventede; Vent!, I'm waiting; I waited; Wait! (cf. NON-FINITE VERB).

FORMAL SUBJECT is **der** or **det** in cases when the REAL SUBJECT is postponed, e.g. *Der* (FS) **sidder** *en gammel mand* (RS) **på bænken**, There's an old man sitting on the bench; *Det* (FS) **er synd**, *at du ikke kan komme til festen* (RS), It's a pity that you can't come to the party.

FRONT is the position at the beginning of a main clause. It is usually occupied by the subject, e.g. *Vi* **er sultne**, We are hungry. But non-subjects, especially ADVERBIAL expressions of time or place, often occupy the front position, e.g. *I morgen* **skal jeg i biografen**, Tomorrow I'm going to the cinema.

GENDER may indicate sex: **drengen** – *han*, **pigen** – *hun* (the boy – he, the girl – she) or grammatical gender: *en* **stol**, *et* **barn**, *et* **hus**, (a chair, a child, a house).

IDIOM(ATIC) indicates a traditional usage that is not readily explicable from the grammar or from the individual elements.

IMPERATIVE is a finite verb form identical in Danish with the stem of the verb, expressing a command, warning, direction or the like, e.g. **Kom!** Come on!; **Vend om!** Turn round!

IMPERSONAL CONSTRUCTIONS do not involve a person but usually **det** or **der**, e.g. **Det sner**, It's snowing; **Der snydes meget**, There's a lot of cheating.

INDECLINABLE describes words that do not INFLECT, e.g. the adjectives **moderne**, good; **fælles**, common, mutual, which take no endings for gender or plural: **et moderne hus**, a modern house; **fælles venner**, mutual friends. Whole word classes may be indeclinable, e.g. conjunctions and prepositions.

INDEFINITE (see DEFINITE)

INDIRECT OBJECT usually denotes a person or an animal benefiting from an action (i.e. the recipient), e.g. **Vi gav** *dem* **pengene**, We gave them the money.

INFINITIVE PHRASE is a phrase consisting of an infinitive accompanied by one or more modifiers, e.g. **at skrive et brev**, to write a letter.

INFLECT means to change the form of a word by means of (inflectional) endings, vowel change or in other ways, e.g. the verb **skrive** (write) inflects **skriv, skrive, skriver, skrev, skrevet**, etc.

INFLECTION (see INFLECT)

INTERROGATIVE is used of questions, e.g. interrogative pronouns and adverbs introduce a question: *Hvem* var det? Who was that?; *Hvorfor* kom du ikke? Why didn't you come?

INVERTED word order denotes the order: verb – subject, e.g. I dag *rejser vi*, Today we are leaving.

MATRIX is that part of a complex sentence that remains when a subordinate clause is removed, e.g. *Birthe lovede*, at hun ville hente os, Birthe promised that she would meet us.

MORPHEME is the smallest part of a word expressing meaning: in the word **bilerne** (the cars) there are three morphemes: *bil* ('car'), *er* (plural morpheme), *ne* (definite plural morpheme).

MUTATED VOWEL is one that changes when a word is inflected, e.g. o → ø in **fod** – **fødder** (foot – feet); u → y in *ung* – *yngre* (young – younger).

NOMINAL means a word or phrase functioning as a noun, e.g. *Bogen* er interessant, The book is interesting; *At læse* er interessant, Reading is interesting.

NON-COUNT NOUNS are nouns that cannot describe individual countable entities. They may be either singular words with no plural form, usually denoting substances ('mass-words'), e.g. **luft**, air; **mel**, flour; **sand**, sand; or they may be plural words with no equivalent singular form, e.g. **klæder**, clothes; **penge**, money; **shorts**, shorts.

NON-FINITE VERB forms are those not showing tense, namely the infinitive and the participles, e.g. (**at**) **løbe**, (to) run; **løbende**, running; **løbet**, run.

NOUN PHRASES consist of a noun accompanied by one or more modifiers, which may precede or follow the noun, e.g. **en dejlig dag**, a lovely day; **en dag, som jeg aldrig vil glemme**, a day I shall never forget.

NUMBER is a collective term for singular and plural. The plural form is usually marked by an inflectional ending, e.g. **en blyant**, a pencil; **to blyant*er***, two pencils.

PART OF SPEECH means word class, e.g. noun, adjective, verb, conjunction, etc.

PARTICLE is a stressed adverb or preposition appearing together with a verb to form a phrasal verb with a single unit of meaning, e.g. **ned** in skrive *ned*, write down; **på** in se *på*, watch; **ud** in skælde *ud*, tell off.

PARTITIVE denotes a part of a whole or of a substance, e.g. *en del af* **pengene**, some of the money; *en flaske* **vin**, a bottle of wine; *et kilo* **kartofler**, a kilo of potatoes.

PEJORATIVE means deprecating, e.g. **dit fjols!** you idiot!

PREDICATE is the central part of the clause, excluding the subject. The predicate comprises the verb plus any object, complement or adverbial: **Han** *spiller* (*klaver hver dag*), He plays (the piano every day).

PREDICATIVE indicates the position after a copula verb: **Skuespillet er** *svært*, The play is difficult; **De bliver** *gamle*, They're growing old.

PREDICATIVE COMPLEMENT (see **COMPLEMENT**)

PREPOSITIONAL PHRASE consists of a preposition plus a prepositional complement (a noun (phrase), a pronoun, an infinitive (phrase) or a clause), e.g. **pigen** *med det lange hår,* the girl with the long hair; **pigen tænkte** *på ham,* the girl thought of him; **pigen gik** *uden at sige farvel,* the girl left without saying goodbye; **pigen sørgede** *for, at bordet blev dækket,* the girl saw to it that the table was set.

PRODUCTIVE implies that a word class or method of word formation can still produce new words, e.g. the suffix **-bar** in **vaskbar**, washable.

PROPER NOUNS are names of specific people, places, occasions, events, titles, etc., e.g. **Jørgen, Randers,** *Løgneren.*

RAISING is the movement of an element from a subordinate clause to the **FRONT** of the main clause, e.g. ***Det* sagde Erik at vi ikke skulle gøre,** Erik said that we should not do that.

REAL SUBJECT is the postponed subject, e.g. **Det er dejligt** *at sidde i solen,* It's nice to sit in the sun (cf. **FORMAL SUBJECT**).

RECIPROCAL indicates a mutual activity expressed either in the pronoun, e.g. **De elsker** *hinanden,* They love each other, or in the verb, e.g. **Vi ses i morgen,** See you tomorrow.

SEMANTIC denotes the meaning of words, phrases, etc.

SENTENCE is a syntactic unit that contains a complete meaning and consists of one or more clauses (cf. **CLAUSE**). Thus the following three examples are all sentences: **Se der!** Look there!; **Hun tager bussen, når det regner,** She takes the bus when it rains; **Hvis du tror, at jeg kan huske, hvad han sagde, da vi besøgte ham i sidste uge, tager du fejl,** If you think that I can remember what he said when we visited him last week, you're wrong.

SIMPLE VERBS consist of one word only (a FINITE VERB), e.g. *Hjælp!*
Help!; (**han**) *sover*, (he) sleeps; (**hun**) *gik*, (she) went.

STATEMENT is a sentence or clause conveying information, as distinct
from a question, exclamation or command.

STEM is the part of the verb onto which inflectional endings are added,
e.g. **dans**e, **dans**er, **dans**ede, **dans**et.

SYLLABLE consists of a vowel and usually one or more consonants, e.g.
ø, rør, rød-e, in-du-stri-ar-bej-de-re.

TAG QUESTION is a phrase attached to the end of a statement, which
turns it into a question: **Han kan lide laks,** *ikke sandt*? He likes
salmon, doesn't he?

VERB PHRASES consist of a FINITE VERB form (optionally) accompanied
by one or more NON-FINITE VERB forms in a chain, e.g. **Han** *sover,*
He is sleeping; **Hun** *må kunne løbe,* She must be able to run.

Latin, Danish and English linguistic terms

In many Danish grammars and works on language, Danish linguistic terms are used in preference to the more international Latin-based terms. This list shows equivalents.

Latin	Danish	English
Adjektiv	Tillægsord	Adjective
Adjektivisk participium	Bøjelig tillægsform	Adjectival participle
Adverbial	Biled	Adverbial
Adverbium	Biord	Adverb
Akkusativ	Genstandsfald	Accusative
Aktiv	Handleform	Active
Apposition	Navnetillæg	Apposition
Artikel	Kendeord	Article
Dativ	Hensynsfald	Dative
Demonstrativt pronomen	Påpegende stedord	Demonstrative pronoun
Diatese = aktiv/passiv	Art	Voice
Diftong	Tvelyd	Diphthong
Direkte objekt	Genstandsled	Direct object
Femininum	Hunkøn	Feminine
Finitte verbalformer	Sætningsdannende verbalformer	Finite verb forms
Formelt subjekt	Foreløbigt grundled	Formal subject
Futurum	Fremtid	Future
Commune (maskulinum, femininum)	Fælleskøn	Common gender (masculine, feminine)
Genitiv	Ejefald, Tillægsfald	Genitive
Genus	Køn	Gender
Hjælpeverbum	Hjælpeudsagnsord	Auxiliary verb

257

Latin	Danish	English
Hypotakse	Underordning	Hypotaxis
Imperativ	Bydeform, Bydemåde	Imperative
Imperfektum/Præteritum	Datid	Past tense
Indefinit pronomen	Ubestemt stedord	Indefinite pronoun
Indikativ	Fortællemåde	Indicative
Indirekte object	Hensynsled	Indirect object
Infinitiv	Navneform, Navnemåde	Infinitive
Infinitte verbalformer	Ikke-sætningsdannende verbalformer	Non-finite verbs forms
Inflektion	Bøjningsendelse	Inflection
Interjektion	Udråbsord	Interjection
Interpunktion	Tegnsætning	Punctuation
Interrogativt pronomen	Spørgende stedord	Interrogative pronoun
Inversion	Omvendt ordstilling/ ledstilling	Inversion
Kardinaltal	Mængdetal	Cardinal number
Kasus	Fald	Case
Komparation	Gradbøjning	Comparison
Komparativ	2. grad	Comparative
Konjunktion	Bindeord	Conjunction
Konjunktiv	Ønskemåde	Subjunctive
Konsonant	Medlyd	Consonant
Maskulinum	Hankøn	Masculine
Modalverbum	Mådesudsagnsord	Modal verb
Modus	Måde	Mood
Neksus	Samordning	Nexus
Neutrum	Intetkøn	Neuter
Nominativ	Grundledsfald	Nominative
Numerale	Talord	Numeral
Numerus	Tal	Number
Objekt	Genstandsled	Object
Optativ	Ønskemåde	Optative
Ordinaltal	Ordenstal	Ordinal number
Ortografi	Retskrivning, Retstavning	Orthography
Paratakse	Sideordning	Parataxis
Passiv	Lideform	Passive
Participium	Tillægsform, Tillægsmåde	Participle
Perfektum	Førnutid	Perfect
Personligt pronomen	Personligt stedord	Personal pronoun
Pluralis	Flertal	Plural

Latin	Danish	English	
Pluskvamperfektum	Førdatid	Past perfect, Pluperfect	Latin, Danish and English linguistic terms
Positiv	1. grad	Positive	
Possessivt pronomen	Ejestedord	Possessive pronoun	
Pronomen	Stedord	Pronoun	
Proprium	Egennavn	Proper noun	
Prædikativ	Omsagnsled	Complement	
Præfiks	Forstavelse	Prefix	
Præposition	Forholdsord	Preposition	
Præsens	Nutid	Present tense	
Præsens participium	Nutids tillægsform	Present participle	
Præteritum participium	Kort tillægsform, Datids tillægsform, Fortids tillægsform	Past participle	
Reciprokt pronomen	Gensidigt stedord	Reciprocal pronoun	
Refleksivt pronomen	Tilbagevisende stedord	Reflexive pronoun	
Relativsætning	Henførende sætning	Relative clause	
Relativt pronomen	Henførende stedord	Relative pronoun	
Singularis	Ental	Singular	
Subjekt	Grundled	Subject	
Substantiv	Navneord	Noun	
Suffiks	(Aflednings)endelse	Suffix	
Superlativ	3. grad	Superlative	
Syntaks	Ordføjningslære, Sætningsbygning, Sætningslære	Syntax	
Tempus	Tid	Tense	
Verbal(led)	Udsagnsled	(Finite) Verb	
Verbalt participium	Ubøjet tillægsmåde	Verbal participle	
Verbum	Udsagnsord	Verb	
Vokal	Selvlyd	Vowel	

Bibliography

Christian Becker-Christensen, *Nudansk Syntaks*, 2004
Christian Becker-Christensen and Peter Widell, *Nudansk Grammatik*, 2005
Robert Zola Christensen and Lisa Christensen, *Dansk grammatik*, 2nd ed., 2006
  Den danske ordbog, 6 vols, 2003–05
Paul Diderichsen, *Elementær dansk grammatik*, 3rd ed., 1962
Barabara Fischer-Hansen and Ann Kledal, *Grammatikken – håndbog i dansk
  grammatik for udlændinge*, 4th ed., 2006
Nina Grønnum, *Rødgrød med Fløde*, 2007
Aage Hansen, *Moderne dansk I–III*, 1967
Erik Hansen, *Rigtigt dansk*, 2nd ed., 1993
Erik Hansen, *Dæmonernes port*, 5th ed., 2006
Henrik Galberg Jacobsen, *Erhvervsdansk, Opslagsbog*, 2nd ed., 1991
Henrik Galberg Jacobsen and Peder Skyum-Nielsen, *Erhvervsdansk, Grundbog*,
  1990
Henrik Galberg Jacobsen and Peder Skyum-Nielsen, *Dansk sprog. En grundbog*,
  2nd ed., 2007
Henrik Galberg Jacobsen and Peter Stray Jørgensen, *Politikens Håndbog i nudansk*,
  5th ed., 2008
Pia Jarvad, *Nye ord. Hvorfor og hvordan?*, 1995
Pia Jarvad, *Nye ord – Ordbog over nye ord i dansk 1955–1998*, 1999
Jørgen Nørby Jensen and Marianne Rathje, *Rigtigt kort*, 3rd ed., 2003
W. Glyn Jones and Kirsten Gade, *Danish. A Grammar*, 1981.
Jørgen Lomholt, *Le Danois Contemporain*, 1982
Tom Lundskær-Nielsen, Michael Barnes and Annika Lindskog, *Introduction to
  Scandinavian Phonetics*, 2005
Tom Lundskær-Nielsen and Philip Holmes, *Danish: A Comprehensive Gramma*r,
  2nd ed., 2010
Annelise Munck Nordentoft, *Hovedtræk af dansk grammatik. Ordklasser*, 2nd ed.,
  1972
Annelise Munck Nordentoft, *Hovedtræk af dansk grammatik. Syntaks*, 3rd ed., 1982
Viggo Hjørnager Pedersen, Hermann Vinterberg and C.A. Bodelsen, *Dansk–Engelsk
  Ordbog*, 4th ed., 1999
Politikens Nudansk ordbog med etymologi, 3rd ed., 2005
Retskrivningsordbogen, 2005
Knud Sørensen, *Engelsk i dansk. Er det et must?*, 1995

Websites

Dansk sprognævn (incl. Kommaregler, Nyt fra Sprognævnet):
    www.dsn.dk
Ordbog over det danske sprog:
    www.ordnet.dk/ods
Retskrivningsordbogen (RO):
    www.retskrivningsordbogen.dk/ro/ro.htm
Sproget.dk (incl. Retskrivningsregler):
    www.sproget.dk

Index

Figures refer to *paragraphs*. Words in **bold** are Danish. Words in *italics* are English.

Printed in Great Britain
by Amazon

84302365R00165